CONTENTS

KISS®

AND

make-up

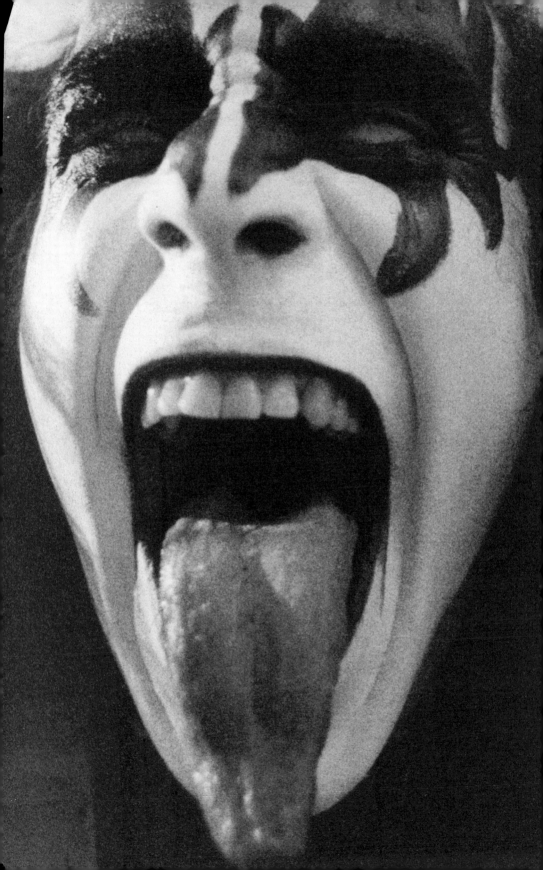

KISS®

AND
make-up

Gene Simmons

THREE RIVERS PRESS · NEW YORK

Published by Three Rivers Press, New York, New York.
Member of the Crown Publishing Group, a division of Random House, Inc.
www.randomhouse.com

THREE RIVERS PRESS and the Tugboat design are
registered trademarks of Random House, Inc.

The KISS logo is a registered trademark.

Originally published in hardcover by Crown Publishers,
a division of Random House, Inc., in 2001.

Printed in the United States of America

DESIGN BY ELINA D. NUDELMAN

Library of Congress Cataloging-in-Publication Data
Simmons, Gene, 1949–
KISS and make-up / Gene Simmons.
1. Simmons, Gene, 1949–   2. Rock musicians—United States—Biography.
3. KISS (Musical group)   I. Title.
ML420.S5629 A3   2002
782.42166'092—dc21
[B]   2001042481

ISBN 0-609-81002-2

10 9 8 7 6 5 4 3 2 1

First Paperback Edition

TO MY MOTHER, who gave me life and taught me to reach for the sky.

TO SHANNON, NICHOLAS, AND SOPHIE, who taught me how to love someone other than myself.

KISS®

AND

make-up

OVERTURE

Someday soon, just after the final chords of "Rock and Roll All Nite" ring out on the Shea Stadium stage, I will pick up my bass and exit stage right. After twenty-nine glorious and tumultuous years, years filled with the highest highs and the lowest lows, America will have seen the last of KISS onstage. America was our home. These were our people. And playing the final show will be bittersweet, to say the least.

Thirty years before, there was no KISS. There was only Gene Simmons, an aspiring rock musician in New York City. Ten years before that, there was no Gene Simmons—only Gene Klein, a Jewish kid who lived in Queens with his single mother. And ten years before that, there wasn't even a Gene Klein—only Chaim Witz, a poor boy growing up in Haifa, Israel. All those people, of course, were me, and I was all those people. I was born in Israel, saw the world change around me when I came to America with my mother, and then began to change myself, first my name, then my face. When I picked up a bass, it was a kind of transformation. When I put on face paint, it was a kind of transformation. And when I took the stage, it was the most profound transformation of them all. In the process, I managed to help steer KISS to the pinnacle of rock and roll: we would eventually stand right behind the Beatles in the number of gold record awards by any group in history.

In my life story, I am the main character. But countless supporting characters have helped to define my life. First, there's the woman who gave me life, my mother, who endured unspeakable horrors in the concentration camps of the Nazis and who used reserves of strength I can only imagine to survive and even thrive. Then there are my bandmates, my second family—Paul Stanley is like the brother I never had, and Ace Frehley, Peter Criss, Eric Carr, Eric Singer, Bruce Kulick, and others helped me to create and sustain KISS (and in some cases, did their best to undo what Paul and I had created and sustained). And last but not least—last and probably most—there is lovely, incomparable Shannon Tweed, and the two children of whom we are the proudest parents imaginable, Nicholas and Sophie.

✦ ✦ ✦

When I sat down to write my life story, I thought about it in terms of the books I had read. The more I thought about it, the more I realized that my story is a story about power and the pursuit of it. I have always read everything I could get my hands on, especially books that taught me new things: religion, philosophy, history, the social sciences, and so forth. There are thousands of books, from *African Genesis* to *World Lit by Fire,* that recount man's endless search for power. Ultimately, all conflict seems to center on it, on who has it and who wants it. I instinctively realized very early on that power was what I really wanted. Fame and riches are fine, but one can have both and still have no power. Power is something I craved from the time I first set foot in America. I was made fun of because I couldn't speak English, or because I was Jewish, but it really came down to not having power.

Someone, perhaps Machiavelli, once said that it's better to be feared than loved. I understand that. Love is evasive. Love has its needs. You have to be giving. You have to be concerned with someone else's happiness. Power is a clearer idea, a cleaner concept. I want to walk into a restaurant and be waited on. I want to have women want me, although not necessarily because I want them. Women understand this notion very well. A woman wants to make herself as attractive as she can, with makeup, clothing, and perfume, because she wants every man to want her, although she may not be interested in any of them. I realize that I'm painting with broad strokes here, but I stand by what I'm saying.

I suppose one of the reasons I wanted power was so I wouldn't get picked on. When I first came to America, I felt like a stranger in a strange land. The Robert Heinlein book spoke to me as no other book ever had. It was my story. I was singled out because I was different, because I didn't speak English well, because I was alone. So I figured that I didn't need anyone, didn't want anyone, and had only myself to depend on. If I didn't do the work and go and get it myself, it would certainly never be handed to me.

◆ ◆ ◆

The story of KISS, of Gene Simmons, is a story of ambition and good fortune, of an immigrant boy's impossible dream realized. But it's also a story of the world's biggest rock band, which means that there's plenty of sex, drugs, and rock and roll. I can't take credit for any of the drugs—I'm straight, never been drunk, not a single time in my life. But the sex? For much of my adult life, I had no girl-friends, although I had plenty of girls. More than plenty. At some point, I began to keep Polaroid snapshots of my liaisons to remember them by. In a certain way, I loved every one of them. But when it was over, it was over. No fuss, no muss. No agony. To date, I have had about 4,600 liaisons. And I have to say that they were all wonderful, that they all enhanced my life in so many ways. Food tasted better. I whistled and hummed. I was alive.

Somehow, through all the craziness with women, despite the sheer numbers, I managed to become a dedicated father. If this seems strange to you, think of how it seems to me. My father left my mother and me when I was still young, and I grew up convinced that I would never have children, in part because I remembered the pain of abandonment, in part because I lived in terror of repeating my father's mistakes. Then I met a girl named Shannon Tweed. The next thing I knew, I was holding my son in the hospital, unwilling to give him up to the doctors. How do I reconcile the cocksman with the family man? The same way I reconcile the shy immigrant boy with the leather-and-studs Demon who climbed onstage to breathe fire. Every personality has contradictions, and a large personality has large contradictions.

◆ ◆ ◆

I have lived my life for myself. I'm not afraid to admit that. But I have also lived my life for the fans: for the faithful soldiers in the KISS Army, those who stood by us through thick and thin, through changing fashion, those who braved bad traffic and bad weather to come out and let us entertain them. When I first sat down to write this book, I was torn by whether I should tell the truth about their band: about the internal rifts and feuds, the personality conflicts and personality disorders. I was torn because I feared that the truth might ruin people's perception of their heroes. And whatever else KISS was, it was about heroes, about magic, about believing in it and delivering the goods. You, the fans, have always deserved the best from us. It's one of the reasons we introduced ourselves at every show with "You wanted the best, you got the best. The hottest band in the world, KISS." In sickness and in health, whether we felt like it or not, we believed we had an obligation to get out there, play our hearts out, and give you everything we had.

I believe that when children grow up, they should find out the truth about their parents. Those of you who believe in KISS need to know the truth. I know that a lot of the things you'll read in this book will be hard to take. I know that some fans may get upset at me. I know that some members of the band will hate me more than ever and claim that everything between these covers is a lie, despite my memory, despite the documentation, despite the witnesses who will attest to the events.

Either way, here's the truth, the whole truth, and nothing but the truth, so help me God.

I was born August 25, 1949, in a hospital in Haifa, Israel, overlooking the Mediterranean. At birth, I was named Chaim Witz: Chaim is a Hebrew word that means "life," and Witz was my father's last name. Just a year earlier, Israel had become independent after roughly 100 million Arabs tried to prevent Israel from appearing on the world map.

The war for Israel's independence followed in the wake of an earlier war, World War II, and the terrible plan of the German Nazis to erase Jews from Europe and eventually from the world. My mother's parents were Hungarian Jews, and my mother had grown

great expectations:

I was posing
with my mother
and a hammer—
for some reason
I loved hammers.

up in Hungary during the 1920s and 1930s. When my mother was fourteen, she was sent to the concentration camps, where she saw most of her family wiped out in the gas chambers. While in the camps, she ended up doing the hair of the commandant's wife, so she was shielded from many of the horrors that befell the other Jews. Having survived that horrific time, after the war she went to Israel. I think the survival instinct was so strong among that generation that, after leaving the camps, they couldn't imagine failing at anything else, and so they set out for this strange new land.

Israel was a new country, only a year older than I was, and its

ISRAEL 1949~1958

We were poor, but I was chilly, so my mother sewed me this coat from the blanket I slept in. I was chewing on a pretzel here at age two.

existence was still very much in question. But I was unaware of all that. It was always such a part of my daily routine that I wasn't able to separate it from any other aspect of my experience. For example, I remember that my dad, Yechiel (or Feri) Witz—who was physically imposing, at least six foot five—would come in on the weekends with his machine gun and put it on the kitchen table. The front lines were fifty miles away, and everybody, every male and most females, was in the army. There were no exemptions. If you lived there, you were in the army.

The gun on the table was one of the few things I remember about my father, because he wasn't around very much. I do recall that he was this large, powerful being with a large, powerful presence. One vivid memory does stand out. Once there was a mouse in the house, and it ran across the room and under the couch, and I remember my dad picking up the couch and holding it up on one

Chaim, Flora, and Feri Witz.

side with one arm while he was trying to shoo the mouse away with the other. I couldn't believe it. A man lifting up a couch? This was like nothing I had ever seen before. It seemed impossible.

I had polio when I was a very young child, probably when I was about three years old. Apparently, I lost most of my muscle control from the waist down. The doctors were worried that it would get worse and sent me to the hospital. In the hospital, I was kept off the ward, in isolation, and when my mother and father came by, they had to communicate with me through a closed window. For some reason, even at that young age, I had a strong sense of what was proper and what was improper, and I knew that it was improper to go to the bathroom in your own bed. My mother potty-trained me early on. She showed me the toilet and explained what it was for. At that time, there were no diapers in Israel, and I learned quickly that the bed was for sleeping, and the bathroom was for your other business. It was very clear. In the hospital, in the ward, I needed to get out of the bed and use the bathroom. I complained and cried and complained some more. I knew I needed to get to the bathroom. I knew that any other solution to that problem was the wrong solution. But the nurse didn't come, and somehow I managed to pull myself over the baby crib and did my business on the floor, while I hung on to the side of the crib. Then the nurse came. She wasn't around when I was in trouble, but the minute there was poop on the floor, she came right by, and she started yelling at me, wondering why I had gone right outside the crib. And my mother stormed right in and screamed at her for not being there for me. "What did you expect him to do?" she said. "Go in his own bed? He's a good boy. He knows better." In her eyes, I could do no wrong.

I was always a loner, even though I had friends. I spent time by myself, observing things, organizing the world around me in my own mind. For example, I was fascinated with beetles. In Israel, they had these huge Old Testament beetles. The beetles here in America are nothing compared to them. These Israeli beetles were the size of small dinosaurs, maybe two inches long. They were brightly colored and beautiful. They looked like jewels. And I used to tie sewing thread around the neck of these beetles and put them in matchboxes along with a little bit of sugar. The beetles would live there until I opened up the box, and then they would fly around, still tied to my thread.

As I got older, I became less of a loner. Instead, I became more interested in showing off around other kids and getting attention. So I changed from the kind of kid who would be a falconer for beetles, letting them fly around at the end of a leash of thread, to the kind of kid who would put a beetle in his mouth and let it walk around in there. Other kids were amazed by that. They thought it was disgusting and brave. Most important, they couldn't look away.

Though I was born in Haifa, my family lived in a place nearby, a little village called Tirat Hacarmel, which is named for the original biblical Mount Carmel. And I remember as a kid climbing that mountain, which is more of a hill, really, rolling hills, similar to southern California's hills. I remember going up the hill and picking cactus fruit when I was a kid, then climbing back down and selling the fruit at the bus depot for half a *pruta,* which is basically half a penny. (Cactus fruit are sweet and juicy on the inside, but have spikes on the outside. Their Hebrew name is *sabra,* and that's what Israelis are called, because they, too, are prickly on the outside and sweet on the inside.)

Living in Israel among all the other *sabras* was strange, especially in school, because Israeli classrooms taught this quirky mix of history, religion, and politics. Think of it: in class, we were taught about an old book called the Bible and were told that the events recounted in this book—incredible events, really—actually took place in the country where we were living. It was a strange notion to swallow and to understand. Because here was a whole book that talked about the creation of life, and Abraham, Isaac, and Jacob, and the flood and the Exodus. And then we were told, "This is where it happened. You're living in the place." It was pretty heavy stuff.

At the same time, I wasn't really all that conscious of being Jewish in Israel, because almost everyone was the same as I was in that respect. Clearly there were Arabs walking down the street, and there were some Christians, but I was oblivious to all that. I was not aware of anything except being Israeli. You'd think that my mother,

having just come through the war and the concentration camps, would have been consumed with what had happened to her, but she wasn't. It was too painful for her to talk about. She never discussed the camps and rarely talked about her childhood in Hungary. All she ever talked about, and only every once in a great while, was that the world is a big place, and there are some good people and some bad people. To this day, I am amazed that she had that self-control. It's proof that my mother, ethically, morally, and in all other ways, is a much better person than I will ever be. She had at that time, and still has, an abiding trust in humanity. She still believed the world is a good place, and that goodness prevails over evil more often than not. I don't know that I would have had that point of view if I had lived through what she had.

When you're a kid, you don't know that people are different races, different ethnicities, different religions. The one thing I did notice about my neighborhood was that it was filled with different languages. Some of the Jews in Israel spoke Hebrew. Some spoke Yiddish, which is a European language that combines Hebrew and German. In my house, the most important language was Hungarian, because my mother didn't really speak Hebrew all that well. And then later, when my mother went to work, it was Turkish and then Spanish, because my baby-sitter was Turkish and the next-door neighbors were Spanish. At an early age I was able to speak Hebrew, Hungarian, Turkish, and Spanish.

I was not aware of America or the rest of the world. But I do remember my mother taking me to a movie. I must have been four. It was my first experience with non–reality-based images. I had never seen a television set, and I had heard radio only occasionally. We

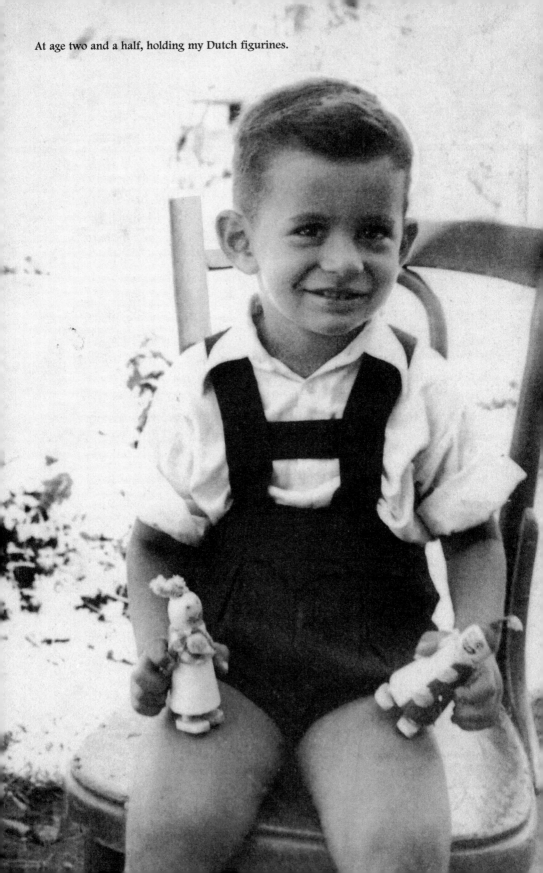

At age two and a half, holding my Dutch figurines.

went to the movie, but we couldn't afford to go inside, so my mother held me in her lap outside of the theater, and we watched the movie, which was shown on a big screen without a roof. It was amazing. I was transfixed. Later, I remembered that it was *Broken Arrow,* with Jimmy Stewart and Jeff Chandler. But at the time, all I could see were huge images of cowboys and Indians and a mythical Wild West where there were outlaws and heroes. Cowboys were the first superheroes, as far as I was concerned, the first characters who were larger than life and more powerful than ordinary people. As important as all of this became to me later—the concept of heroes, and the magic of the movies—what made the greatest impression on me was the sound of American English. That might have been the first time I heard English, and it sounded funny to me. It was one of the languages that, as a kid in Israel, we mimicked. To my ears, the American language had its own sound, with lots of *y*'s, and lots of soft *r*'s. These sounds didn't exist in Hebrew. That was my fake English, and it sounded pleasant to me.

◆ ◆ ◆

From the beginning, it seemed, my father and mother would separate. A simple conflict lay at the heart of my parents' bad marriage. My mother, Flora, was extremely beautiful as a young woman. She had classic movie star looks, like Ava Gardner. In the village where they came from in Europe—Jand, Hungary—she was considered quite a catch, but not as big a catch as my father. He was highly valued because he was the tallest in the village, probably six-five or six-six, although I remember him as even bigger. In my memory he was six-nine, a giant. Though his name is Yechiel in Hebrew, he was called Feri in Hungarian. When they met and married, they were young, in their early twenties, and during the first few years of their marriage, my mother gradually woke up to the idea that my father wasn't going to be the kind of provider she needed. For some reason, he could never make ends meet. He could never run a business successfully. He was not really a pragmatist. He was more of a dreamer. And for a carpenter, being a dreamer was roughly equivalent to being unemployed. He would make pieces of furniture that he loved but nobody else liked, and he would find to his surprise that he couldn't sell them. But it was more important to him to do what he wanted to do. And I remember he whittled me a scooter with his own two hands. Not an electric scooter, but the push kind, the ones with wheels and a little platform. He made it for me for my birthday. It was always impressive to see what he could make, and I'm sure that my mother was happy that he got off on his own creativity, but at some point you have to begin to submit to practical needs as well: namely, how do you make money? He didn't know the answer, and she kept asking the question, and they fought all the time.

Even if we had been living in a secure country, with a secure middle class, they probably still would have fought, but we were at the edge of this new frontier, in this new country, with new neighbors, new languages, and new rules. So my mother's anxiety about these issues intensified. Whether because of her pressure or my father's own self-esteem issues, their arguments would sometimes devolve to physical violence. Not terrible beatings, and not one-sided either: I remember that every once in a while one of them would push the other. At one point—I must have been four or so—they were bickering back and forth, and I jumped on my father's leg and started biting him near his knee. I can't even say for certain that it was a serious fight, but I was just trying to protect my mother.

Things didn't get better, and the fact that they weren't getting better made things worse. My father left Haifa for Tel Aviv, to look for work and take some time away from my mother. When he was gone, my mother started working at a coffeehouse called Café Nitza. I'll never forget it, because when you pulled up to it, you saw a kind of Mama Beulah figure, a large, fat, happy black woman sipping coffee. Up until that point, I think, I'd never seen a black face of any kind. She was so big and so happy, that face on the sign. I remember as a kid going to see my mother and getting my first cup of coffee and a poppyseed cake. I remember being hit by the caffeine, and I thought I was going to pass out. I couldn't believe what was happening to me. Everything started moving at a different speed; in my mind, I thought I was slurring my words.

My mother liked working. It gave her self-esteem, and she was very disciplined and a very hard worker. But still she wanted to make her marriage work. One day she told me that we were going to see my dad. So we took a trip to Tel Aviv, and we searched in vain for him for a little while. He wasn't where he was supposed to be. He wasn't in any of the places my mother expected to find him. So we went to the movies. I don't know if my mother suspected he might be there. I don't know if she was just going to relax for a little while. But in the lobby, I caught sight of my father. He was at the top of the stairs with a blond woman. I turned to my mother and told her, "There's Dad with a blond woman." At the time, I didn't think of it in terms of jealousy. That didn't enter into it at all. It was more like a game, looking for my father, and I had won the game by spotting him at the top of the stairs with this blond woman. My mother knew differently. We went to his apartment, and somehow she got a

I looked up to my father—he was everything I admired.

passkey, and we went inside, and she went through his pockets and found condoms in one of them. We went back to Haifa, and the two of us continued with our lives, and that was the last of my father's role. He didn't surface again. I have no idea whether my mother tried to make contact privately, and she won't talk about it to this day. For me, as a child, that was the end of that. The last visual image that I had of my dad was at the top of the stairs with that other woman.

After that, it was just the two of us, my mother and me, and she devoted herself to raising me. She went out on a date or two with some guys and would always do her best to explain to me what was happening. I didn't react very well, probably because I thought that I would lose her affections to somebody else. I became jealous and guarded, and I let her know in no uncertain terms that nobody else was permitted in the arrangement. One way or another, it worked, because my mother stayed single until I was about eighteen or nineteen.

Shortly after my mother and father separated for good, my mother and I moved from Tirat Hacarmel to Vade Jamal, another village in the Haifa area. At that time, I was five or six and starting to get a sense of the kind of country I was living in. For starters, it was a poor country that was just finding its way. Israel worked on a food-stamp system, and you could have meat once a week. Even milk wasn't something you could just go and buy. You had to get your stamp. There were certain amenities we simply didn't have. I never saw toilet paper or tissues. We wiped with rags. They were washed. Showers were unheard of. I bathed in a metallic bathtub, and my mother would heat the water up on the stove and then pour it into the bathtub, pot by pot, until it filled up.

Despite that, I was mostly oblivious of the idea of rich or poor. There were bullet holes all over the walls in the apartment where we lived, because three years earlier the Arabs and the Jews were fighting the War of Independence in the streets. But I was oblivious to the bullet holes. It just looked like a building. I do remember one incident: every once in a while my mother would save up money to bake a *babka*, which is a thick pastry. When she made the frosting to cover the cake, she would let me stick my finger in the pot and taste it. I remember being horrified that there was a big hole in the middle of the pot. And I was embarrassed to say anything to my mother at the time, because I thought she would feel embarrassed herself. But when I did happen to mention it, she started laughing, because in fact, the *babka* pot that you cook in actually has that big hole in the middle. To me, though, it was just a broken pot, and a sign of our poverty.

◆ ◆ ◆

I was my mother's only child. There were no other children, no husband. As a result, she protected me fiercely. We were a team, and she was intent both on raising me right and on ensuring that other people treated me with respect. Some of my most vivid memories are of my mother defending me, which she did passionately. I guess it was her way of announcing to the world that she valued her son and expected the same from everyone else.

My mother used to have these huge thigh-high boots, the kind that plumbers wear, as opposed to the stylish boots that are more familiar to Americans. They were very clunky, and I remember watching those boots go through the dirt as I walked along behind her. One day walking along behind those boots, I saw a neighborhood boy who had a bad habit of throwing rocks. Or more to the point, he had a bad habit of throwing rocks at me. I was minding my own business, and suddenly a rock hit me in the head. My mother moved faster than I had ever seen her move. She chased down this kid and picked him up off the ground by his hand and smacked him so hard that he was swinging like a sack of potatoes. This kid was crying, but she couldn't, or wouldn't, stop hitting him. She just kept slapping him. Then she took me by the hand in front of his parents, as if to say, "Yeah, what are you going to do about it?" Nothing came of it. We walked away.

Another time my mother's protectiveness actually landed us in the police station. This was slightly later, after I had started school in Vade Jamal, and after I had established myself as the loud kid, the show-off: the kid who always had to go the farthest, the highest, the fastest. There was a fig tree that grew over into the school grounds, although it was rooted in the yard of the woman who lived next door. The kids loved to climb up the part of the tree that was in the schoolyard, then climb down into the neighbor's yard. When she came out, all the kids would clamber down and scurry away. I was usually the last one down, because I was in the highest branches. One time I was too slow coming down, and the woman caught me. She had a banana stalk in her hand, and she started hitting me with it. I don't remember how badly she hurt me, only that I was scared and that she knocked the wind out of me. My friends brought me home after school and told my mother about the beating, in front of me.

The next thing I knew, we were back in the street again, and I was behind my mother and her boots, and we were going to the woman's house. We got to the house, and my mother banged on the door, and the woman came out. I remember being struck by her size. She was big, bigger than my mother, and had a hard look. She must have had a hard life. My mother asked just two questions. The first one was "Did you hit my son?" The woman said, "Yeah, he climbed my tree, and anybody that does that is trying to steal my figs, and I will hit anybody that I see." The second question was "What did you hit him with?" My mother spoke levelly, as if she were just trying to collect information. The woman said, "I'll show you what I hit him with." She brought out the banana stalk.

My mother grabbed the stalk out of the woman's hands and started beating her over the head with it. At first, Mom

My father at age forty-four.

was swinging it with one hand, and then she had it two-handed, as if she were playing baseball, and she was bringing it down on the woman's head, hard, the way you do with a sledgehammer over a spike. This woman was being drilled into the ground. The woman's legs gave way, and she was on her butt against the doorway, but even then my mother kept banging her over the head. By the time my mother got through with this woman, I was just amazed, because I'd never seen blood literally spray out of a person's head like a sprinkler system. It was just spouting out. It looked almost comical. There was blood everywhere. The woman was covered with blood, and my mother was covered with blood. It was hard to believe. It felt almost like a cheap horror movie.

In short order, because it was a small town, the police were there. There was a police station around the corner from the school. The cops took my mother and myself—we walked, because there were no cop cars—two blocks to the station. The sergeant behind the desk had a huge mustache; you couldn't see his mouth, it just hung over his lips. "Did you—" he said to my mother, and before he could even finish, she nodded. "Yes," she said. "Yes, I hit her over the head." The sergeant asked her why, and she told the story and explained her thinking: whether her son was right or wrong, she said, no one was allowed to lay a hand on him. And then she got carried away, because it was emotional in the retelling, and she must have felt defiant, and she started to yell at the sergeant and told him, "If you even so much as look at my son in the wrong way, I'll split your head open, too." The sergeant repeated that with an expression of disbelief, and the rest of the cops started laughing. Then he let us go.

◆ ◆ ◆

When I look back on Israel, I find that most of my memories are about my mother, or clothing, or food—the basics. I left when I was still a child, so my personality didn't really come into its own there, but every once in a while a memory comes up that surprises me with its strength and explains something about myself. For many years, for example, I couldn't stand the sight of spiders. I dimly remembered an incident from my childhood, but it wasn't clear. Then it came back to me: one morning my mother was getting ready to go to work, and I was getting ready to go to school, and she put my hat on my head. It didn't quite fit—there was a lump in it. She took off the hat, saying something about how my hair must be crumpled underneath. While she was talking, the biggest spider I ever saw crawled out of the hat and ran away. I shrieked, and for years I couldn't get over the idea that there were spiders waiting for me. I had a habit of looking under clothing and hats and in pockets to see if anything was crawling inside.

There's a similar story with chickens. Across the street from us lived a Moroccan family who always treated me as one of their own. One of the daughters in that family was named Jonet. She was a little older than I was—she must have been twelve to my five or six. She would always treat me to these huge cucumber, butter, and bread sandwiches when I came over. That was how we did things then: you'd have your bread, and put on it a piece of vegetable and lots of butter, and that was your sandwich. It was great. I was always looking forward to spending time at her place.

Her family had this chicken, a royal chicken with red plumage, and I always used to give it crumbs from my pockets. As soon as the chicken saw me walking in, it would start clucking. I guess it figured that it was feeding time at the zoo. One day I walked into Jonet's place expecting to get a sandwich. But she said she had to go, and she was pulling the chicken by a leash. It was fluttering its wings, and cluck, cluck, cluck, it wouldn't go. She tried to force it, but it resisted. So I said, "Let me pick up the chicken, he likes me." I reached for the chicken, but she said, "No, don't do that, he's going to peck your eyes out." I ignored her and picked up this giant chicken, and it settled into my arms like a newborn baby. And we walked. I didn't know where we were going, but I was brave enough to carry it. After a little while, though, the chicken started to weigh on me. It was probably five pounds. So I asked Jonet how far we were walking. "Very close," she said. "It's just up here around the corner."

As we rounded the corner, a large man with an apron came and grabbed the chicken from my arms. He held it by the neck and snapped it, then produced a knife and cut its head off. I saw the body of the chicken running around while the head was in the man's hand. It was the most hideous thing I had ever seen. Because of this memory, I couldn't eat chicken in any way, shape, or form. Especially if the head was connected, with the wings and all that. You'd think this would be a trauma that would pass, but until my mid-thirties, if I was going to eat chicken, it would have to be amorphous and not look like a chicken.

With all this, it was a good time. My needs were simple because they had to be. As long as I had jam and bread, I was happy. To this day, I find fancy food, like French pastries and baby carrots, disgusting. Give me a nice piece of cake, and I'm in heaven.

One day my mother and I received a care package in the mail. Inside there were cans of food and a sweater. It was the first time I had ever seen canned goods. My mother explained to me that it had come from her uncle Joe and her brother, George Klein. This was the first I had ever heard of a brother. In fact, she had two brothers. In Hungary, before the war, they had gotten wind that something bad was on the way, so they had gone to New York City. I asked my mother why they were sending us things. As I said, I didn't have any strong sense of privation. I didn't feel poor. I had food and clothing. Then she opened up the cans, and I tasted my

rocket ride:

1958~ 1963

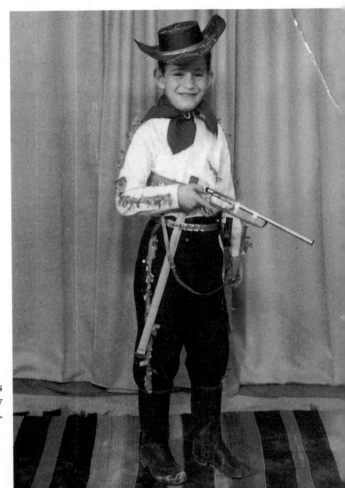

When I dressed up in this outfit, I felt like I really was a cowboy.

first canned peaches, which I thought were just astonishing. I went to her, with the peaches still in my mouth, and said, "Where did this come from?" She said, "America."

It wasn't the first time I had heard that word, but it was the first time I could attach a concrete sensation to it—in this case, the peaches in my mouth. I remember thinking it was a funny-sounding name, partly because I was giving it the Hebrew pronunciation, with a hard *r*. I went around the house saying "Amerrrica" for days.

Pretty soon the word began to collect other associations. One of the first was cowboys. Once I recognized that America was the land

coming to america

of cowboys, that was enough to make me think more about it. I was eight and a half by then, and movies were bigger than the entire world, and a big part of movies was the cowboy myth. This was before rock and roll, before the Beatles. At that point, cowboys were the ultimate cool. They got the girl, they were the loners, they rode off into the sunset. And cowboys represented America, at least for all the kids who weren't there. If you were a cowboy, you could exist in this pure heroic world. You could live by the gun. You were the judge and the jury, and you meted out justice with your hands. And you just moved on, and the girls loved you. You went off into the sunset.

In one school play, I dressed up as a cowboy, with a toy gun my mother bought me. It was the only costume that made sense. In fact, I was this small kid playing cowboy, with not an ounce of cool in me. But I was dreaming about cowboys, and through that, I was dreaming about America.

I don't think I consciously understood it at all, but I would look up at the movie screen and see this other place where everything was just much more dramatic and much bigger. The thing about America that always came through loud and clear was its size.

The word was *big*. The people were big. The ideas were big. The women were big. Their breasts were big. The horses were big, and they had buffaloes there, which were big, and big trains. Everything was big. And for me, it was about to become a reality.

One day my mother told me to get dressed, because we were going to the airport. I had never seen an airport. I had never seen jets or planes or anything. So I was transfixed. Then as we started to walk down the tarmac, it occurred to me that maybe I should show a little interest in this process. So I said to my mother, "Where are we going?" And my mother said, "We're just going one stop." I thought we were going on a trip. So we got on the plane and stayed there. The trip seemed like an eternity—partly because it was a long flight, and partly because I was as sick as a dog. I had never felt so terrible before, not in my entire life. I just kept vomiting and vomiting. I must have thrown up everything I ate that morning, and everything from the day before and the day before that. Finally, we landed in Paris. I remember stopping in Paris only because my mother went out to the duty-free area to buy herself some perfume. Then we got back on the plane, and I was sick again, and finally we landed at LaGuardia Airport in New York.

For me, as a kid, this was a new world, and I was trying to soak it all up. Later, though, I learned two stories about my mother's experiences in this immigration process that helped me to understand it better. At the time, only a certain number of people were allowed to come to the United States from Israel. My mother was very striking as a young woman, and apparently she convinced one of the authorities, either with her looks or with her people skills, to move our papers out from the bottom of the pile and to the top. That way we were able to get out of Israel and come to the United States. That's the first story.

The second one involves the fact that my mother had to take an oath before leaving Israel. She saw the American official at the embassy, and he couldn't speak Hebrew, and she couldn't speak English. They fumbled around and eventually hit on a common language, German. He asked her a series of questions about her political beliefs. They were trying to gauge her suitability for coming to

America. The first question was, "Are you now or have you ever been a member of the Communist Party?" Those were the kinds of things that people were asked in those days. Literally: "Are you a member of the Communist Party? Do you have secret plans to overthrow the American government?" Who's going to say yes? She said no. So the interview went fine, and then it came time for her to take this oath, and the official said, "Please raise your right hand." I guess my mother was a bit flustered at that time, and Jews don't do the same swearing on the Bible that Christians do, so she stuck her hand straight out the way the Nazis do. He started laughing, and he told my mother, "No, don't worry, you'll never have to do that ever again." That was very profound, I think. That marked the change we were about to undergo. The Nazis had hung over her like a shadow ever since the war. It was so painful that she didn't like to talk about it. But now we were going somewhere that would help to make all that a distant memory.

◆ ◆ ◆

When we got to New York City, my mother and I went to stay with her brother Larry and his wife, Magda, in Flushing, Queens. I was, at that time, no longer Chaim Witz. I had taken the name Gene for my first name, because it was more American than Chaim, and I had taken Klein because it was my mother's maiden name. In Old Testament Jewish law, it's a matriarchal society, so once your father leaves or dies, your mother's maiden name becomes your name. So I was not Chaim Witz, Israeli. I was Gene Klein, new American. And I do mean new American. I was eight and a half years old when we arrived, and there were so many things that I just couldn't understand, things that were so foreign to me. One of the first things I remember seeing was a Christmas billboard for Kent cigarettes, with a picture of Santa Claus smoking. He had this big cherubic face, and in the background the reindeer were up in the sky waiting for Santa to join them. Since I had never really heard of Christ or Christmas or Santa Claus, I immediately thought, "Oh, that's a rabbi smoking a cigarette." I figured that he must have been a Russian rabbi, because of all the snow in the background.

The other impression I had was that the place exceeded my imagination in every possible way. There's this stereotype of foreigners who come to America—they keep their heads up, so they can see all of these unimaginable vistas, streets that never end, rows of houses that never end. Coming from Israel, there was nothing to prepare me, and that's exactly how I was. I walked around with my head up and my eyes wide open. As usual, the best way I can describe how I felt is with a scene from a movie, although it's a movie that would come out a number of years later: *Moscow on the Hudson,* with Robin Williams. He plays a guy who comes to America from Russia, and he's fresh off the boat, and he goes into a supermarket and walks up to one of the floor managers and says, "Excuse me, which way is coffee?" in his broken English. And the floor manager, polite as can be, says, "Aisle 13." Aisle 13? What does that mean? So the guy says again, "Aisle 13, sir. All of Aisle 13." So when Robin Williams goes down to that aisle, there are literally hundreds of brands of coffee. He can't believe his eyes. He just starts repeating the word, "Coffee, coffee, coffee!" and eventually he collapses, and all the coffee falls on him.

Passport photos of my mother and myself, in 1958. She was thirty-two and I was eight and a half.

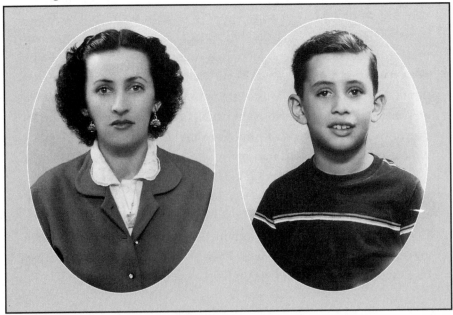

That was my experience of America. The stores were like football fields full of food. I had never seen anything so big. In Israel, there was no such thing as brands. You wanted milk, you got milk. You wanted eggs, you got eggs. Here there were hundreds of kinds of breads, hundreds of kinds of meat. And when you walked outside, people were wearing hundreds of kinds of shoes and hats, driving hundreds of kinds of cars.

I would like to say that I quickly grew sophisticated in America. But the truth is far different. When I first walked into my uncle George's house, which, like his brother Larry's, was also in Flushing, Queens, it must have been around dinnertime one night, and the television was tuned to the news. In those days, the television sets were huge—six feet long or so—and most of the piece was furniture, because it was the centerpiece of the room; it was considered bad taste just to have a TV screen. So here I come, fresh off the plane, and there's a close-up of a man's face on the screen reading the news. I actually went around behind the furniture to see where the guy was. That was my first impression of television, which later bloomed into a full-fledged love affair. But at the time, it was just another thing that I didn't really understand.

The refrigerator was another source of amazement for me. I opened it up and found these huge bottles of soda, and I didn't even have a word for them yet. (I called them *gazoz,* the Hebrew word for soda.) Then there was Bosco chocolate syrup, which I used to squirt directly into my mouth, and ketchup, which I loved so much that I used to make ketchup sandwiches. My cousins would just sit at the table and watch me eat, because of the combinations of food that I would invent. Wonder Bread was like cake to me. We would sit down to dinner, and I'd just start eating slice after slice of Wonder Bread. And my aunt and my mom would say, "No, no, you have to eat right." And I would think, "Eat right? What's wrong with this?"

That first year, my life changed, and changed again. My uncle Larry had two daughters, and they were older than I was, and though they were kind to me, they viewed me as a curiosity. One of my cousins, Eva, let me ride her bicycle, which I thought was a gift from heaven. I rode it around the block what must have been a hundred times. A native-born American kid would have just crossed the street, but I had never crossed the street before, and there were cars going by, and I didn't know what to do. In Israel we didn't have stop signs, red lights, or green lights, at least not where I lived. So I kept going around the block. I didn't feel limited, though. It was fantastic just to ride around and around the block.

Then one day I saw two kids on the other side playing marbles. Up until then I hadn't had much interaction with other kids, because I would start talking to them, and pretty soon I would get this strange look and this series of questions, "What? Are you stupid? Can't you speak English?" And I couldn't. I could barely understand anything. But these kids playing marbles intrigued me, because I had four or five marbles that my cousins let me have, and I also had skills—back in Israel I had been very adept at playing marbles. And the Israeli style of playing marbles was different: in America you used your thumb as the aiming mechanism, but in Israel you played standing up. I knew that I could hit a marble standing up, from maybe four or five feet away. These guys saw me coming across the street and knew that I was a rube, and they tried to take my marbles away. They explained the rules, and I quickly understood that there was a circle, and anything you hit out of the circle with your marble was yours. If your marble stayed in there, you lost your turn. By the end of the day, I won all their marbles, well over a hundred. I've still got all those marbles saved in the same Dutch Masters cigar box that my aunt Magda gave me. Those kids didn't think I was stupid in the end.

I loved being with my uncles. My uncle Larry was a baker. He made cakes, so he was my hero. One of his best, and one of my favorites, was this amazing poppyseed cake. And my uncle George was a prosthodontist. He made teeth for people who wore false teeth. He also made fake testicles for people who had lost their own. I'm not making that up. Both Larry and George worked hard and made good livings, and they were very generous to my mother and me. Still, about a year after we came to America, my mother decided that she needed to strike out on her own, rather than stay with her brother. My uncle Larry was happy to have us, but we were living in the basement, and she wanted to go to work and make her own way. So within a year, she put me into a Hasidic yeshiva—the Jewish equivalent of a theological seminary—in Williamsburg, Brooklyn, while she worked at a button and buttonhole factory. The factory was nonunion, a sweatshop, and she made a penny for every button that she sewed onto a coat. She was making about $150 a week, which was a lot of money at that time, and an awful lot of buttons. She had to lift the coat, sew on one button, and then the next, and then lift each completed coat and hang it on a hanger. It was seven until seven, six days a week, of back-breaking work.

While my mother was at the button factory, I was staying with a family in Williamsburg, the Schainers. They were part of the Hasidic Jewish support system, people in the community who accepted boarders to give kids a chance to go to yeshiva. They didn't have any kids of their own; they were an older couple, or seemed older, although they were probably in their forties. They were very kind to me, and I remember seeing the first private telephone in someone's house. It was another wondrous sight.

My schedule was grueling. It wasn't the button factory, of course, but at seven o'clock in the morning, wearing a yarmulke and dressed in black, I started in on a very thorough Jewish religious schooling. The first half of the day was spent on the Old Testament, Torah studies, and Bible stories. Then we had a half-hour break, and by twelve-thirty we were back in school for fundamental academics: reading, writing, arithmetic, and so on. At six, when we were already tired from the school day, we would move from one building—at 206 Wilson Street in Williamsburg—to another building, at South Third Street and Bedford Avenue, and gather for a group meal. Then after the meal, we would have more class, evening Bible study, until nine-thirty. Then when I would go home to the Schainers, I would have homework. This was six days a week, not five. On Saturdays we were expected to go to temple, both in the morning and in the evening. With this kind of schedule, one thing was for certain: you were never going to get into trouble. I lived in a poor area, but it was a happy neighborhood. We didn't know any better.

Slowly I learned how to get around in this new world, and I

learned to speak English, which wasn't always easy. One of my early language lessons was with the phrase *Come here*. I thought it meant "Come here," but what I didn't realize was that there were two different phrases. One was *Come here,* and that meant "Come here." The other was *C'mere,* and that meant "I'm going to kick your ass." Originally, with my extremely limited English, I wore a name tag with my address, saying, "Please point me in the direction of this address." Even when I was able to get by, after about a year, I still sounded like Latka, Andy Kaufman's character from *Taxi*. I would say, "What time it is?" instead of "What time is it?" and I had a very thick accent. I remember other kids constantly making fun of me. "What's the matter?" they would say. "Are you stupid? Can't you even speak English?" That always struck me as bizarre. I always knew the difference between being stupid and simply not being able to speak a language. It's okay, though. Later on in life, they would all work for me.

◆ ◆ ◆

America was many things to me. It was a new language. It was new family. It was economic opportunity. But above all, it was entertainment: television, comic books, and the movies. Kids who grew up during the fifties say that they were raised by television, and sometimes they say it in this self-pitying tone, like they missed out on something. For me, it was the best experience I ever had.

That first summer, out in Queens, was all about television. All the other kids wanted to go out and play baseball. I didn't care about baseball. Once I discovered television, why would I ever want to leave home? It was free, and there were endless, endless shows, and they weren't confined to the Earth. There was *Planet Patrol,* which went into outer space, and *The Vikings,* and *Superman.* All those images are indelibly etched in my mind forever. And magically, I started to speak English with a Walter Cronkite flavor to my accent.

Television led naturally to movies. When I did get a chance to go, I went to a theater in Williamsburg, in Brooklyn, where for twenty-five cents I got to see three movies and cartoons. The theater was right under the elevated subway, and when I first started to go to yeshiva, I remember wanting to go to the movies so much. I had never been inside a movie theater in my life. In Israel they set up benches and a screen outside, and we watched at night. So one day I just stood outside the theater, looking at the poster on the wall. There was a John Wayne movie—there were always John Wayne movies—and *Gorgo* was playing. That was a *Godzilla* rip-off. At ten A.M. in the morning, there I was, waiting for people to start going in. Eventually the theater owner came by, and a truck delivered the film canisters. The owner took one look at me and said, "If you carry this all the way up to the projection booth, I'll let you come in, and you can have popcorn."

The film must have weighed as much as I did. The canisters felt like a body bag. But I carried them up, all the way up, one step at a time, with both hands. I remember thinking my hands were going to fall off, because I'd never lifted anything so heavy. But I got it done, and the rest of that day I was the king. I sat all the way up in the top tier and ate popcorn until I almost threw up. It was one of the most amazing days of my life.

Television had the same effect, except it was easier because it was free and at home. At first it didn't matter what I watched. It was all America. Over time I developed favorites based on costumes, and the bolder they were, the better. On television I never missed *Superman*. I'd watch *The Mickey Mouse Club,* but I didn't like the girls on the show. They did girl things. They danced around and cooed and couldn't run as fast as the guys, and the guys would always have to watch out for them, and they would just get in the way. The guys did Spin and Marty stuff. They were adventurers. I do remember watching *The Vikings* on television, which was a series based on the movie, I suppose. I remember Jet Jackson, this guy with a big fast jet. And I remember the cartoons, especially the Warner Bros. cartoons. I enjoyed *Tom and Jerry,* but there was never a sophisticated story line, only the chase. Although they were beautifully drawn and the gags were funny, the different levels that Bugs and Daffy worked on were astonishing. There were a lot of in-jokes, double entendres, sexual innuendos. Bugs Bunny dressing up as a woman, marrying Elmer Fudd. It was just the most outrageous stuff. Many years later, after home videotaping became popular, I used to tape Saturday morning cartoons and watch them over and over again. Even if I had company at the house—other musicians, actors, celebrities—I was intent on watching these cartoons. People didn't understand my obsession, but then a few years after that everyone acknowledged these cartoons as seminal works of postwar American art. But I always knew they were.

◆ ◆ ◆

Overall I was drawn to anything with adventure, anything that would let me go to new places and do bold things and save the world. Pretty soon I started to have a love for science fiction and fantasy films. *Gorgo,* the *Godzilla* rip-off I saw in Williamsburg, was only the beginning. I loved *Conga,* which was a rip-off of *King Kong.* I loved *The Crawling Eye,* which was an English film with this hideous octopus-looking thing with one eyeball in the middle of its head. That scared the pants off me.

The third ingredient in this new consciousness was comic books. One day during one of the half-hour play periods at 206 Wilson, I saw my first comic books. They were *Superman* and *Batman* comics, and I was hooked. I knew Superman from TV, but I had no idea who this Batman was. But the other kids all seemed to. I went down the street to the house of one of the other yeshiva kids, and he had a pile of comics, not just superheroes but *Challengers of the Unknown* and *House of Mystery* and many more. I would read and reread them, and they took me far away from where I was.

Meanwhile all around me society was changing and shifting. This was at the very beginning of the civil rights era, and if there were signs of progress, there were also persistent signs of unrest. After a year in the yeshiva, my mother and I moved from Brooklyn back to Queens, to Jackson Heights, where I attended a public school on Junction Boulevard and Ninety-third Street. That marked another chapter in my American education, because it was my first contact with black kids. In fact, my two best friends were black, because they were the tall guys, and they stood in the back of the line with me. The fact that they were black and I was white never dawned on me. It wasn't something that I had much experience with in Israel, and it wasn't emphasized around my house. But slowly I began to get the sense that there were racial lines drawn between people.

I remember going to one of the black kids' houses after school. His name was Walter, and he was my friend. His mother would fix us sandwiches, and we would play games. As darkness came, his mother would reappear in the room and remind me that it was time to go home. I had another black friend named Alfred, and some afternoons he would lend me a second bicycle, and we would go riding around near LaGuardia Airport. As we headed for home, we would get close to Junction Boulevard, and he would say, "Well, you better not come bike riding in there, it's not safe." I didn't understand, even after he explained it to me. I was very naïve at that time, even willfully so, because I was not a street kid. I was a television kid. I lived in the world of *Superman* and *The Twilight Zone*.

One of my best friends in Newtown High School was black, and he and I would hang out after school and sing doo-wop. Two or three of us would get together and harmonize—nothing fancy, just a chance to sing. And after Martin Luther King was shot, he showed me a small ax he had hidden in his shirt and told me that maybe he and I shouldn't hang out with each other, because his friends were really angry. But I remember feeling scared, telling him that I was sorry about what had happened, and that I didn't have anything to do with it. He said, "Yeah, but my friends don't understand. They're really angry." That was the end of our friendship. Educated Jews, well-read Jews, were very interested in the civil rights movement, because they saw the parallels between the way the blacks were treated in America and the way the Jews had been treated throughout history—we had been slaves in Egypt and they were slaves in America. But an intellectual and emotional interest in social conditions didn't always translate to the street.

◆ ◆ ◆

However complicated the social conditions of mid-1960s America were—and they were very complicated—I could always lose myself in television. Not that I watched indiscriminately. At the time, live TV did nothing for me. There were variety shows that my mother would watch, but they didn't interest me. The camera stood still, which was a pretty severe technical limitation, and as a result you couldn't really be swept away. A still setup with a guy talking and the camera standing still? I'm snoring. But the one thing that did interest me was the fact that on some of these shows, girls would scream for the performers. I hadn't put it all together yet—the girls on *The Mickey Mouse Club* who always seemed to be wasting the boys' time, people screaming on TV. But it felt like something major.

Then one day I was looking out of the window at 99 South Ninth Street in Brooklyn. I was twelve years old, probably. And I saw a Spanish girl jumping rope. She had long black hair that hung down past her waist. It was straight and it shone like vinyl, and every time she jumped, the hair would slap against her backside. I didn't see that girl's face. I have yet to see her face. But that was the first time I had this odd tingly feeling, and over the next few months, as it happened over and over again, I figured out that something strange was going on, in my mind and in my body. It's almost like when you're developing a cold. My muscles started to ache, and I started to feel bizarre, like I'd never felt in my life. Different parts of my body got engorged, and I started growing hair in places where I didn't have hair before, and I got scared. I would run to the bathroom with scissors and try to cut the hair off. I couldn't speak of those things to my mother: *I'm feeling weird, there's this girl I like, and I'm starting to grow hair between my legs. Oh, my God, the world is ending.*

Gradually, I started to see all this as a good thing. My mother and I would watch *The Ed Sullivan Show* on Sunday nights—that's when she was home—and every once in a while we would see a teen idol on the show, Bobby Rydell or somebody like that. And we'd hear the girls in the audience scream. When I was ten or eleven, that didn't make any sense to me. When I was twelve, even though I still thought it was bizarre, I liked it. It struck me that these teen idols had a kind of power over these screaming girls, and also that there was something extremely pleasurable about watching these girls lose control. Still, it was a very respectable kind of screaming, almost subdued. Just a year and a half later, when I was a bit older, I would be watching *Ed Sullivan* again. But the screaming wouldn't be quite so subdued. And onstage there wouldn't be a single teen idol with slicked-back hair but four teen idols with shaggy hair and funny accents. When I saw that, I understood everything about the world in a flash.

I was oblivious to Elvis. I never saw him on television, so in some sense he didn't really exist for me, and while I was vaguely aware of him as a recording artist, I didn't think much of him. He was just another one of those guys who sang, and besides "Hound Dog" and "Jailhouse Rock," it really wasn't the kind of music that I was interested in. It was crooning, and it was too smooth. So when Elvis appeared on *Ed Sullivan*, wriggling his pelvis, it wasn't a major turning point for me. But then in 1964, my mother and I were sitting around one Sunday night, in the middle of our usual ritual: dinner and *Ed Sullivan*. I was eating homemade hamburgers that my

crazy crazy nights: the beatles

Here I am making time as a teenager.

mother used to make, and peas. I wasn't a fan of most vegetables, but I didn't mind peas, so she must have just loaded me up with them whenever she could. So there I was, with the hamburger, the peas, and Ed Sullivan, and Sullivan started saying, "Ladies and gentlemen, tonight on our show, we have the Beatles."

I didn't know what he was talking about. Cockroaches? Bugs? Was this one of those novelty acts that sometimes came on the show, like a flea circus? Then they came onstage, and the entire Beatles phenomenon just hit me like a ton of bricks, all at once, as hard as anything had ever hit me. They had these haircuts that at the time I

the sixties and
1964~1969

The Long Island Sounds in 1965. Stan Singer is on drums and Stephen Coronel is playing guitar on the right.

thought were silly. *Oh my God,* I thought. *They're dressed like girls.* That was my first thought. My second thought was that they looked like monkeys. (That was, apparently, a popular notion, because I think it's where the Monkees got their name.) Through two thoughts, I wasn't sold on the Beatles. But then my mother walked into the room, and she remarked on how ridiculous their appearance was, and at that point I did an abrupt about-face. I said, "No, Mom, I think they look cool." I liked the idea that I thought they were cool and my mother didn't. I liked the difference. I wanted there to be a difference. It was a form of rebellion. And at that moment, all the things I had wondered about for months started to make sense: these guys in these silly girl haircuts and the girls screaming for them at the top of their lungs. My first thoughts about pop music were born on that night, and they were simple thoughts: *If I go and start a band, maybe the girls will scream for me.* Don't let anyone tell you any different—that same impulse launched a thousand bands.

In fact, the first record I remember owning came very early, before the Beatles, before *Ed Sullivan* and everything else. On WOR-TV in New York, the twist was in full swing, and Chubby Checker had an afternoon TV show, sort of an instructional spot to teach kids how to do the dance. I remember being so fascinated by the whole phenomenon that I actually went out and bought a teen magazine that had capsule biographies of the big stars of the day. I found out that Chubby Checker's real name was Ernest Evans, that he was a chicken plucker, and that Dick Clark's wife had named him Chubby Checker after Fats Domino. I had never heard of Hank Ballard and the Midnighters, who originally did the song. I didn't know anything, really. But I started to twist and to participate in these twist contests.

Wednesday afternoons after school we all stayed for dance contests. I'd go up and dance with the black girls, because they knew how to shimmy and shake. The white girls talked too much and dressed too dowdy. The rest of the guys stayed off on one side. The white girls thought that was dangerous at first, but soon they too would come up and start dancing. I won the twist contest, and my prize was a Nat King Cole forty-five with "All Over the World" on one side and "Rambling Rose" on the other side. Initially, I wasn't that crazy about it. But eventually, I came to see the point, since music—not just the twist, not just Nat King Cole, but all music—was my entrée to the soft, milky thighs of girls. I would soon realize that music was the key that made girls welcome me with open arms and eventually open legs. This is the big secret of being in a rock and roll band. There are no messages, there's no inner being striving to express itself through music. We all picked up guitars because we all wanted to get laid. Plain and simple.

At first my dreams weren't grand. I didn't think about conquering the world of girls—I thought about improving my standing with the girls down the block. How do you get noticed by the girls down the block? Simple. You play in a band that plays the school dance. So I put together a band with two friends from school, Danny Haber and Seth Dogramajian, both of whom have unfortunately passed on. We went to school together at Joseph Pulitzer Middle School in Queens, New York, and we were all close friends, because we were all obsessed with comic books. Seth and I used to publish amateur fanzines about comic books and science fiction. We would write articles, review movies, and talk about characters from television shows. His fanzine was called *Exile;* mine was called *Cosmos.* But after the Beatles, it became clear to us that, as much as we loved science fiction, it wasn't going to get us where we wanted to go with the girls. So we formed a band called the Lynx. I didn't even think about how to spell it, but I had the animal in mind. At school, when we performed at a talent show, we were introduced as the Missing Links, which of course changed the spelling. The first two songs we did were "There's a Place" by the Beatles and "Cathy's Clown" by the Everly Brothers. We picked them for their three-part harmonies, because all of us wanted to sing. Danny and Seth played guitar, and I just stood there singing. I hadn't picked up the bass yet. I'd like to say I was the front man, but the truth was that it was a three-man band.

Somehow the Missing Links won the talent show. We loved being onstage and having everyone watch us. When it came to being the center of attention, we were naturals. After that talent show, a couple of things happened. First of all, I started to have friends, many of them people whose names I didn't even know. Guys would walk up to me in the hall or on the street and say, "How you doing, Gene? What's up?" Also, all of a sudden I started getting into trouble in class. Up until then I was a pretty good student, pretty well behaved. Even though I was always the tallest guy in class, I was never in any fights, never got sent down to detention. After the Missing Links won the talent show, though, I started to get the evil eye from teachers, because girls were turning around during class and asking me questions. There was one girl named Stella, and she was in Mrs. Cassola's class with me. During class one day she turned around and said, "Hey, Gene, will you show us that weird thing you do with your tongue?" I didn't know what she meant at first. It must have been something she saw me do at recess. But gradually I got the idea that she wanted me to stick out my tongue and wiggle it around. The second I did that, they started giggling, and the teacher came right over. "Gene Klein," she said, "did you stick out your tongue?"

"Yeah," I said, "but the girls asked me to do it."

"Go to the principal's office," she said. As far as I was concerned, I was being railroaded. Stella had asked me to stick my tongue out, so I stuck it out. But I realized that the teacher thought it was something sexual, because her face turned red.

When you have a band and then you get in a little trouble, your reputation soars. Even the tough kids in school started giving me respect, although it was an odd sort of respect. This one guy named Danny was a weightlifter. He was huge and looked sort of like Harvey Keitel; he must have been older than the rest of us. He always had his troops around him, and he would walk down the hall pushing everyone else out of the way. For some reason he never picked on me, and I'm certain the reason was the Missing Links and this small but persistent bit of local fame I had stumbled into. The closest he ever got to beating me up was to call me Doof. That was okay with me, since I didn't even know what the word meant. But he never laid a hand on me, and he even offered to protect me—"If anyone else ever lays a hand on you, you let me know, all right?"

You'd think I would have used the opportunity to start hanging out with the guys, get a little gang of my own. But I wasn't interested. I just wanted to get back to my beloved television.

After school everybody else would hang out in the schoolyard and smoke cigarettes and get into trouble. I'd run home, turn on the television set, and do my homework, and I was set. I was back doing what I loved. In fact, not only did I not hang out after school, but I hardly ever had visitors come over to my house, because when they did come over, I'd ignore them and just watch TV. My house was not a fun place to go to; all I had were comic books and science fiction and fantasy magazines. The other guys were interested in bikes and baseball bats and going outside and doing sporty things. They were chewing gum and spitting, and they'd start talking in hushed tones about Mickey Mantle, and I tried, maybe for a little while, but I found that I just couldn't care at all. Mickey Mantle next to Superman? Hands down, Superman. Are you kidding? Mickey Mantle couldn't fly.

Tuesdays and Thursdays were the most exciting days of the week, because that's when the new comic books came into the candy store, and I'd be there as soon as I could. The store owner knew me by name, and he would tell me what was coming up and ask if he should save me a copy: *Fantastic Four, Thor,* and all of those movie magazines, like *Famous Monsters of Filmland.* Soon I had a stack of comics and magazines higher than me. In fact, my comics collection became the basis for

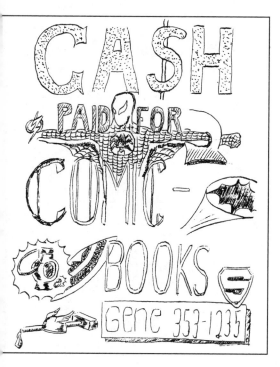

Even at a young age, I had entrepreneurial tendencies. I was able to make a lot of money buying other people's comic books and finding ones I could resell.

my next business. My mother had gotten me a mimeograph machine, which I used to publish these science fiction and fantasy fanzines, and soon it occurred to me that I could use the same machine to make some money. I started printing up fliers that said "Willing to Buy Comic Books" with my phone number on them. I had a set price: a dollar a pound, and that meant that I would get between fifty and a hundred comic books for a dollar. The people who were selling to me didn't have the expertise or the energy to go through the collections themselves, so I would look through thousands of issues, and usually I would find one or two books that were genuine collectibles. One collector's comic book could fetch me a hundred bucks.

✦ ✦ ✦

Despite the fact that I spent my afternoons and evenings in front of the television and with my nose buried in comic books, my music career started to take on a life of its own. Seth and I eventually brought in another guy, whose name was Stephen Coronel. I had known Steve for years, and he ended up being in a number of bands with me, including Wicked Lester, which was a precursor to KISS. This was around 1965, and the four of us, along with a drummer named Stan Singer, began to play more than just the

Fantasy News was a fan magazine done by someone I knew. I drew the artwork for the cover.

school dances. Even though we existed largely because of the Beatles and in the wake of the Beatles, we didn't play a single Beatles song. They were much too complex. Instead, we tried our hand at some soul standards, like "In the Midnight Hour" and "La Bamba" and anything else that was easy to play. The lesson I had learned with the Missing Links, I learned again and again. It's great to be a guy in a band.

Then just before I turned fourteen, everything changed again. This time, it wasn't music, and it wasn't girls. It was women, and it was a whole different thing. I had a paper delivery route in Jackson Heights, Queens, where I would throw papers to people's doors every morning, and then once a week I had to collect the subscription money from customers. Around Christmas I was going from house to house, getting payments, getting some tips. One customer was an older woman. In retrospect, she must have been in her early twenties, but to me she was a grown-up, and she was on the other side of the line: kids over here, grown-ups over there. Because she was a grown-up, I was mostly oblivious to her, but not totally oblivious, because I remember thinking to myself that she was attractive. Anyway, before the Christmas holiday, I went to collect the money, and she answered the door dressed in one of those frilly nightgowns and crying. I tried to leave. I said, "I'll come back later." She insisted that I come inside, and she started talking a mile a minute about her husband, and how he was away, and how she was lonely. She was clearly drunk.

She kept saying she would get my money for me in a second, but plenty of seconds went by and she didn't make any attempt to get me my money. And then everything happened in a flash. All of a sudden, I was down on the couch and she was on top of me. I don't even remember, to this day, how my pants came off. I wasn't exactly a Casanova: I had my hands up near my shoulders, with my palms out like I was trying to stop an oncoming car, and all of a sudden it was over. Then she gave me a tip and I left.

I was terrified, both during and after. Whenever I saw her again—and I saw her many times, because she was still on my paper route, not having had the good sense to move away after this episode—I would take her money and run. There was no one I could talk to about it, really. Sexual discussions with my mother were off-limits. I did eventually mention it to one of the guys at school, another self-styled rebel. And he must have talked it around, because soon everybody seemed to know. In the schoolyard, the girls would point, and I acquired some additional celebrity to go along with my band celebrity, because I had *done it*.

I was oblivious, for the first thirteen years of my life, that I was endowed with a large oral appendage, my superlong tongue. It really was longer than everyone else's, and I was soon to find out that having a long tongue came in handy with the girls.

One of the girls who seemed to like me was named Connie. She was Italian Catholic and she kept asking me to walk her home. I thought she simply wanted to be my girlfriend, but in retrospect it is clear that she had carnal intentions. One day when we were walking home after school, she explained to me what girls were like. I was stunned and fascinated. "You want me to put what? Where?"

She explained that she couldn't get pregnant that way. When I escorted her to the entrance of her apartment complex, she led me downstairs to the basement where the laundry room was. It was dark and empty. We were alone. She lowered herself to the floor and pulled me on top of her. Between passionate kisses, she hiked up her dress, lowered her panties, put her right hand behind my head, and gently pushed me down, between her thighs.

I was scared. I had heard stories, especially from the Italian guys on the school grounds. "Hey, you crazy or sumthin? You put your face down there? You're gonna get sick!"

She immediately started moaning and I became aroused like I never had. I thought she wanted me to kiss her there. I did. It sent her into further ecstasy. And then, as if a sign from heaven told me everything I needed to know, I heard a voice plead, "Oh, Gene, your tongue, give me your tongue!" I did. No sooner did I make contact with her than she went into violent convulsions, wrapped both of her hands behind my head, and rammed her pelvis into my face. She squirmed her entire body and used my tongue like a hot knife through butter.

Although the entire event sticks in my mind as having lasted a long time, it probably only took her thirty seconds to achieve orgasm. This was my baptism by fire. I owned her. She lay there on the basement floor in complete surrender. For the rest of my life, I would remember that early encounter and what I could do with my tongue.

But it wasn't over, not yet. A few moments passed and we talked a little as I lay beside her. While I was in midsentence, she reached over and put her right hand between my legs. She raised herself up, undid my jeans and pulled them down, and immediately wrapped her mouth around me. Though I was barely conscious, I noticed that she held me with her left hand and was manipulating herself with the right.

Sadly, this was to be the only encounter between us. She soon moved away. And if she reads this, I hope she remembers it fondly. I certainly do. I started having off-the-cuff conversations in school about my encounter. When I told one of the guys about it and stuck my tongue out to show him what I had done with it, he remarked how goddamned long it was.

I never knew. I never thought it mattered. But when I started showing girls my length, they were clearly impressed.

The tongue incident ushered in a whole new era in my love life. I had only just turned fourteen, but since I was tall, I kept being invited to Sweet Sixteen parties, even though I was a little younger. There were all these girls whose names I still remember, Belinda and Irene and Barbara and Andrea. They were the cool girls, the ones the guys wanted to go out with at night, and for some reason they wanted me at their parties. Those parties were filled with the kinds of things I had never seen before: turning down the lights and playing records and spin the bottle. There was also slow dancing. Irene, I think, was the first girl who picked me to dance; it was ladies' choice, and we were moving together, and the lights were down, and everybody started kissing. Then all of a sudden she stuck her tongue in my mouth. I thought I was going to throw up or drop dead. And then while she was sticking her tongue in my mouth, she took my hands and moved them down below her waist. I had a queasy feeling, that same tingly feeling I had from the girl jumping rope, but stronger. Then I got the hang of it, and I stuck my tongue into her mouth, and all of a sudden she started moaning. Then the song ended. We parted, then everybody went over to the table to have chips.

While I was thinking over what had just happened, two other girls came up and asked me to dance. I didn't have a clue what was going on, but apparently word had gotten around that I knew what I was doing, and they wanted to try having me stick my tongue in their mouths, too. The seeds of what would later be KISS were all planted during this period: television, the Beatles, superheroes, science fiction, girls. Everything about America was coalescing in my mind.

Being in a band also opened up certain social situations. For example, I didn't know what a country club was—we were still relatively poor. But in the summer my next band, the Long Island Sounds, got invited to play at various country clubs around the area. We walked into these places, and we were amazed. Everyone there was being served. They had drinks that they took with them into the swimming pool. They drove nice cars.

After one of the dances, a girl invited me to come back the following Saturday for a swim date. I came back happily, and the two of us went swimming, which was really just an excuse for making out in the pool: our heads were above water, but our bodies were under water, and we were hugging and necking and kissing. Her parents were nearby, but they couldn't see us or pretended that they couldn't. I must have been nervous, because in the middle of this, I felt as though I had to let out some gas. In fact, a major amount of gas. I thought I was pretty sophisticated, and that I could do it so that it would come out silent—in class, at least, I never let a raspberry go full steam; I finagled the cheeks left and right and kind of squirmed for the sake of subtlety. In the pool, I figured that it was even easier, but for some reason logic escaped me, and it didn't occur to me that the gas would rise. All of a sudden, like the Creature from the Black Lagoon, the water started bubbling, there was a huge noise, and the beast emerged. The girl untangled herself from me and swam away. I never saw her again.

Cosmos Stiletto, which I edited and published, was the merger of two magazines, *Cosmos* and *Stiletto.* My friend Stephen Coronel did the artwork for this issue, #11.

◆ ◆ ◆

When I wasn't in New York, I was in New Jersey. By that I mean that during the summers my mother sent me off to summer camp. She had started doing better and had managed to save a bit of money, and one summer she announced that I was going off to Surprise Lake Camp. The big surprise at Surprise Lake was that there was no lake, just this little pond. I stayed there for three weeks, which seemed like an eternity, mainly because there was no television. I thought it was a prison. To me, it was like yeshiva again, where everybody ate communally, where you had to line up just to get something else to drink. The last thing I wanted to do was hike, and the second to last thing was play sports. One day I left the campground and went into the nearest town, which was Monticello, I think, and I bought a *Fantastic Four* comic book. That was my support network for the rest of the summer; I kept rereading it and rereading it. Eventually, I learned to make do with the camp's arts and crafts program, because they had a mimeograph machine, and I learned how to publish a newspaper.

I also sang in the camp talent show, which would have been pleasant if it weren't for the fact that it was the site of one of the most horrific things that ever happened to me. Those summer camp talent shows are all the same. Someone tap-dances. Someone else juggles. A group of people form a choir. I had some kind of singing group, and we were onstage, and since it was the middle of summer the bugs were everywhere, more so because there were spotlights onstage. Right at my moment in the show, the rest of the stage went black, and I was in the spotlight by myself. I opened my mouth to take a deep breath, and I swallowed a giant moth that died violently, squirming all the way down my throat. I couldn't wait to get back to my bunk and read the *Fantastic Four* comic book again.

Camp was the first place I became aware that the world also has homosexuals. There were public latrines, where everybody would line up and then do their business. There were no walls between the boys, just this trough. Next to me was a guy who I think might have been my age. He kept looking over at me, and at my member, and asking what bunk I was in, and commenting on this and that, and asking me if I wanted to come over to his bunk. I said, "Do you have any comic books?" This took him aback a bit. He didn't have comic books, he said, but he was there. "Well," I said, "I don't want to go if you don't like comic books. Unless you know where I can get some TV?" This totally threw him. TV? Why? "Because I want to watch *Superman*," I said. This was a classic example of miscommunication: he was trying to pick me up, and I was trying to watch TV and read *The Fantastic Four*.

✦ ✦ ✦

Even though I was playing music at home and at camp, in Queens and all around Long Island, it didn't occur to me that I might be able to make a career out of being in a rock band. I had always worked, making deliveries or in the butcher store, and I saved like a madman. I never spent a dime on anything. I took great pride in the wad of cash I had accumulated. So I was never afraid of finding a job or making money. I knew how to do that. But as the band began to take up more of my time, it seemed like I might be able to find some way to make a go of it professionally. To make sure I didn't do anything stupid, Mom agreed to let me pursue my band, or whatever else I wanted, as long as I had something to fall back on. She told me that I would need to go to college and get some kind of degree, in case my other plans didn't work out. It never occurred to me to challenge this condition. My mother's approval was extremely important. She was the reason I never smoked or drank or got high—not when I was a teenager, not to this day. Because of her horrible experiences in the concentration camps of Europe, I was always very clear on the fact that I didn't have the right to break her heart. She had suffered enough. As a result, I'd always try really hard in whatever I did to never embarrass her or in any other way hurt her. She gave me life. The least I could do to repay her was to give her happiness.

I could have gone to school downstate or stayed in the city, but all my life I had grown up surrounded by Jews and the Jewish experience. On television I saw a much broader and more diverse world, with blacks and Christians who were from different places and spoke differently and wore different clothes. Up until that point, I hadn't been out of Israel and New York, except for my brief trips to summer camp, and everyone there was Jewish, too. The few experiences I had had with other kinds of people, like the black friends I had in sixth grade, were all positive experiences, and I wanted to explore them some more after I graduated from high

flaming youth: my college years 1970~1972

school. I packed up and went upstate to South Fallsberg, New York, where I attended Sullivan County Community College.

When I got to Sullivan County, I made sure that both my roommates there were black. My mother was scared something would happen to me, not because they were black, exactly, but because she had lived through the Holocaust, where she had almost been wiped off the face of the Earth. Anyone from the outside was a threat to her. She tried to strong-arm me; she said that if I didn't move out, she would disown me. Eventually she came upstate, and we had a heart-to-heart conversation. "Mom," I said, "I know you love me. I know you're trying to protect me and do what's best for me. But I have to try to figure this out on my own." It wasn't easy for her, but she let me go my own way. Once I was there at college, I tried to confront my own racism, or what there might be of it, by seeing whether I could live with these two guys. Were they any different just because they were black? The three of us got along fine. We played records for each other, we hung out together, and we ate together. There was a difference culturally. Some of it was in the speech; I couldn't quite understand some of the patois, and some of their cool references were completely alien to me. One of the guys' friends actually made money, he said, by being a gigolo. This seemed bizarre to me. Women paying for men?

South Fallsberg was a tiny community. The entire town had ten streets in all, and the school was the center. Primarily it was a hotel and culinary school, where people came from all over the world to learn to cook and run restaurant kitchens. I went up there to get a liberal arts education and to get away from my Jewish roots. I ended up smack-dab in the middle of the Jewish mountains—the Catskills.

WHY I WEAR A YAMUIKA AT HOME —
BUT FEEL EMBARRASSED WEARING
IT IN GRAND CENTRAL STATION —
SOME THOUGHTS -

WAKING UP IN THE MORNING — AT least MY EYES OPEN TO THE SOUND OF THAT PIERCING ALARM CLOCK — DAMN, DOES IT HAVE TO BE SO SHRILL? IT FORCES ME OUT OF BED — IF ONLY TO TURN IT OFF... I'M TEMPTED TO GO BACK AND SLEEP FOR ANOTHER 10 MINUTES, BUT I THINK OF SCHOOL AND GETTING THERE ON TIME... (SOMETHING I LEARNED WELL IN HIGH SCHOOL — PROBABLY WOULD'VE GOTTEN AN "A"___)
IT'S 6 IN THE MORNING AND IT'S DARK — LIVING IN QUEENS HAS ITS DISADVANTAGES IF THE SCHOOL IS IN STATEN ISLAND... AFTER FINISHING BREAKFAST THE USUAL IN THE JOHN (CONSISTING MOST MORNINGS OF 1. PISSING — USUALLY LASTING A MINUTE? 2. BRUSHING TEETH AND 3. ASSORTED MOVEMENTS, LIKE COMBING MY HAIR) I SAT DOWN TO A BREAKFAST OF CHOCOLATE DOUGHNUTS AND MILK —

CLARIFICATIONS—   1
MY MERITS, ENCOMPASS THOSE THINGS WHICH SEEM IMPORTANT TO ME BUT WHICH ALSO, ADMITEDLY, OTHER PEOPLE CONSIDER IMPORTANT. THEY ENCOMPASS THOSE THINGS THAT I'VE BECOME ADEPT IN, IF AT LEAST FAMILIAR,
MUSIC COMES TO MIND BEFORE ANYTHING ELSE. I WRITE BOTH LYRICS AND MUSIC AND THEY ARE FINE EXAMPLES OF THE GENRE COMMONLY REFERRED TO AS 'ROCK'.
I PLAY BOTH THE SIX STRING GUITAR AND 4 STRING BASS — WELL ENOUGH TO PLAY WHAT I WRITE. THE RESULTS (E.G. ON STAGE) USUALLY PRODUCES APPLAUSE OR VOCAL NOISES EXPRESSING BASICALLY THE SAME SENTIMENTS.
I AM, FOR ALL INTENTS AND PURPOSES, A TRIVIA EXPERT. THE EXPERTISE IS LIMITED TO HORROR MOVIES, COMIC BOOKS (OF THE SUPER HERO VARIETY) AND RECORDS —
I AM ALSO QUITE A TYPIST — ABLE TO REACH (TALL BUILDINGS WITH A SINGLE BOUND) A SPEED OF CLOSE TO 90 WORDS PER MINUTE.

Some musings from when I was going to school in Staten Island.

I wound up being a lifeguard at the Pines Hotel during the summer. I had learned to swim and gotten my swimming credentials at Surprise Lake. When I then took the test to become a lifeguard, the Pines Hotel hired me. That was the place where I had my first sexual escapades in which I actually took the bull by the horns. There was a black maid who cleaned all the rooms, including the rooms of the staff who worked at the hotel. We had these little rooms, just big enough to fit a bed and a sink in. One day I was leaving my room, and she was saying "Okay, are you ready? I need to clean up the room." As we brushed past each other, I got aroused and closed the door behind me. She didn't object. She was young enough but older than I was. I have always had respect for a clean room, never more so than that day.

Being a lifeguard was a job, and I assumed it was an easy job—in an Olympic-size swimming pool, you're never going to have to save anybody. Right? Wrong. One day I was sitting by the pool, watching over the place, and this classic Jewish couple came along—she about three hundred pounds, he about a hundred pounds, she torturing him verbally, he barely alive. To me, they might as well have been a hundred years old, although they were probably in their forties. She decided to take a dip. All the way in, walking toward the pool, she was talking her head off to him, talking, talking, talking. He wasn't even looking at her; I'm sure he had heard it all before, a million times. She dove into the deep end of the pool—and promptly sank to the bottom. I looked up at him, thinking, *Please God, make him dive in and get his wife.* But he didn't move a muscle. Nothing. I had to jump up, get in there, get her up, and stick my hip under her, which is a kind of life-saving method. She was fighting me every step of the way. Even when I got her to the side of the pool and tried to hoist her up, I thought, *Okay, he's going to come over and help me hoist this three-hundred-pound whale up out of the pool.* But he did nothing. When she finally got up, with the help of other people, she went and lay down next to him on the recliner. She didn't look at him. She didn't verbally abuse him about not helping her. They both just stayed there quietly staring ahead. I thought it was the most bizarre thing I had ever seen. He didn't lift a finger to save her, and she didn't berate him for not saving her. That's marriage for you.

People had their young daughters with them, these horny Jewish girls who were coming up there to meet boys. During the weekends, I'd work at the hotel, and at night there would be Holiday Inn dances where AT&T telephone operators would come for the weekends. Once my friend Stephen Coronel came up to visit me on the weekend. We danced with girls and so on and got a room and picked up two girls and brought them back to the room. One of the girls fell asleep, and the other one was ready to be active with me, but I got engrossed in a movie. As I was watching it on the floor, Steve took my girl and started to do his business, finishing up what she had begun with me. I felt a little robbed of the experience and a little mad at Steve. But the next morning when we woke up and she was long gone, Stephen complained of a tingling sensation. He cockblocked me but caught the clap.

On campus the guys lived at the Green Acres Hotel, which was a run-down property that had too many vacancies to stay afloat on its own, so it let its rooms be taken over by the state university system. The girls lived at another hotel down the way. I romanced one girl who was quite a beauty. I have forgotten her name but not her face. One weekend I arranged for her to come over and meet me in my room. I had the habit of inviting more than one girl, thinking most girls wouldn't show up, and that if you asked more than one, the chances were good that one of them would show up. So in addition to this beautiful girl, I invited a girl named Nancy.

I took a shower at two o'clock. I got dressed. Three o'clock, which was the appointed hour, was drawing near. And there I was in my dorm apartment. I had my hot plate. I had my cans of beans. I had my Twinkies. I had all the things that were necessary to impress a girl when she came over to your room. The knock came at the door. I opened it, and it was the first girl. We didn't waste any time. My mattress was on the floor, and I took her down for the count. At some point, there was another knock on the door. I'm not sure that I heard it; even if I did, I wasn't about to answer it. My roommate opened up the door, and there was Nancy, the other girl. She was so shocked that she started running down the hallway crying. I jumped up, put on my pants, and ran after her, and I eventually cornered her in one of my other friends' rooms, where I apologized to her profusely. She came back. By that time, the other girl had gone, and Nancy's tears turned to passion. She stayed with me that night in my room, and I took her virginity.

She was, I think, the first girl whose virginity I ever took. They say this is a big moment for girls; for boys, it's slightly different. I don't remember anything more than just being excited by the moment and continually but softly trying to break through. I felt like a doctor with a scalpel, because that's how you had to be. Later that night I got up to go to the bathroom, flipped on the light, and almost had a heart attack, because there was blood all over the sheets. I wasn't prepared for that. I thought she was going to die. But I gave her a hot bath, and we stayed awake most of the night. The next day was a Sunday, and we basically just cuddled and watched TV. This initial drama turned into a relationship, and we would meet in the afternoons. She started thinking of me as her boyfriend, and I didn't do anything to discourage her. But I have to say that even when I was seeing her, I dillydallied. I took a theology class with an Episcopalian clergyman (I was a theology major) and one day his college-aged daughter came to visit him and attended his class. I was eyeing her throughout the session, and afterward I immediately cornered her and asked her how long she was visiting.

"Just for the week," she said.

"Do you want to meet me tonight?" I said.

That evening she picked me up in a truck. We drove out into the cornfields and had each other. But these were side projects. I still had an emotional urge to go back to my girlfriend, and so I did.

When summer came along, I decided to stay upstate instead of going home to New York City, and I started working at Zackarin Brothers, which was a hotel supplies warehouse. I was a gofer for the manager. I was still with Nancy, and she and I moved into an apartment right next door to Zackarin Brothers. We lived in the same apartment building as her best friend, Maria, and her boyfriend, who was a chef. Between all the cakes he baked and brought home every day and the food that Nancy made for me, I ballooned up to 220 pounds. My average day went something like this: wake up, eat some cake for breakfast, go next door to work, make some money, come home for lunch, repeat until satisfied. During the weekends I would play with my band, Bullfrog Beer. It was a great time. Around us things were in turmoil—the country was being torn apart at the seams. But I have to say that it didn't affect me too much. Vietnam wasn't a factor. I saw more of it on TV than I ever encountered in life. Every once in a while, the school would be closed, and people would be marching up and down the street. I never marched with them. I always wanted to go to school, because I had taken out a bank loan. I thought they were preventing me from going. Besides, I didn't feel that most of the marchers had it in their hearts politically. Protest was more of a social event, and most of the hippies were just rich white kids who didn't want to work for a living.

♦ ♦ ♦

College was a great experience. My musical career was coming along. My experience with women was proceeding to my liking. But when I got my associate bachelor's degree and my time at Sullivan County ended, I moved back down to New York City, back in with my mother, and then went to school at Richmond College in Staten Island, which was part of the New York City university system. I was finishing up my education, getting my degree, which was part of my deal with my mother. But in my heart, I was planning how to make it in a rock band.

When I first started to play in bands, we were following in the footsteps of a class of bands slightly older than us that had already made names for themselves. Billy Joel's first band, the Hassles, were already local heroes, and I was aware of them. I was aware of the Pigeons, who later became Vanilla Fudge. I was aware of Aesop's Fables and the Vagrants. In general, these bands were Guido mods, Italian versions of English bands. They had shag haircuts and thick New York accents and emulated the prevailing fashion, which was dictated by bands like the Who and the Kinks and the Faces. Imagine a guy named Tony trying to be Rod Stewart, and you'll understand that scene pretty well. For the most part, having a band was simply a tool for getting access to other things, mainly girls. Still, I was lucky in that I was in bands with friends who were obsessive record collectors. Stephen, for example, bought records like crazy, and he listened to everything from the Ventures, to obscure British invasion bands, to Mitch Ryder and the Detroit Wheels.

Around that time, in the middle of 1970, I met Paul Stanley. He wasn't Paul Stanley yet, but Stanley Eisen, and he was circulating around the New York rock scene at the same time I was, trying to make a name for himself as a guitarist and a songwriter. He had even played in a band with Stephen Coronel. We were on parallel tracks, and for a long time we operated independently of each other: I was playing in bands as a bassist. I had picked up the bass when playing for the Long Island Sounds in high school. Everyone else wanted to play guitar, so I thought it would be a good idea to play something different, set myself off from the rest. I was trying to get gigs and write songs, and he was trying to do the same. Our parallel tracks even intersected, although we didn't learn about it until much later. For example, at one point I came down from upstate because I needed to replace a guitarist for a band I had there, and I went to see Stephen Coronel in Washington Heights. There was another guy there named Stanley Eisen, and Steve told me that the two of them were putting together a band called Uncle Joe, with two guitar players and a drummer. At another point, after Wicked Lester was up and running, I placed an ad for a guitarist to play on some demo recordings. This same guy, Stanley Eisen, who would later become Paul Stanley, was one of the guitarists who answered that ad. I didn't make the connection, though.

Finally, the two of us met. Brooke Ostrander, Tony Zarella, Stephen Coronel, and I were starting to rehearse, and Paul walked in. Paul came from a traditional middle-class Jewish background. His family also lived in Queens, where his father worked for a furniture company. And while we obviously had quite a bit in common, there were also some key differences. Paul's parents were very well read, liberal, and assimilated, while my mother was cautious and not as well read. In some ways, Paul's family was more like the families of the cousins I stayed with when I came to the United States.

I'd like to say that Paul and I hit it off instantly, that a flash of inspiration passed between us, containing the seeds of what would eventually become the KISS empire. But the truth of the matter is that when we first met in upstate New York, Paul didn't like me at all. He thought I was abrasive. I think it had something to do with the fact that after we shook hands, I looked him straight in the face and said, "Oh, so you write songs? Let's hear them." I certainly made no attempt to be confrontational. But he got that impression. He got this expression on his face, like *Who does this guy think he is?*

Paul and I have known each other now for thirty years. He has been the brother I never had. So it's somewhat difficult to remember that first meeting. But I can see how my manner may have been a bit off-putting; my enthusiasm sometimes comes off as a kind of arrogance. And I can see why he might have perceived me that way: I didn't have a father, or a father figure, or a big brother, so the only one I was ever able to turn to for inspiration was myself—or, when I wasn't able to generate it, to Superman, or King Kong. In a lot of ways I was delusional, and still am. I am one of those few guys who can look in a mirror and believe I am better looking than I actually am. This has always been the case. As a result of this delusional self-confidence, when I got dumped by girls, it meant nothing. I would think, *She doesn't understand,* and go on to the next girl. Being relentless has its rewards. Every time I would succeed, I would think, *See, I'm right.*

What accounts for this? Perhaps it's because I was an only child. Perhaps it's a result of my mother always being there and always saying the things that parents are supposed to say. She had survived so much hardship in the concentration camps that when she had me, she spent every minute of her time telling me the things that children should hear. *You can be anything you want to be. You're better than everybody else. Don't let the people outside get to you.* When my mother would answer the phone and I was in the bathroom, it was, "The king can't come to the phone. He's on the throne." I guess you could say she spoiled me. While this was great for me, it wasn't always great for the people who met me. They didn't know what to take with a grain of salt and a sense of humor.

As I quickly learned after Paul joined Wicked Lester, he wasn't so different from me. Immediately, he started hanging out with the rest of us, trying to write songs and push us up the ladder of local bands. But there was some tension in the band, particularly between Paul and Steve. They didn't get along, and I couldn't understand why. One day at his house Steve turned around to Paul and said, "Who the hell do you think you are? Do you think you have some kind of aura around you?" And Paul said, "Yeah. I do think that I have an aura around me."

So call it whatever you want: ego, aura. I think you have to have a screw loose to do this—to be in the rock star business. Look at nature. Animals duck or flinch when they hear a noise. It's instinct. But there is always one animal that holds its ground and raises itself up to its full height. You see this with little dogs that bark at larger animals. Either this dog is out of its mind or it thinks it's a much bigger dog than it is. You think the dog is crazy, but you also admire it for being fearless. If you think about it, any normal person would be scared to death getting up onstage and being scrutinized by an audience. But that never fazed me. And Paul too was driven toward this same goal: he has always been the kind of person who, though he is very intelligent, has to feel passionately about something or he doesn't do it at all. He went to an arts magnet high school: he had to pass tests and show high achievement to be admitted. Then at college, after just a few months, he left. It wasn't his thing. He loved rock and roll. Either of us alone might have made it, or might have cracked under the strain of all the disappointment and rejection. The two of us together, though, were unstoppable.

None of this is to say that success was quick in coming. It wasn't. Our early gigs were nightmares: no crowds, no money. I remember one show at the Richmond College Armory. It was a dance, but nobody came. It rained nonstop and leaked through the roof. Paul caught the crabs from a dirty mattress on the floor. Another time we played a Jewish B'nai B'rith in New Jersey. We rented a milk truck and had to drive for hours just to be incidental music in the background while all these Jewish American princesses walked around showing off their new dresses. All I knew was that we were getting paid $150 and having a chance to pick up some of these girls during our breaks. That wasn't a great success, although I did manage to corner one girl, who started making out with me behind the curtains. But then Mom and Dad came and she had to leave. It was only five minutes, but I got a taste of her.

The early hardship produced at least one benefit: it made us focus on our songwriting, which we knew was the only thing that would advance us as a band. Wicked Lester was, by that point, an all-original band. That wasn't so common then; most bands were still doing R&B hits and Beatles covers, with maybe the occasional original thrown in. When we played, audiences would get into the music and then ask us what song it was. "Who did that?" they would say. When we said we did, they couldn't believe it.

◆ ◆ ◆

Before he died, Jimi Hendrix built a studio named Electric Lady, named for his Electric Ladyland album. It was located in downtown New York, and it was one of the most advanced studios in the world, with state-of-the-art equipment and an A-list clientele. Out in Queens somewhere, Paul had met a guy who worked in the studio. His name was Ron, and he told Paul to call him up at the studio and let him know when our band was playing. Paul did, but the guy never returned his calls. Frustrated, Paul put in a more aggressive call, told the secretary that he had been calling Ron, and that if Ron didn't call him back, his band was going to have to dissolve, and the blood would be on Ron's hands. As it turned out, the Ron that was getting all these messages wasn't the Ron that Paul had met at all, but rather Ron Johnson, who ran the studio. When we got him on the phone, we figured it was an opportunity we couldn't miss. "We have this band," we said, "and we're really good, and you should come down and see." He did, and he said that we had the most potential of any band he had seen, since Three Dog Night, which was a big deal at that time. At that point I was working at the Puerto

Rican Interagency Council by day and then going to work as a checkout guy at a deli on Fifteenth around Union Square.

Ron Johnson decided that he wanted to do some demos for Wicked Lester. But he wasn't quite ready for us. Paul and I hung out in the studio and did some session work. We sang background vocals on an album by Lynn Christopher and other people who actually were making records. We did demo work and got some real hands-on experience: we learned how to work a microphone and a multitrack recorder and so on. After a few months, Ron Johnson made good on his promise and started recording Wicked Lester with the hopes of shopping a demo to record labels. He liked our songs. He liked our look. He believed in us. Despite our brief apprenticeship, we were completely oblivious to the process of making a record. We didn't know a thing. We spent fifteen-hour sessions at the studio with barely any sleep, and at the same time we had to keep going to work or to school. But somehow we got through it. It's a miracle that we did, because we made every mistake you could imagine. When you're recording a song, you punch in the vocal track only so that you can lay down the vocal track without affecting the rest of the song. The engineer who was on duty that night instead pressed a button that recorded over everything—the drums, the guitars, the bass. After we finished with the vocal, he came and told us that we had to rerecord the whole song.

It was also our introduction to the soap opera of the music world. One of the other engineers on the session was married, but he was seeing a very exciting blonde on the side. She was always in the studio. One day the wife showed up, and she and the blonde proceeded to tear each other's hair out. The poor engineer was in the middle, being pummeled by both sides. Everything was dramatic, bigger than life. Another time we were downstairs getting ready to record, and a stunning woman walked by. I went to talk to her, because I was always the advance scout, and convinced her to come up to the studio. Once we got there, she got right down to business. Before we knew it, she was servicing the entire band at once! This is something we had never seen except on sexy videos—mistresses and wives and catfighting and groupies crowding into the studio.

Paul and I never left the Electric Lady. During recording sessions, we would try to pinch our behinds tight so we could hold off the inevitable moment when we would have to run to the bathroom; we just wanted to look over the shoulder of the engineer and digest as much of the scene as we possibly could.

We finished the record, which had songs like "Molly," "What Happened in the Darkness," and "When the Bell Rings." Ron started shopping it around, and pretty soon we got an offer from Epic Records. They liked what they heard, and they asked us to play at CBS Studios. We went down there, set up the amplifiers and the drums in the studio, and played the songs for them as best we could. Afterward the record execs put their heads together. Then one guy surfaced and told us, "Well, the band's okay, but we don't want the lead guitar player." That was Stephen, my childhood friend. I was given the task of telling Stephen that he couldn't be in the band. I think we had a sense that this was going to happen with Steve, but he couldn't believe it. He felt betrayed. He wanted to know how I could do that to him, how I could let him be treated that way. It was difficult to explain, but I managed. This was one of my early lessons in the cruel division of the personal and the professional in the music business. Stephen and I remained friends after that, but it wasn't quite the same. He reacted well to my being friendly, and my attempts were genuine. I told him that I had every intention of recording the songs that he and I had written, and I did: "She" and "Goin' Blind" both appeared on the second KISS record. Steve has had good royalty payments from those compositions over the years. But the truth is that there's no healing of a wound that runs as deep as that: you're about to get to the finish line of a race you think you're winning, and somebody pulls the rug out from under you. The decision wasn't malicious. It really was survival. But it was one of those life-defining moments—he could have been in KISS, but it just wasn't meant to be. He formed a band called Lover, and as KISS was growing, I would go and see him at these little clubs. The two of us would go to dinner. Those were always interesting dinners, because I liked him very much as a friend, but the undercurrent of wistfulness was very strong.

But you get it on both ends. After Steve was let go, there was a protracted period of waiting, during which time we decided to get another guitarist, a guy named Ronnie who was a talented session player. We got Metromedia Records to come down and see us at the studio. As we were getting ready to play, we started to set up around the stage, but Ronnie was still sitting in a chair. We were flabbergasted. "Get up," we said. He said, "I'm a musician, I'm not a performer like you guys. You guys jump up and down—that's circus stuff. I'm a musician." Needless to say, he didn't last long in the band.

As the months dragged on, Paul and I realized that Wicked Lester was unraveling. At one point we looked at each other and said, "You know what? This is not it. Whether we get a contract or not, this isn't what we want." In Wicked Lester there were all these three-part harmonies that sounded like the Doobie Brothers, and there wasn't nearly enough guitar. Paul and I had started writing other material, songs like "Deuce" and "Strutter," and we decided to put together the band we had always dreamed about. It's not that our tastes had changed, really; rather, we became braver about making the band reflect our tastes. I remember going to see the New York Dolls early on. We knew that they looked like stars, and that's what

```
                    nothing here
Today is October 13, 1972 and it's a Friday ----
and Gene Klein (that's me) on behalf of Wicked
Lester and the record of the same name, is giving
Steven Coronel the sum total of $200 for his per-
formance on the same record. Until the actual pa-
pers are drawn up by Peter Thal, this is like a sub-
stitute for the interim... which just means the money
is being given out before the paper that's supposed
to make it legal is drawn up... anyway, underneath
this is for Steve to sign to make this whole thing
look nice, see?     Stephen Coronel
                    -signature----------------------


                    nothing here
```

This is a letter to my best friend, Stephen Coronel, asking him to leave Wicked Lester. In the early days I negotiated, wrote, and typed all our documents.

we wanted to be: stars. We were in awe of them. But when they started playing, we looked at each other and said, "We'll kill them."

Initially, our idea was to fire Tony and Brooke and remake Wicked Lester in our image. But when we announced this to the other guys, they weren't happy about it. Our drummer, in particular, said that he was not leaving the band and would honor the contract. So we had no choice but to quit ourselves. We had a contract with Wicked Lester, but we didn't have a contract with each other, so Paul and I just left.

At just around the same time, we suffered another major blow to our fledgling recording career. We had a loft on Canal and Mott Streets that we used as a practice space and a crash pad. One day we came in to practice, and it was like we had stumbled into the wrong room. The place was empty. Picked clean to the bone. We couldn't believe it—our equipment had been stolen, down to the last little piece. We had only the guitars we were carrying, so Paul and I went down to the sidewalk and played like street performers.

◆ ◆ ◆

I wasn't optimistic about the band that might or might not rise from the ashes of Wicked Lester. Paul wanted to start another band with me, but I told him that I was going to go upstate, back to Sullivan County. I planned to look for a guitar player and start another band, and I promised to call Paul when I got back. He said, "No, no. I'll come along." So we went hitchhiking up there. We had a mission, as I remember: we were looking for this hot guitarist who was the big guy on the local Sullivan County scene. Right at the beginning of the trip, we got picked up by these two black guys. We were dressed in fur and leather, the whole aspiring-rock-star deal. We thought they would kill us. But they were nice guys, as it turned out. We started talking, and they weren't going as far as we were. So we got out and flagged down the next car we saw, and it happened to be a VW bus with these two girls in it. They weren't attractive. They were unattractive. But they were nice, and they invited us back to their place. It was a farmhouse, and it was filthy, one of those hippie crash pads. Not only was it filthy, with dogs everywhere, but it was stifling hot. It was like a furnace in there, because the heat wasn't regulated, and it was the middle of winter.

Paul and I went to sleep in one room, and the two girls were in the other room. In the middle of the night one of the girls got up and went to feed the dogs, and I woke up and saw her naked silhouette. I was going to go up to her and see if I could transact a little business, and Paul elbowed me. He was always more cautious in these situations than I was. "Cut it out," he said. "You're going to get us kicked out into the cold." So I went back to sleep. But then in the morning she came into the room and opened the front door. The blast of cold air was so invigorating. I went to stand by the door, and I took the occasion to tell her about what had happened the night before. I said, "You know, last night there was a moment when I woke up and saw you, and I was aroused, and I thought about making an advance, because you were quite beautiful." I made a long speech, and at the end of the speech, she said, "I'm sorry. Hold on a second." She reached into her bag and pulled out a hearing aid and put it in her ear. I had to repeat this whole long speech a second time, just as flowery as the first one. At the end of it she looked at me, and I was afraid that she was going to tell me that she hadn't turned the hearing aid on. But instead she said, "Oh, you wanna fuck?" I did, so we went out to the barn, and we lay down on some blankets, and we began to get acquainted. But her hearing aid was on, and every time my head came near hers, I heard feedback noise from the hearing aid. It scared the pants off me at first—actually, they were already off, but it was incredibly disconcerting. Eventually I got used to it.

We never found the hot guitarist in Sullivan County. It didn't really matter. The trip was like a rite of passage, a way for Paul and me to bond and to reassert our devotion to creating the best band imaginable. What began to rise to the top, ironically, wasn't the musical aspect of the band but the entire package: the showmanship, the costumes, the hair, and so on. We weren't wearing makeup yet, but we were heading in that direction, thanks in part to this unshakable faith, on both our parts, that this was the right way to get noticed in the rock world. Glam rock hadn't hit yet and rock music was still mostly the province of hippies, guys in jeans and girls with long hair. How you looked wasn't as important as the music you made and the way you felt about each other. We didn't buy into that. I still remembered the first thing that struck me about the Beatles when I saw them on *Ed Sullivan,* and it wasn't their music. It was the way they looked: perfectly coordinated, cooler than cool. They looked like a band.

Even in Wicked Lester, the entire band toyed around with more theatrical models of rock and roll. Steven drew some sketches of the different personalities that we imagined for ourselves. Brooke was going to wear an undertaker's hat. Paul was going to dress up as a gambler, with a cowboy hat and twin guns and so on. I was going to dress up like a caveman and drag my bass behind me. Steven was going to be an angel with wings. After he sketched out the plan, he actually went ahead and built his costume; he made an angel rig with movable wings in back. Clearly the plan needed to have some of the wrinkles ironed out. But we were on the same wavelength, which was that we needed to keep pushing the visual appeal of the band. We weren't content to just stand there and strum our guitars. That wasn't enough. We wanted to make a big splash.

A band is like a puzzle. Some of the pieces get filled in right away, and some of them take a little longer. At first Paul and I had a vague idea of what we wanted our band to be like, but as time went on we began to home in on what we were trying to achieve. We saw plenty of bands doing things we didn't like, and every time we saw them, we were able to refine our vision. Paul and I were primarily songwriters and singers. We could play instruments, but at demo level. We needed the rest of the band to fully realize our vision.

After the Mott Street disaster, we got ourselves a loft at 10 East Twenty-third Street. It was the same kind of thing, half practice space, half crash pad. What we mainly did, when we weren't sneaking girls up there, was sit around and brainstorm about the kind of musicians we needed. First on the list was a drummer. One after-

let me go, rock times in NEW YORK

noon I ran across an ad in *Rolling Stone* that said, "Drummer available—will do anything." I called the guy on the telephone, and even though he was in the middle of a party, he took my call. I introduced myself and said we were starting a band and that the band was looking for a drummer, and was he willing to do anything to make it? He said that he was, right away.

He answered almost too quickly. So I slowed him down. "Look," I said. "This is a specific kind of band. We have very particular ideas about how we're going to make it. What happens if I ask you to wear a woman's dress while you play?" He covered up the phone and repeated my question to a guy in the background, who laughed. I went on: "What happens if I ask you to wear red lipstick or women's makeup?" By now, the people in the background were beside themselves. But the drummer answered my question. "No problem," he said. "Are you fat?" I said. "Do you have facial hair?" Because if he did, I explained, he would have to shave it. We didn't

and roll: hard
CITY 1972~1973

One of our first shows—in the early days we would play eight shows a week. This was the original leather outfit I wore with a skull and crossbones on the chest. My sweat would eat through the leather, so I cut out a hole in the chest to get some air.

want to be like a San Francisco hippie band. We wanted to be big stars, not medium stars who looked like hippies. We were going to put together a band that the world had never seen before. We were going to grab the world by the scruff of its neck and . . .

I guess I went on too long, because at some point the drummer stopped me. "Why don't you just come and see me?" he said. "I'm playing at a club in Brooklyn Saturday."

Saturday came, and Paul and I took the subway all the way down to the end of Brooklyn, to this small Italian club—whose clientele could easily have been actors on *The Sopranos*. There were maybe twenty people there, all of them milling around, drinking beer, and watching this trio on stage. The bass player and guitar player looked like soldiers in the Genovese family. The drummer was something else entirely. He had a shag haircut that looked like Rod Stewart's on a good day, and he had a big gray scarf. He outdressed everybody in that club, and he looked like a star.

They were playing mostly soul covers, and when they did "In the Midnight Hour," the drummer started to sing, and this Wilson Pickett–style voice came out of him. Paul and I said, "That's it, that's our drummer." His name was Peter Criscuola, and we shortened it to Peter Criss. We brought Peter into our loft on Twenty-third Street, and we began to play as a trio. It was 1972 and things were moving more quickly now: we had songs we were happy with, and our look was starting to crystallize—we were even starting to wear makeup, although it was far cruder than it eventually became.

This new version of the band still needed to go before Epic to see if they were interested. The record label sent down the vice president of A&R. He came to the loft, where we had set up a little theater—ten rows of four seats—to simulate the feeling of playing in front of a live audience. He sat down, and we played the three songs that we were most confident about: "Deuce," written by me, "Strutter," written by Paul and me, and "Firehouse," written by Paul. The set went well, although we weren't sure that the A&R guy exactly understood what we were about. I was wearing a sailor's uniform, and I had my hair puffed out and painted silver. At the end of "Firehouse," there's a stage move we had worked out where Paul grabbed a fire pail filled with confetti and tossed the contents over the audience. He went for the pail, and as he flung it toward the seats, I saw a look of terror on the A&R guy's face. Clearly, he thought the pail was filled with water. He leaped to his feet and headed for the door. To get there, he had to get past Peter Criss's brother, who was hanging out at the loft. He was a navy guy who was spending the afternoon with us, and he had been drinking hard. As the A&R guy went past him, the brother made a kind of gurgling noise, then threw up on the A&R guy's shoes. "Okay," the A&R guy said on his way out, "I'll call you."

Around this time Paul and I recognized that if we were going to change the band—hire new players, write new music—we should probably have a new name. One day Paul and Peter and I were driving around, brainstorming for new names. I had thought of a few, like Albatross, but I wasn't happy with any of them. At one point—we were stopped at a red light—Paul said, "How about KISS?" Peter and I nodded, and that was it. It made sense. Hindsight is 20/20, of course, and since then people have talked about all the benefits of the name: how it seemed to sum up certain things about glam rock at the time; how it was perfect for international marketing because it was a simple word that people understood all over the world. But we just liked the name, and that was that.

I had been equally matter-of-fact about changing my own name. In those early days when I was rehearsing, working, and traveling back and forth from Queens to Manhattan, I had plenty of time to ponder all sorts of things, like what the name of the band should be, what we should look like, and how the hell we could pull off the stunt of becoming the biggest band in the world. Most important, did the name Gene Klein have that certain ring to it?

I decided it did not. On one of those subway trips I dismissed the name Sidcup Kent for the new group and took on the name Gene Simmons for myself. It was as simple as that. Complete commitment. One day I was Gene Klein. The next day I was Gene Simmons. I would never be Gene Klein again.

We weren't finished hiring the band yet, though. We still needed a lead guitar player, and so we put an ad in *The Village Voice*. While Peter had fallen right into place as the drummer, the search for our guitarist was significantly more problematic. We went through audition after audition. One guy came in with a Spanish *The Good, the Bad, and the Ugly* cloth over him. His wife was with him, and before he played, she explained that he was a highly trained musician who had spent time with the masters. When he sat down and started playing, it was flamenco. We couldn't believe it, and we told him to stop. "Oh," he said. He was faintly offended. "This is in the grand tradition of the masters."

"In the grand tradition," I said, "good-bye."

Everything was like that. One after the other, loser after loser. Even the winners were losers. One guy, a guitar player from another group, came in and really floored us. He was a fantastic player and a great guy. The only problem was that he was black, which wasn't a problem for us personally but was a huge problem for us as a band. He finished his audition, which was just phenomenal, then went downstairs, and we had an impromptu band meeting in which we decided that no matter how good he was, he just didn't fit our image. He was black, we were white, and we wanted to put together something that looked like the Beatles on steroids.

I volunteered to go down there and tell him the truth, and I didn't mince words. I told him I liked him. I told him that we should hang out. And then I told him he couldn't be in the band because he was black. I couldn't believe the words that were coming out of my mouth. To his credit, he understood. In fact, he fired it right back at me. If the Temptations uncovered a great white singer, he said, they wouldn't make him an offer, no matter how good he was.

Meanwhile we still didn't have a guitarist. One guy named Bob Kulick had played around town, and we really liked him. He was close to making it, and we were giving him the golden rules. Number one: you practice all the time. Number two: no phone calls. While we were talking to Bob, in walks this strange-looking guy with two different-colored sneakers. One was orange and one was red. We had chairs in the back lined up so you could come in and sit and wait your turn. Completely oblivious to the fact that we were still talking to Bob, this new guy plugged into the Marshall amplifier and started playing. "Hey," I said, "are you out of your mind? Sit down and wait a second, will you?" It was like he didn't even hear me. He just kept playing. We excused Bob Kulick and told him that we would call him later. We sat this new guy down. "You'd better be good," I said, "because two notes into it, if you suck, you're out on your ass." He just stared straight at me, without any defiance or remorse. We played "Deuce" for him twice, and the third time he got ready to play his solo. And it just fit. Here was this troublemaker who couldn't match his sneakers and didn't have the good manners to wait his turn, and he just fit.

"What's your name?" I said. He said it was Paul Frehley. "Well," I said, "we can't have two Pauls in the band."

Then he actually turned around and said, "Call me Ace."

I said, "Call me King." I wasn't joking. Neither was he.

◆ ◆ ◆

That was the foursome. That was the Beatles on steroids that Paul and I had envisioned. From the start, it was a tricky mix. People say that certain couples are like oil and water—well, we were like oil and oil and water and water, the four of us. Between Ace and Peter, with their various insecurities, it was a nightmare from the very first day the band ever got together. It was all about getting up and doing what needed to be done. It never was about friends. It never was about hanging out. It never was, and to this day it still isn't.

Early on it was very clear that Ace would enter the band warts and all: he had some very bad self-esteem problems and was a drinker. But in those early days Peter was actually the most volatile. Mostly it was a cultural divide, one that I couldn't imagine crossing. When we first met Peter, we knew it was going to be a different world because Peter walked up and said, "Hi, I'm Peter Criscuola, and I've got a nine-inch dick." Paul and I looked at each other quizzically. We were amused, but we didn't know what to make of it. Obviously guys say stuff with bravado to each other all the time, but half the time it's to get a rise out of you or a joke. But the way he spoke, his tone, his attitude—they were all bizarre. The same kind of thing happened with Ace. We were at one of our first shows, and the truck was loaded up, and we were ready to leave. Ace wasn't doing anything. He always had guys who lifted things for him. And he was peeing. We're waiting for him, and the truck's lights are on him. He walks over and says, "This is what my dick looks like when it's soft." He wanted to show us that he had the inches.

Pretty early on Paul and I were aware that we had just met two types of people that we had never been around before. They drank and were attracted to violence. There is a romantic figure in Italian neighborhoods, and that's the unlawful guy, whether it's the local bully or the Mafia guy. That's the hero, the icon of all icons, not Michelangelo, not Da Vinci. Peter was from that culture. Both Peter and I spent part of our lives in Williamsburg. I was shielded from the neighborhood by the yeshiva, but Peter would run through the streets and go up to kids and demand their pocket change. Peter loved that because of his self-admitted Italian posing. The idea of a

Jewish kid running up to you and demanding your pocket change is laughable. It's just not what you learn when you grow up. I remembered that as a ten-year-old every once in a while I would have to run down the street to get away from the gangs and get safely inside the yeshiva. Peter liked to joke that he could have been one of the guys chasing the Jews. There's another way to describe the difference between the two cultures, and it's an old joke. What's the difference between a Jewish mother and an Italian mother? The Italian mother tells her kids, "If you don't do what I tell you to do, I'm going to kill yuz." The Jewish mother says, "If you don't do what I tell you to do, I'm going to kill myself."

After one of our shows, Paul and I went to return the milk truck to the rental place. Peter had driven home. Ace was nowhere to be seen because he never helped us load or unload the trucks. After Paul and I finished the work, we had arranged to meet at two or three in the morning in Chinatown, where Peter was having a birthday party. His wife, Lydia, was there, his friends were there, and he was sitting at the head table, presiding over the crowd. When Paul and I walked in, we looked like freaks. We still had makeup spread on our faces. At that point we didn't have makeup remover. We just tried to wash it off with soap. So we came in late and tired. We just wanted some fried rice and stuff. Peter called for the waiter, who came out of the kitchen and asked us what we wanted to eat. At that point Peter started making fun of the waiter to his face with this mock Chinese speech. "What kind of fucking way is that to talk?" he said. It was very embarrassing to Paul and me. "Please don't do that," we said. "He's just trying to take the order."

Peter blew up. "Fuck you," he said. "If you don't like the way I talk, why don't you get the fuck out of here!" He must have had something to drink, or at least I'd like to think so.

Paul and I said, "Okay, if that's the way you feel, we'll leave."

"Hey," Peter said. "If you walk out that door now, I'm leaving the band."

We looked at each other, shrugged our shoulders, and walked out the door. Peter was yelling all the way out. It was Lydia who talked sense into him, and he came back after two weeks. He was all about false bravado. The smallest dogs bark the loudest.

We came to understand that Peter just wanted to be part of the excitement, and that he took every setback very personally and very hard. His best friend was Jerry Nolan, who ended up drumming for the New York Dolls. The old Dolls drummer had died from a heroin overdose, and when they went out to hire a new one, Peter hoped that he would get the gig. He didn't, and he didn't take the disappointment well. As we were getting ready to go play the Diplomat Hotel, which was our first major coming-out concert to the industry, Peter was depressed and threatening to leave the band again.

Paul and I had a war council, and we decided that we should do everything in our power to keep the band together, at least until we got a record deal. Then if things still weren't working out, we could always let Peter go and hire another drummer. It was all about pragmatism. We racked our brains trying to think of a way to improve Peter's mood, and I finally came up with an idea. Just before the show, we were all outside, in full makeup, and Peter was bellyaching again. "I don't know," he said. "I don't feel like playing. I'm not sure what I want to be doing with my life."

Just then a Mercedes-Benz stretch limousine turned the corner and headed down the street. It stopped in front of us, and Paul and I turned to Peter and said, "This is for you." Knowing that he was depressed, we had rented it for him.

It worked like a charm. His face lit up. "Now I feel like a star," he said. "Let's go kick some ass."

We piled everything into the limo, the guitars and the girls and the four of us. It was like one of those old college stunts where everyone crams into a phone booth. We were barely able to breathe. But we went in style. That's how it went all the time: the ship would start sinking, and Paul and I would plug the leak and keep paddling.

✦ ✦ ✦

We wanted the entire band to sing, and we wanted everybody to write. We wanted everyone to be a star. We wanted to do it like the Beatles, but with a twist, because we were taller and didn't have those little-boy looks. An early photo from around that time shows us in semidrag, with heavy makeup. But as time went on and glam became a bit more familiar, we started to rethink our dedication to dressing in drag and wearing makeup.

The first thing we did was go to all-black costumes. I had never seen a band all in black. When we started to design the mature version of KISS, we were doing things that no one had ever done in rock and roll. For example, the idea of having a big sign with the band's name on the stage, which later became a cliché with almost all heavy-metal bands, started with KISS. You didn't have bands getting up there with big flashing signs telling you who they were. That was Las Vegas stuff. And that was precisely what we were doing. Other bands would come out, and the audience wouldn't know who they were. There were no signs. Sometimes they'd put their name on the drum set, but even that was fairly low key. From the beginning, we envisioned everything bigger, grander, more over the top.

We also started to put more thought into the makeup and specifically into the idea of creating a character for each band member. Later on in our career, when we went to Japan, the reporters there wondered if our makeup was indebted to the Japanese kabuki style. Actually mine was taken from the Bat Wings of Black Bolt, a character in the Marvel comic *The Inhumans*. The boots were vaguely Japanese, though—taken from *Gorgo* or *Godzilla*—and the rest of the getup was borrowed from *Batman* and *Phantom of the Opera*, from all the comic books and science fiction and fantasy that I had read and loved since I was a child. As KISS became more comfortable in this second skin, we started to see how powerful our new look really was, and how it moved far beyond glam rock, which was already feeling as though it was running its course.

The first official KISS gig I ever got for us wasn't as KISS but as Wicked Lester. In the early days, I used to go to ridiculous lengths to get us booked into shows. Sometimes I would literally go door to door, knocking and waiting until the manager came out, then trying to convince him to hire us. There was a nightclub called Coventry (originally Popcorn) in Astoria, Queens, and I managed to get Wicked Lester a spot there. It wasn't the weekend slot, though. It was the middle-of-the-week slot, Tuesday, Wednesday, and Thursday, which was pretty much a dead zone. We gave our picture to the club, and by this time we had decided to be reborn as KISS, thanks in part to Epic's decision to drop Wicked Lester. I remember very clearly when our picture went up on the outside of this club, Ace took a marker and wrote our new name right on the picture. The way he drew it was pretty crude, but it resembled our logo, with the two *S*'s like lightning bolts at the end of the word. It didn't make much difference for the show, which had a crowd of maybe three people: Peter's wife, Lydia, a girl named Jan who I was seeing, and Jan's friend. But it was a booking, and soon there were other bookings, including a club called the Daisy in Amityville. Those shows were packed, but mostly because it was a drinking club, with cheap beer and a biker crowd. It was the kind of place where you might see a pregnant woman with a drink in one hand and a cigarette in the other. It didn't matter to us what the places were like or how big the crowds were. We were on cloud nine.

◆ ◆ ◆

I had all sorts of odd jobs while the band was crystallizing. While I was in high school, I had learned to type, and in college I even started a little business, typing term papers for fifty cents a page. So when I came back to the city from college and was trying to get the band started, I took a job with Kelly Girls, later the Kelly Agency, which supplied temporary secretaries and typists to businesses all around the city. It was decent work, and also a great way to meet girls, since there were very few guys there. Through Kelly, I ended up getting a job at *Glamour* magazine, and within a few weeks I became indispensable, not only because I could type ninety words a minute but because I knew how to fix the hectograph and mimeograph machines. Pretty soon I got moved from *Glamour* to *Vogue*, where I worked as the assistant to the editor, Kate Lloyd. That lasted about six months, although at the same time I was working as a cashier at a deli. With all this work, I couldn't get to the practice space until nine or ten at night, but I made it, and we would rehearse until two in the morning. I never had a moment's rest. It got so busy that I moved my bed and my television set into the loft, so I could wake up and go to work without traveling for an hour by subway. I always worked, so I often had to pay the rent or lend the band money for food or the subway.

In fact, my social life started to center on the loft, because I would arrange for the girls to meet me after rehearsal and spend the night. Not every girl dared venture into 10 East Twenty-third Street; those who did were the few and the brave, because this place was a hole. It didn't have any windows. We had put up floor-to-ceiling egg crates to dampen the sound. Some of these egg crates had broken eggs in them, so it was a field day for cockroaches. And you could hear them, the pitter-patter of little feet. One night after I turned off the lights I had a girl on top of me on the bed, naked. All of a sudden she let out a bloodcurdling scream. Well, something must have crawled over her, because she jumped up, ran into a wall, and fell down in the pitch-black room. When I turned on the light, she was trying frantically to jump up on the bed; she wasn't willing to let her feet touch the floor. "Get my clothes," she said. "Get my clothes. I felt something on my back." That was the last I ever saw of her.

As soon as I graduated college and got my B.A., I taught sixth grade for six months in Spanish Harlem. It was a fine experience in some ways, and less satisfactory in others, but it didn't last long. Then I started working for the Puerto Rican Interagency Council as the assistant to the director of a government research and demonstration project called Improved Services to Puerto Ricans in Northeastern U.S.A. and Puerto Rico. The project was a way to track government funds and how they actually went down through government and local authorities and to determine whether they did actually get to the Puerto Rican population. Because of a government rule, I was the non–Puerto Rican working in there. But as it happened, the director liked me enough, because I could do anything. As I said, I could work the mimeograph and the hectograph machines. I also used the offices after they were closed and on weekends to send out our mailers. I used the typewriter and the layout and the stencils, and Peter knew a printer downtown. Ace did nothing. So we were able to put together a very professional-looking promotional package with a photograph, a one-page bio sheet, and everything else. I got the year-end issues of *Billboard*,

Record World, and *Cash Box,* which were music-industry trade magazines, and copied out a huge list of record company executives, managers, music reporters, and so on. Then I sent out our mailer. I must have sent out a thousand of these mailers to everybody and their cousin, and people responded. Because in those days you didn't get professional-looking packages coming in off the street. Now every band does it. But in those days it was unheard of.

I took something from every job I had. When I was a teacher, I learned how people took in new information, and what kinds of information excited them. When I worked for the Interagency Council, I learned the importance of making a professional package. Just before the band took off, I worked for the Direct Mail Agency, a company that invites people to send them complaints about wanting to be taken off mailing lists for junk mail. The DMA then puts together a list of these people and sells it to the junk mail companies, so that they can save money by not bothering to send their junk mail to the people who have already identified themselves as unreceptive customers. They're making the junk mail people more market-savvy.

◆ ◆ ◆

We were primed to break—all we needed was one final stroke of luck. Paul and I took the step of planning a Friday the Thirteenth show at the Diplomat Hotel, which was on West Forty-third Street, a block from the Forty-second Street subway. It was a run-down hotel, but it had a grand ballroom. We had no stature on the local scene—while other bands were making the rounds, playing these clubs, we were in our loft practicing. So we needed this show to be a big deal. Paul and I arranged to get the Brats, a big local band that could pull three hundred people wherever they played. They looked like larger Italian versions of the Faces, a cross between the mods and the mob. We met with them, and I told them that they had to go on at eleven P.M., no sooner. We paid them $350, which was a lot of money. There was another local band, Luger, that had a small following, and we made them go on at eight P.M. and paid them $150. Then we took out newspaper ads and made fliers; our total cost was about $1,000. We were counting on a crowd of 750 or maybe 1,000, each paying about four dollars a ticket. Since we had done most of the organizing ourselves, we stood to make a decent amount of money from the show. But it wasn't about the money.

I had read that Elvis's manager, Colonel Tom Parker, had actually banned Elvis's hips from television. It wasn't the network that did that—it was Parker. Because he wanted people to make a to-do about it, he manipulated the media and the audience. We were trying something similar. On our own, KISS couldn't pull any tickets. But with these other bands, we could. I wasn't a lawyer and we couldn't afford one, but I composed and typed up contracts that restricted the movements of these other bands, contracts that required them to appear onstage at a certain time and not before or after; the whole place would be ours for a key window. When the invitations went out, they read, "Heavy Metal Masters: KISS," and we sent along complimentary tickets, backstage passes, and so on. According to the invitations, we would appear onstage at nine-thirty. We figured that the record executives wouldn't be able to separate the crowd; even though everybody was coming to see the Brats and Luger, we could pretend they were there for us.

Then we went into phase two of our plan. We packed the front row with sisters and girlfriends wearing KISS T-shirts, which we made at home. Paul and Peter stayed up one night and poured glue and glitter through a KISS stencil, which was good for only two or three wears. Ace did nothing. So the entire front row was filled with girls wearing these black T-shirts with "KISS" on them.

The place filled up with record company executives and producers, just everybody, including Bill Aucoin, the producer of *Flipside* and *Supermarket Sweep*, a game show. Before MTV, before anything else, *Flipside* was a groundbreaking show for televising popular music. When he arrived at the Diplomat, he saw a rabid crowd of a thousand people, including the girls in the front, and the band hitting the stage at nine-thirty sharp in full makeup sticking out their tongues. You can imagine the effect.

By that time, we had already done some recording on our own. Ron Johnson at Electric Lady owed us some money for the sessions we had worked on, and he'd asked if we wanted to take the money or use it to do a demo tape of our new band. Paul and I jumped at the offer to do a demo—on the condition, we said, that we got to work with Eddie Kramer. Eddie had engineered Led Zeppelin, Jimi Hendrix, Humble Pie, and lots of other big-name rock bands. He was already a legitimate guy. So he engineered our tape of five songs. We now had a professional-sounding tape plus an event. So if Bill Aucoin and some of the other people came and saw us and said, "We're interested, can we hear a tape?" we could put a tape on the table that would blow them away. It sounded like a record, and we had it in hand when we went to do the Diplomat show.

When Bill Aucoin came over to talk to me after the show, I still had my makeup on, and one of the girls I had been seeing was sitting on my knee. She thought I was just flirting with her, but I was completely aware that I had to have the garnish around the food—otherwise it wouldn't look as good. So while he was talking to me, I was in full makeup, with a girl wearing a KISS T-shirt sitting on my lap and cooing in my ear. Bill Aucoin didn't know that I already had a relationship with her. He didn't need to know.

Aucoin asked us if we had a management contract. I said no. We were naïve, as it turned out, because the contract we had signed with Ron Johnson was also a comprehensive management contract. But we were also lucky, because that contract was up. We were free to sign with Aucoin, and we did. When we joined up with Bill, we also joined up with another guy who would be influential in the early development of the band, a guy named Sean Delaney. Sean was a fairly young guy who had tried to have his own career in rock and roll. He had a band called the Scat Brothers. The Scat Brothers never made it, and he became part of Bill Aucoin's management company, which was called Rock Steady. Paul and I thought that we had a pretty good idea of what we wanted to do with KISS. But we didn't know the first thing about turning our vision into a career. That's where Bill and Sean came in. Without them, we were a high-spirited young band with enough enthusiasm to carry us along for a while. With them, we were poised to become superstars.

The band was designed as a democracy. That was the blueprint—it was the Beatles model. But like the Beatles, it was clear that Paul and I were in the front seat, because we were writers, and Ace and Peter were in the backseat.

Paul and I didn't think of ourselves as leaders, necessarily. When we met Bill Aucoin, he recommended a four-way split. In order to keep things smooth, he said, we should divide the money equally. Better to do that, he said, than to quibble over shares and

nothin' to lose:

half-shares. Plus, if everything went according to plan, there was going to be plenty of money for everyone. We took Bill's advice. Whenever there were decisions, we made them democratically, which didn't always make sense. If Paul and I wanted to do something and Ace and Peter didn't, we were in a stalemate. To get our way, we had to emotionally batter them, and often they felt as though Paul and I were ganging up on them. That may have been the perception at times. The truth was that Ace and Peter simply were not qualified to make decisions about band matters that depended upon organization and structure. They were not willing to put in the time to think things through. We would have a meeting about a tour or a photo shoot, and then the very next day Peter would come up to me and say, "Gene, when are we going to have a meeting about the tour?"

"We had it," I said. "Yesterday. You were there."

"Yeah," he would say. "But I didn't understand anything you were saying."

In this respect, Bill was more like me and Paul. I didn't realize it immediately, but Bill was gay. Paul knew it from the start. I didn't see it. Paul asked me if I minded having a gay manager—I said, "No. Why do you ask?" I was oblivious to it. Bill's appearance and style

From a KISS photo shoot in the early 1970s.

the birth of KISS
1973~1974

were clearly suited for the corporate world. He dressed in suits and ties and presented himself well. He would show up with a beautiful blonde every now and then. He was not, for lack of a better word, a queen. Over time I got the sense that something else might have been happening in his life. At any rate, it wasn't something I minded or have ever minded. He did the work he needed to do. He focused on the band. That was all that mattered. We also met Joyce Biawitz, who would comanage us with Bill. She would later marry Neil Bogart. She was a powerhouse.

Once we had Bill's attention and Sean's help, we went from nothing—playing our Friday the Thirteenth show at the Diplomat Hotel—to a record deal in about three weeks. This is where Neil Bogart entered the picture.

Neil Bogart had been born Neil Bogatz and grew up as a poor Jewish kid in a rough section of Brooklyn. He had always wanted to be in show business, and after attending the High School of the Performing Arts—that's the school in the movie *Fame*—he worked as a singer on a cruise ship and had some odd jobs as an actor. Eventually he came back to New York and went to work for an employment agency. Soon he was in the record business, first at MGM Records as a promo man, then at Cameo-Parkway, then at Buddah. He was still a young kid at this time, about twenty-five years old. At Buddah he started the careers of bubblegum bands like the Ohio Express, who recorded "Yummy Yummy Yummy" and "Chewy Chewy." In 1973, with the help of Mo Ostin at Warner Bros., Neil started his own label.

When Bill heard about this, he sent our demo tape over to Neil immediately. Kenny Kerner and Ritchie Wise, a popular production team who had worked on big rock and roll records—"Brother Louie" by Stories and "Imagination" by Gladys Knight and the Pips, among others—heard the tape and told him they would love to produce KISS. As a result of their enthusiasm and his own, Neil signed us without ever having seen us. Bill kept explaining to him that he had to see the band live, that the stage show was an integral part of our act, so finally Neil arranged for us to play in front of him at LaTang Studios, at Fifty-fourth Street and Seventh Avenue.

It was a small room, with about twenty people, and we came

out wearing makeup and played at maximum level. We blew out everybody's ears. It was an absolutely ferocious performance, and at one point I jumped off the stage and ran up to Neil and forced his two hands to clap together. He must have been scared out of his mind, because with the heels on, I was close to seven feet tall, and he was about five-seven. And by the end of it he was so overwhelmed that he was exhausted. He had two concerns: first, that the makeup was going to get in the way of the band's success. He thought the glam thing was over. More specifically, he worried that we were projecting a gay vibe, particularly Paul. We talked to him for a while and explained our vision of the band, which was to go beyond glam to something else. As far as the gay thing went, our feeling was that we dressed the way we felt inside, and the gay vibe wasn't really part of that. In a strange way, our greatest asset was the fact that we took our look seriously. Superman wore tights and a cape, and no one ever questioned his sexuality because he didn't see his costume as campy or funny—it was just what superheroes wore. This explanation seemed to satisfy Neil.

Afterward, we were talking to him about his new label. "It's going to be called Emerald City," he said. I told him I didn't like it and that he should change it. There I was, a guy who had never recorded, telling the new label president that I didn't like the name of his company. He was taken aback. "You don't?"

"No," I said. "I'm in a rock band. It sounds like *The Wizard of Oz*."

"No," he said, "it's about magic."

"But when I think of the Emerald City, I think of a girl, of Judy Garland going down the Yellow Brick Road." He ended up changing the name to Casablanca.

Neil came from a hit singles background and, more specifically, from a show-business mentality. He wasn't qualified to make musical decisions—for all intents and purposes, he might have been tone deaf—and he was never a pure music guy. But he was a concept guy, and his influence on our career was tremendous. Someone else would have wanted singles from every KISS album, and that would have been correct according to the prevailing business models. But what we did (and by so doing arguably became one of the biggest bands of all time—right behind the Beatles for gold albums by a group, yet without a number-one single or album in our entire career) was to go steady. The *Billboard* chart is an indication of what a record did in only one week. A band can come in and have the number-one record, and then it's gone the next week. Neil pushed us for product. He made us go back into the studio and record albums to keep our name in stores, of course. He pressured us for hit singles, of course. But he also let us find our own pace, and we turned out to be marathoners. The guy who runs the fastest is not the guy who wins the race. It's the guy who keeps the steady pace.

◆ ◆ ◆

If our career was in good hands with Neil, our act was in excellent hands with Bill Aucoin. We rehearsed downtown at a rat-infested loft that Bill provided for us. He was very forward-thinking. He had been a television director and producer, with his *Flipside* show. Now he and Sean Delaney set us up with a video camera so we could see ourselves performing. Initially we resisted. It sounded stupid— why would we want to do that? But it was eye-opening. We actually saw ourselves and thought, *Wow. We look cool.* I remember sitting there afterward in stunned silence with the rest of the guys and really feeling the effect. The other thing Bill did was to put Sean Delaney with us as a kind of coach. This happened very early on: we would do our stage act, and he would stand off to the side, stopping us at certain points. I don't recall whether he served as a choreographer or just observed us and told us what was working. But we had open lines of communication, and when he made a suggestion, he could show us exactly what he meant on the tape. We could see our act coming together and our poise growing by leaps and bounds. We knew we were part of something special.

How did we know? From seeing other bands, and realizing how much better we could be. Paul and I went to see other bands in concert, not as casual fans but as students. If a band came out with a certain kind of lighting or built a certain kind of set, we would file that away in our minds and make a note to do better. At one point,

The wedding photograph of my mother, Flora, and my father, Feri. They were married in Jand, a small village in Hungary, when they were in their early twenties.

Chaim Witz in Israel, age six and a half.   Gene Klein in high school, age fourteen.

I am singing here with my high school band the Long Island Sounds. Seth Dogramajian is on the left, and Alan Graff is playing guitar on the right. We played after-school dances at Joseph Pulitzer Middle School.

Paul, Peter, and I auditioned here for Don Ellis from Epic Records. We were still Wicked Lester at this point, but in our hearts we were already the band that would become KISS. This is an early version of our makeup.

My mother has come to every single New York City KISS show throughout the years. Here she is with me at Madison Square Garden in 1977. While I was onstage raising hell, she was in heaven, elbowing everyone around her in the audience and saying, "That's my son, that's my son."

When I hit the stage, I was transformed. Offstage I was reasonably glib and paid attention to business. Onstage, I was all hell and brimstone. I became the Demon.

The Japanese fans loved us—we were like the characters in their superhero shows come to life.

Taking a break from the Japanese tour in 1977.

Opposite: I started spitting fire during "Firehouse." I would come stalking from stage right holding a metallic sword on fire at the handle. My mouth was full of kerosene. At center stage I would pause and hold the sword still. Then I'd rush it to within six inches of my face and spray the kerosene at the flame. When the flame met the kerosene it would ignite. The fans saw what looked like a huge fireball shooting out of my mouth.

Throwing up blood seemed to incite fundamentalist Christians. They actually believed I was a Devil worshipper, or perhaps even the Devil. The combination of the makeup, my tongue, and the blood meant something to them. I always found it curious when they said, "You look just like the Devil." When was the last time they had seen the Devil? How do they know what he looks like?

Here I am with my serpent friend. This photograph was taken during the filming of *KISS Meets the Phantom of the Park* in 1978 at a live concert film shoot held at Magic Mountain, in California.

we went to see the Who. They were touring behind *Quadrophenia,* and we went down to Philadelphia to see the show. Lynyrd Skynyrd was opening, and throughout their set the audience was talking and milling around. Then the Who came out, and the entire crowd got to their feet and started pumping their fists in the air. Paul and I got up too, but it was mostly out of respect for what they had done. The truth was that we brazenly thought we could do better. We knew we could. The bands that struck us as having something special weren't necessarily the most popular bands. In fact, the one we kept returning to was Slade, the British glam rockers who had hits with "Cum on Feel the Noize" and "Mama Weer All Crazee Now." We liked the way they connected with the crowd, and the way they wrote anthems. But we knew they would never make it in America, because they were just too British. In fact, the lead singer, Noddy Holder, was Welsh, and it was hard to understand anything he was saying. We wanted that same energy, that same irresistible simplicity. But we wanted it American-style.

◆ ◆ ◆

The first KISS album was recorded in September 1973 at Bell Sound Studios, which was on Fifty-fourth and Broadway, in a not entirely reputable part of New York City. The studio was seedy and dirty, although it was easy to get to from the subway. Although Bell Sound had perfectly good equipment—it was a twenty-four-track recording studio—its feel was totally different from Electric Lady's. That was a connoisseur's studio, built by Jimi Hendrix and treasured by professional musicians. Bell Sound was a commercial endeavor, and many different kinds of recording were going on there all the time.

We got right to work. Paul and I were especially interested in paying attention to the process, learning how a record was created. Our producers, Ritchie Wise and Kenny Kerner, worked with us on the first two records, and they were great teachers: efficient, professional, without any illusions about what we were doing, which was trying to capture the energy of a live show on a vinyl disk. If there were any difficulties, I don't remember them, because I was so impressed that we were actually making a record. In fact, the strangest thing about that time was the change in my workday. I was accustomed to going to work at *Vogue,* or at the Puerto Rican Inter-agency Council, as a straphanger—I would wake up at six or seven and come into the city by subway. As soon as we started recording, I was able to sleep until eleven, wake up and have a leisurely lunch, and then head into the studio. Of course, I wasn't coming back until late at night, but it felt like I was suspended in time.

The studio work went quickly. KISS worked then the way KISS has always worked: the rhythm tracks went down first, and then later on we added vocals. The songs that we brought into that session included some reworked material from the Wicked Lester period, as well as some new compositions. Over time that first album has really held up well, mainly because the songs were so strong:

Paul putting on his Starchild makeup.

"Firehouse," "Strutter," "Deuce," "Cold Gin," and "Black Diamond," amazingly, are all products of the same recording sessions.

When the record was finished, we went to shoot the cover photo. Our image was extremely important to us, and we wanted to get it right. The record company had paired us up with Joel Brodsky, a well-respected rock photographer who had taken cover shots for dozens of acts, including Leslie West, the Nazz, Gladys Knight and the Pips, Carly Simon, and the Ohio Players. He was best known for the cover of the Doors' *Strange Days,* a surreal, carnivalesque shot with a strongman and a midget. He had a studio in midtown Manhattan, and we all showed up there a little early, because we wanted to leave time to get into makeup.

From the second we walked in, things were different from what we were used to. First of all, we were accustomed to doing our own makeup, but they had hired someone to do it for us. That's why Peter's makeup is completely different on that first album from what it eventually became. But that was only a minor hiccup. Once we were all made up, Brodsky put us in front of the camera and then draped a black cloth over us so you could only see our heads. That was intentional; it was what we called the *Meet the Beatles* effect, just four heads coming out of the darkness.

Then Brodsky asked us who wanted to hold the balloons. We didn't understand, until he explained his concept. "I get it," he said. "You're clowns. I'll go get the balloons." It took us a while to explain to him that we were completely serious. It's easy to see why he was confused—up until that point, you didn't have popular bands coming out with makeup on. Alice Cooper was a front man in makeup, and obscure bands like Roy Wood's Wizzard and the Crazy World of Arthur Brown wore makeup. But to have a real rock band with four guys, all of them in makeup, was unprecedented. It didn't have as much in common with rock and roll as it did with the movies or Las Vegas. But we convinced Joel Brodsky that we were serious.

The album was recorded. The cover photo was done. Then Bogart suggested that the drums should magically levitate—and something else: one of us would have to spit fire. We gathered in Aucoin's office, and a magician stepped up and spit fire clear across the room.

We were asked which of us would like to do it during the concerts. No one else raised a hand, but I curiously found that my own right arm was thrust high in the air. The guys were happy I'd be the one.

All we had to do now was wait—and play as many shows as we possibly could. We joined the bill for a big New Year's show at the Academy of Music, which later became the Palladium. There were a bunch of bands, including Iggy Pop and the Stooges and a band called Flaming Youth, a name Paul later borrowed for a song. The headliner was Blue Oyster Cult.

It was a very exciting time. I had a liaison with one of the girls in Flaming Youth, and I was in a rock band about to play its first show. We had yet to release our first album and we had a half-hour to go out there and do our stuff. We finally went on fourth, and we just killed the crowd. We played with fury from the first explosion of the opening chord of "Deuce."

By the third song, "Firehouse," the stage was covered by fog. Sirens were going off, flashing lights were blinding people, and the entire place was on its feet, fists pumping in the air. And if they thought they had seen it all, we would give them more. I emerged from the fog in full KISS gear, carrying a sword with the hilt lit on fire and my mouth full of kerosene. I came to center stage and I spit out the kerosene. A huge ball of fire erupted out of my mouth, and the audience went nuts. I stood there, legs spread apart, soaking in the adulation. It was then that I smelled something burning. I had wanted to look extra cool on our opening night, so I sprayed extra hair spray on my hair so it would really puff out. Sean Delaney ran out and wrapped my head in a wet towel, and they went out of their minds! We came. We saw. And we damn well conquered. We were the sensation of the show, and a few weeks later, when a British magazine called *Sounds* published a New Year's roundup of shows across the world, they printed a picture of me.

◆ ◆ ◆

It wasn't exactly fame yet, but it was getting closer and closer. Audiences would scream when we came onstage. We would be recognized in the street. And sometimes we would even be recognized by girls. When I was a freshman in high school, there was a senior girl who was one of the most popular girls in school. She was in the student government and was the president of this club and a member of that society. She was so stunning that when she walked by, I'd lower my head, only to bring it up a second later to check out her lines. Everything about her spelled arousal. So I was walking down Forty-second Street, after KISS had been around for two or three years and everybody knew us, especially in New York. And I heard this squeal in back of me and then this voice. "Gene, Gene, it's me, it's me, it's me."

I didn't recognize her at first, but then it came to me. She was still beautiful.

I played it cool. "Oh," I said. "So you like the band." She nodded. "Well, I have to go now," I said. "Do you want to come over tonight?" It was as simple as that.

"I'd love to," she said. And that night I made up for all those nights of imagined passion. Being in KISS had its side benefits.

In February 1974 the Michael Quatro Band dropped out of a tour in Canada. Michael Quatro was the brother of Suzy Quatro, who made a name for herself as a glam-rock star. As a result of their sudden departure, we were named the replacement band on the tour. It was only a few cities, and small Canadian cities at that, but it was a real tour, and that meant everything to a band that had never been out of the New York area. Within a week we were on tour.

The first place we went was South Edmonton in Alberta, and I had my first authentic groupie, a girl with green hair. She didn't

shout it out road and on the

KISS performing on *In Concert*, hosted by Dick Clark.

know who KISS was. We were just a rock band. I grabbed her, and she spent the night with me. I was in heaven. This girl was spending the night with me just because I was in a band. No courting, no relationships, no dates, no "what does it all mean?" The very thing that women want out of a relationship is this kind of heaviness of "life and meaning." All I wanted was no meaning. Twenty-four hours of experiencing life with a warm female body.

Early on the other guys in the band would tease me for not being selective. They would say, "She ain't so hot," or, "I could have had her." But I didn't care. For me, it was not a contest—your girl is

loud: on the rise 1974~1975

prettier than mine or mine is prettier than yours. All I cared about was satisfying my carnal needs; I always seemed to have the "urge to merge." The lifestyle really appealed to me; bedding down a girl whose name I barely remembered was something I wanted to do all the time. Some girls seemed to have a kind of fascination with my tongue. Others had a fascination with the whole concept of KISS. In fact, more than one asked me to leave on my makeup and my costume while we went to bed—or to the bathroom, or to the floor of the dressing room. It wasn't always the bed.

The band ran on adrenaline because we had nothing else to run on. We were in the back of a station wagon, four of us, and Sean Delaney was driving. We would torture him. Peter and Ace would strip off their pants and stick their dicks against the window of the station wagon we were touring in.

Sean tolerated all of this. We checked into motels, and he was like a camp counselor. When we had girls, he would storm into the room and tell them to leave. "Get out! These guys need to sleep!" One time a girl wouldn't leave. Sean was pulling her by her hair, and she wouldn't leave: "Fuck you! You can't tell me what to do." Then this other language poured out of him. With his body language, he was very flamboyant. But it was all so entertaining. Brand new. New cities, new foods. Grits. "How y'all doing?" What are you, on *Gunsmoke*? I had never heard that kind of language except on TV, and I thought cowboy hats went out in the eighteen hundreds.

Even though the girls on the road were starting to pile up, I was still seeing a girl named Jan, off and on, and it was at her house that I heard our music for the first time on the radio. There was a deejay in New York at the time named Allison Steele. She went by the name the Nightbird, and she was the kind of deejay that they don't have anymore, the kind who would dig around in a pile of records until she found something she liked. I was over at Jan's house, down in her basement in bed with her, and we were listening to the radio, and Allison Steele came out of one record and went into the next one. I thought it sounded pretty good, and it took almost a minute before I realized it was KISS. A few weeks after that, the album came out in stores. This was in February 1974.

✦ ✦ ✦

Once our stage act was refined by the short tour, we were ready for our first big industry showcase, which was happening out in Los Angeles. Neil flew us out west and rented us cars, and for a little while we soaked up California. It was a new experience, the West Coast. All the girls were pretty, and they had the sun in their hair, and the weather was always nice enough for them to show a little skin.

The showcase would happen at the Century Plaza Hotel. Neil had packed the place with record executives and businessmen. They weren't sure what to expect, but it's fair to say that they weren't expecting KISS. Soft rock was starting to become more popular at this time, and the bands that were on everyone's minds were acts

Our coming-out party for Casablanca Records at the Century Plaza, with Alice Cooper and Jan Walsh.

Getting ready to perform on *In Concert.*

like the Little River Band and John Denver. When we came out, their jaws dropped. By now we were used to this reaction, and we played it for all it was worth. That's what made it rock and roll, in some sense: scaring the suits.

Neil loved it, but he realized we needed more exposure, and pretty soon he got us booked on a show called *In Concert,* which was hosted by Dick Clark. The other guests that night were Kool and the Gang and Melissa Manchester; that gives you some idea of how eclectic the rock and roll scene was at that time. There may have been bands who, before playing on these TV shows, mingled with the other bands and made friends. We weren't one of them. For starters, we were defiantly out of step with the times. The other thing that set us apart, though, was our makeup. We had to apply it ourselves, and it took a few hours, so the ritual of getting ready for the show actually prevented us from having much contact with the other bands.

While we were getting ready for the show, Dick Clark came backstage to say hello to us. He shook our hands and wished us luck. To this day, he remains one of the classiest people I have ever met in the record business. I can't tell you how gratifying it was to be a young band and have Dick Clark treat us with respect. Paul and I have talked about that occasionally over the years, and it's been kind of a guide for us, especially in dealing with our fans. We try never to be rude, never to turn away kids looking for autographs.

Being polite backstage, though, didn't mean that we weren't going to tear the roof off the place when we finally got onstage. We played three songs, "Deuce," "Firehouse," and "Black Diamond," and each one was more powerful than the last. The show was absolutely wild. At one point I went right at the cameraman while breathing fire, and on TV all you can see is my face approaching and then the ceiling, because the cameraman jumped off his platform and ran. We didn't see the show until two months later. By that time we were back on tour, in Asbury Park, New Jersey. After the show we'd gone back to the motel to change before heading out for the night. Someone turned on the TV set, and there we were, on national television.

That whole first tour was a blur. We were making seventy-five dollars a week, which was nothing, although it seemed like all the money in the world since we were making it playing music. We opened for many bands: for Savoy Brown and Manfred Mann, for Foghat and Golden Earring. And we founded a proud tradition of being thrown off of tours. In part this was because we would leave the stage a terrible mess when we were through with it: there would be fake blood all over, and parts of the set would be singed. Once while opening for Black Oak Arkansas, I accidentally set a corner of their curtain on fire. Bands really wanted us off the tour, though, because they couldn't follow us. In theory, we were the opening act and they were the headliners. But when we were finished with the crowd, they would have a stunned, uncertain look in their eyes. There was no way to go on after us.

We felt triumphant on tour, like we were on our way to the top. But we didn't forget the people who helped us, particularly our road crew. One guy named Paul Chaverria, my bass roadie, was a little tiny guy, no more than five-five, but he could be an attack dog. Once Paul Stanley was trying to get into the arena, and a security guard wasn't letting him by, and Paul Chaverria just lit into this guard like nothing you've ever seen. Then there was Junior Small-ing, a big black guy who worked as our road manager. A guy named Moose loaded Ace's guitar, and another guy, one of our drivers, lost his life years later when he swerved to avoid a family on a bridge. They were characters, roadies like you'd expect to see in a movie. But they were amazing: competent, devoted, and uncomplaining. We couldn't have done it without them.

For a number of shows we opened for Argent, a band led by Rod Argent, who had previously been a member of the great British invasion band the Zombies. Argent had charted with at least one huge hit, "Hold Your Head Up," and the band had a number of albums under their belt. We were novices compared to them, and as the junior band, we had to follow lots of arbitrary rules, one of which was the no-encore rule. According to Argent, we could go out there and play only eight songs, and then we had to close up shop. The only problem was that the audiences wanted us for longer than that. Argent fixed that by shutting off our power after eight songs.

We'd be playing our hearts out, and the crowd would be screaming along, and then suddenly the lights would go dead. It was demoralizing. During one show our set went well as usual, and the audience was in a frenzy. We got to the end of our eighth song, and they were screaming as loud as they could, and we all braced for the lights to go dead—but they didn't. They stayed on. So we played an encore, and the crowd was still screaming. At that point we didn't really have any more songs, so we actually went back and replayed some of the songs from earlier in the set. Finally, after the third or fourth encore, we came off, drenched in sweat, completely confused about Argent's change of heart. It turns out that we owed our good luck to Junior Smalling, who had gotten into a little argu-ment with Argent's road manager and pushed him into an anvil case and locked it shut. Needless to say, we were thrown off that tour too.

It was a wild time. Later in our careers we would fly first class or on our own jet, but in the beginning we flew commercial, with regular civilians. I remember talking to people about what I did. My hair was big and bushy. We wore platform heels with leather pants and studded belts with spiders encased in the belt buckles and black fingernail polish. "What do you do?" they would say.

"I'm in a band."

"What's the name of your band?"

"KISS."

"Oh, really? That's a strange name for a band."

As the band became more and more successful, we got letters from people who were wearing our makeup. They started to get involved in the mystique. We soon realized that we had created alter egos. The fans wanted them, not us. They wanted Superman, not Clark Kent. So we started to hide our real faces, which only fueled the mystique.

◆ ◆ ◆

The first album was selling okay—fifty to sixty thousand copies, thanks mostly to our touring. But Neil Bogart wanted to sell more, and he always had ideas for how to do it. One of his earliest ideas was for a kissing contest. This was an old radio and deejay gimmick, to sponsor a kissing contest and have a bunch of young couples come out to a mall or car dealership. They were marathons—the couples would kiss as long as they possibly could, with only five-minute breaks every hour. The way Neil saw it, we were perfectly positioned to capitalize on this phenomenon because of our name. He suggested that we rerecord that old Bobby Rydell song, "Twistin' Time," which would be changed to "Kissin' Time" and used to promote a series of contests around the country. The winners would get two big prizes: an all-expense-paid trip to Hawaii, and an appearance on *The Mike Douglas Show*, a daytime talk show on network television.

It wasn't a song we would have chosen, but Neil was insistent: he was a real promoter, and he believed it would be a successful gimmick. We finally agreed, but only on condition that we rewrite the lyrics. It would have been a death sentence to record the song with the lyrics from the 1960s. It wasn't our style or our time. Paul and I sat down in the studio with paper and pencil and remade the song to fit our fans—mentioning the cities where we were big, the places people wanted to hear about. Then we recorded it. The whole process took about an hour.

All in all, I'd say that we went along with it reluctantly. It certainly wasn't rock and roll, and we knew that, but we managed to do a decent job recording it, trying to get as much of our personality into it as we possibly could. We also extracted a promise from Neil that the cover version of the song would never appear on any actual KISS albums, that it would be a one-shot deal to promote the contest. Of course, it didn't work out that way—the song later found its way onto some albums and rereleases.

As a promotional single, "Kissin' Time" was moderately successful. At the beginning of May, it was released—"Nothin' to Lose," a real KISS song, was the B-side—and broke into the Top 100. Neil's master plan called for us to follow the regional kissing contests and appear with the national winners on *The Mike Douglas Show*. Needless to say, we weren't the show's usual fare, and we played up our strangeness. One of the other guests was the comedienne Totie Fields, and at one point she said, "Who are you supposed to be?"

"I'm evil incarnate," I said, giving my best scowl.

"No, you're not," she shot right back. "You can't fool me. You're probably some nice Jewish kid from Long Island." She was a trouper; I later thanked her on my solo album.

Nice Jewish kids or not, we performed "Firehouse," and it was a real spectacle: plenty of pyrotechnics, plenty of makeup, and so forth. As a performing group, we were hitting our stride.

◆ ◆ ◆

We were exhausted from touring, but we had careers to build, so as soon as the first album began to lag, we went right back into the studio to record our second, which was titled *Hotter Than Hell*. In many ways it was a continuation of the first album. The songs were drawn from the same pool of material, mostly written by Paul and me, with a couple of contributions from Ace. We had written some on the road and used some from the original KISS demo. The producers were the same: Kenny Kerner and Ritchie Wise, who had done a fine job on the first album and were easy to work with.

In fact, there was only one difference between the first album and the second. But it was a big difference, a three-thousand-mile difference. Because Kerner and Wise had moved out west to California, we had to follow them to cut the second album. The culture shock was tremendous. We felt out of place in a million small ways, because we were a New York band with New York attitudes. The record label rented us cars, but that was just asking for trouble. Ace and Peter drank too much and drove too fast and cracked up their cars, and I didn't drive at all. The one benefit was the girls. While we were recording, we lived at the Ramada Inn, and it was a real rock and roll hotel, with girls going up and down the halls all day and a swimming pool stuffed with them. We didn't spend many nights alone.

Recording was smooth, more or less, although Peter and Ace were a handful. Ace had his usual problems showing up on time, and Peter was, as Peter has always been, deeply insecure about his role in the process. There's one song on there, "Strange Ways," that was written by Ace, and while we were recording, Peter insisted on playing a long drum solo. It was the kind of thing that bands like Led Zeppelin were doing, but mostly in their live shows, and Peter was no John Bonham. It just didn't work. When we heard it, we all thought it was ridiculous, and we insisted that it come off the record. Peter dug in his heels. If the solo went, he said, he would quit the band. This wasn't the first time he had given us an ultimatum, and it wouldn't be the last. We responded to it the way we always responded to his ultimatums: we ignored them, cut the drum solo out, and did what we knew was best for the band. He didn't quit.

Norman Seef, who had been a brain surgeon in Africa before he became a photographer, did the cover shoot for *Hotter Than Hell*. He was entirely competent and professional, but he was a guy who believed that when you do a photo session, you have to create a certain ambience. He probably explained this philosophy to us on the phone, but before we went down to his studio, we didn't know quite what to expect. When we got there, it was like stepping into another world. He had a number of girls, and they were walking around half naked with silver paint all over them. There were mirrors on the ceilings and pieces of furniture suspended from wires. The whole feel was very surreal, like *The Twilight Zone*. Everyone got drunk—except for me. Paul got so drunk that at the end of the shoot we had to carry him out and lock him in the backseat of our car, so he wouldn't wander away. The photo shoot was also interesting because a few days earlier, Ace had decided to see how well and how fast he could drive his car down a winding Beverly Hills mountain. As it turned out, he couldn't do it very well. He smashed up the car and his face. For the photo we had to superimpose the left side of his made-up face over the scarred right side.

The album was released in late October 1974. It was the second album we had put out that year, and after its release we went right back on the road. That meant more cities, more venues—and most of all, for me, more girls. By this time I understood exactly what I wanted out of the touring experience. I wasn't drinking. I wasn't using drugs. I could stay in the hotel and watch TV, and I did plenty of that, but I had my limits. When I had had my fill, there was only one more thing to do, and that was to go out and chase skirt.

I got a reputation for being indiscriminate, and I suppose it was earned—I didn't have very specific tastes in women. If they were female and in my presence, I was interested. During that tour, though, I surprised even myself. In a conservative town in the deep south, we had a limo driver who must have been in her sixties. She was a full-figured gal in a chauffeur's hat and uniform. I kept calling her Grandma, and she kept calling me Sonny. I must have been twenty-five, twenty-six maybe. The next day at about eight in the morning, there was a knock on the door.

"Who is it?"

"Open up, Sonny. It's Grandma."

"What time is it?"

"Eight A.M."

"I thought we weren't leaving until ten."

"You're not. Open the door, Sonny." So she came in, and we were all over the floor, the bed, everywhere else in the room. And so help me God, in the limo on the way to the airport, the other guys in the band were looking at me because I must have smelled like a lobster. I wasn't saying a word. And she turned around while she was driving and said, "Here's my nineteen-year old daughter"—or granddaughter, I don't remember which it was. "She's coming into town, want to hook up?" Then the guys figured out what had happened, and they looked at me like I was crazy.

Another time we were playing in Atlanta, and there was a policewoman offstage while we were running through our sound check. Afterward she motioned to me with her finger. I walked over and said, "Officer, you know you can't make me come with just one finger." I was being cocky.

"Very funny," she said. Then she asked me for my autograph. "It's for my daughter," she said. "She's fascinated by your tongue. I don't understand her tastes, but what am I going to do?"

"Who are you trying to fool?" I said. "It's not your daughter. It's you. You want to come and get it? I'm in room 190." Naturally I didn't expect anything. But later that night there was a knock on the door, and the woman was standing there in her full police outfit. When she walked in, it was like a scene from a movie. She took her hat off, and her long hair fell down. Then she unbuckled her belt and took off her gun. Then the scene faded to black. The next day we both came downstairs, and she was dressed like a policewoman again. The guys all lined up against the wall: it was as if someone had yelled "spread 'em."

When I wasn't chasing girls, I was trying to keep Ace and Peter out of trouble. It took some doing, especially in Ace's case. Originally Peter and Ace had roomed together, but after a while they didn't get along. Peter asked me if I would mind if he roomed with Paul and I roomed with Ace. It didn't bother me. We were all in the same band. One night I was going down to the hotel bar to see if there were any girls for the taking. I asked Ace if he wanted to come along. "No," he said. "You go ahead. I'll be down in a little while." I went by myself, and of course there were girls, and I started talking to them. After a while, though, I started to wonder where Ace was. I called up to the room, and no one answered. Then I got a little worried. I got one of the hotel managers, and we went to the room and knocked on the door, but there was no answer. Finally we smashed open the door. Ace was in the bathtub, passed out and slumped down, with the water rising. His mouth was just above the water. He would've died in a minute. He smelled like a pickled herring. We pulled him out of the water naked and put him

to bed. I stayed up all night to make sure he didn't roll over and fall to the ground, which he did anyway, or throw up and choke on his own vomit. By the next morning I was exhausted. Ace wasn't—he bounded out of bed, bright-eyed and bushy-tailed. Hey," he said, "I stayed in last night and went to bed early. What did you do?" He didn't remember a single minute of the ordeal.

✦ ✦ ✦

Despite our best efforts—and we were still growing as a touring band, both in confidence and in ability—*Hotter Than Hell* wasn't a commer-

In the chair at the Georgette Klinger salon, getting ready for a *People* magazine spread in 1975.

cial success. The album barely made it into the top 100, and soon Neil Bogart was calling for yet another album. This time we came back to New York to record it. It was called *Dressed to Kill,* and Neil had decided that he would produce it with us, back in New York, at Electric Lady studios.

The objective for the third album was to push KISS to a higher level. For previous albums, Neil had boosted sales with novelty singles or television appearances. This time he wanted an anthem. He told us he wanted a song like Sly and the Family Stone's "I Want to Take You Higher," something that would get the whole audience involved, screaming, pumping their fists. Paul had an unfinished song he had been working on for months, and I had a piece of a song that I hadn't finished either. We put the two together, and before we knew it, we had this new song, which eventually became "Rock and Roll All Nite." The song was simple, which was very appealing, and it had a chorus vocal that was sung by a large group of people in the studio—not just the four band members but engineers, families of people from the record label, about twenty people in all. We felt the energy of it immediately—it was like those old Slade songs that we had liked when we were just starting out, but with this very accessible, middle-America feel. We had a feeling it was going to be big.

For the cover of *Dressed to Kill,* we used a photographer named Bob Gruen, who had earned some fame for taking pictures of John Lennon and had worked with dozens of other rock stars. The original idea was to have us in full makeup on the streets of New York, but Bob thought that it might be more interesting to put us in makeup and normal business clothes. We liked the idea, but there was only one problem—none of us had normal business clothes. So we borrowed suits from people, and they weren't exactly perfect fits. If you look at the cover photo closely, you can see that my pant legs and jacket are a little too short and a little too tight.

Dressed to Kill was released in March 1975, and the single of "Rock and Roll All Nite" went to radio a week later. It wasn't the success we had hoped for. It didn't do terribly—I think it peaked at number sixty-eight—but we had really thought that it might break us into a different level of radio play, and it didn't. At the same time, we were laying the groundwork for our next album. About a week after *Dressed to Kill* was released, we made plans to record some live shows. There was already talk of possibly putting out a live KISS album, because we still felt that we were a much more powerful band onstage than in the studio. We loved being on tour, and it showed.

I remember two sisters who showed up at my hotel room door in Indianapolis in early 1975, both of whom wanted to spend the night with me. The better-looking of the two was noticeably pregnant. Despite that, we all stripped naked, got into the shower, and became fast friends.

In another city after another show, I opened another hotel room door to find another lovely young lady. My guess was that she was eighteen. I always made it a point to ask the girls how old they were. It may not have been the most gentlemanly thing to ask, but my intentions were certainly honorable. She came in and quickly had her way with me, and I with her. Then there was another knock at the door, and I yelled for whoever it was to leave. My young lady friend said that I could answer the door, it was okay with her. When I opened the door, a woman was standing there, attractive and in her early forties, who identified herself as the mother of my companion. I must have looked as if I'd seen a ghost, but the mother said there was no problem and asked me if it was okay for her to come in and join the fun. I looked over at my young lady friend, and she just giggled and nodded her head yes. Life was good.

In a midwestern city—I can't say which, but it's on a lake—a prominent radio promotion man invited KISS to be his guests at his home for dinner. We were told to go, because we needed radio support to sell records. The dinner was uneventful and quite boring—until the promo guy got up and started making a long speech. Sitting across from me was his beautiful wife. When she brushed her high heels against me under the table, initially I thought it was accidental and moved my leg away. I had already arranged for a guest to meet me at my hotel after dinner and had no intention of coming on to this man's wife. She brushed up against me a second time and smiled suggestively. Then the promo guy took some of our guys on a tour of his home, and his wife quickly took me by the hand and led me to the far end of the house into a bathroom. There she dropped to her knees without a word and showed me how fond she was of me.

Some of the memories are bittersweet. When KISS played Las Vegas for the first time, we had finished the concert and quickly made our way back to the Stardust Hotel. Standing in the lobby, waiting for the elevator, Peter nudged me and whispered, "Wow— look at that girl over there." She was stunning: long blond hair, short tight miniskirt, and high heels. She smiled. I immediately reached out, grabbed her hand, and pulled her into the elevator

Dressed to Kill cover shoot, with Neil Bogart, at Electric Ladyland Studios in 1975.

with us. She came willingly. Neither of us said a word while the elevator went up to my floor. When we got inside my room, words didn't seem necessary. We devoured each other.

Afterward she told me that her name was Star, that someday she would be a star, and that her last name was Stowe. We stayed up all night long, and when morning came and it was time to leave, she asked me what she should do. I remember saying something about sending photos of herself to Hugh Hefner. I was out of touch with her for about six months. Then one of our road crew showed me an issue of *Playboy*. The centerfold was Star Stowe; she described herself as a "one-band woman" and said some very nice things about me. I contacted her, and for a time she was my companion on the

The beautiful Star Stowe in 1975. Fin Costello, the photographer, is on the left.

road. We had terrific times. We went to movies together. We went to clubs. We ate. We danced. We couldn't keep our hands off each other.

After a time I lost touch with her. Years later I ran into her at one of our concerts. She had been through some hard times, had not saved any money, and seemed sadder than I had ever seen her. Later on I looked her up and was stunned to find that she had passed away.

The relative failure of the "Rock and Roll All Nite" single disappointed us slightly, but it didn't scare us, because we knew exactly what we had to do. We had to go right back on the road, which was where we were strongest and connected with our audience most powerfully. This time there was an extra wrinkle: we had decided to record some of the shows and release them as a live album. We had the three studio albums, but we never felt as though they captured the band. They were merely documents. For the full KISS experience, we needed to let fans have a taste of our live show—not only the theatrical elements but the power of the band.

rock and roll and DESTROYER

The recordings that would become *Alive!* were drawn from a number of concerts, including shows in New Jersey and Iowa. The majority of the album, though, was taken from a late March show at Cobo Hall in Detroit. In some ways the decision to tape the Detroit concerts was the easiest one we ever made. A city is never just a city. It is always defined by the people who live in it and by what they do for a living, which then in a very real way affects their lifestyle. Because New York is a cosmopolitan city, it was the birthplace of Studio 54. Southern cities were more repressed in some ways and wilder in others. Detroit, being the hub of the auto industry, was antifashion, much more meat and potatoes. I wouldn't be surprised if McDonald's sold more hamburgers in Detroit than anywhere else. It's very blue collar, a real middle-American metropolis. The big stars that emerged out of Detroit through the late 1960s and early 1970s— the MC5, Ted Nugent, Bob Seger, and Grand Funk Railroad—were similar bands: loud and passionate, with minimal pretention and a bit of grittiness. Detroit is all about no-nonsense music. From our

We were one of the biggest bands in the world.

all nite: ALIVE!
1975~1976

very first record, Detroit had taken us to heart immediately. People in New York and Los Angeles misread us—they affected a certain sophistication and felt that we weren't up to their standards. But Detroit understood our mix of fun and energy from the start.

After the Detroit show, we were presented with an award and went to a party thrown in our honor. There was plenty of action at the party—lots of booze, music, and women. I wasn't interested in the booze; I had had my fill of music for the day; and I even had my female companion for the night, a writer from *Creem* magazine who was doing a feature article about the band. I was ready to leave with her, when I spied the waitress moving through the crowd with a plate of brownies. My sweet tooth got the better of me, and I pounced on those suckers. I must have eaten six or seven of them before I had my fill. Within five minutes I became Gene in Wonderland. Immediately my head shrank to the size of an apple. My feet ballooned to the size of boards. My hands grew bigger the longer I stared at them. I grew frightened, took the hand of my female companion, and ran out to the waiting limo.

Once inside I became very thirsty for milk. I had to have some, and within a block of the concert hall, in a seedy part of Detroit, we pulled up to an all-night diner. Inside it was quiet, and there were a few people with their heads down, either eating or drinking coffee. I stepped up to the counter, thinking that my voice couldn't be heard because my vocal cords must have shrunk along with my head. I screamed at full volume, *"May I have a glass of milk, please?"* It scared the pants off the waitress. Everyone at the place, now startled, looked up. I was embarrassed. I thought they were all looking at how small my head had gotten. I left the diner, dove back into the car, and thanked God my female companion knew where the hotel was. She got us there, and as I was walking down the hallway, propped up by her, every step felt as though I were walking through a funhouse mirror.

When we got to the door to my room, I couldn't fit my key in the lock. My key was now the size of an anvil, and the keyhole no bigger than the eye of a needle. The only saving grace that night, when we finally got into bed, was that I was finally proud of my manhood and couldn't imagine anything getting bigger.

Alive! almost did not come out. Casablanca had taken a bath on a record called *Best Moments of the Tonight Show,* a double album that consisted of highlights from Johnny Carson's talk show. (Ironically enough, this record was put together by Joyce Biawitz, our former comanager and the woman who would soon be Mrs. Neil Bogart.) Even though we were the label's prize act, there wasn't a whole lot of money to go around. There have always been rumors that the *Alive!* record was substantially reworked in the studio. It's not true. We did touch up the vocal parts and fix some of the guitar solos, but we didn't have the time or money to completely rework the recordings. What we wanted, and what we got, was proof of the band's rawness and power.

Alive! was released in September 1975 and immediately moved up the charts. Sales eventually went to four million. Amazingly, the live record produced our first big single, a concert version of "Rock

We received an award for breaking the attendance record at Cobo Hall in Detroit (held by Elvis). From left to right, Bill Aucoin, Peter, me, Paul, Ace, and Joyce and Neil Bogart, with Steve Glantz, seated.

and Roll All Nite." Almost overnight we went from being a working band with a record contract and a devoted following to being national superstars. The lasting effect of the live album went beyond KISS, in fact—it affected the entire rock industry. Before *Alive!* bands didn't really release concert albums as legitimate product. They were almost always put out to fulfill contracts. We were one of the first bands to really care about the idea and to package it accordingly: when the album came out, it had a gatefold showing all three studio records and pictures of handwritten notes from all the band members. Within three years, many more of these elaborate live packages appeared, including *Frampton Comes Alive* and *Cheap Trick at Budokan* (which included a little homage to us in a song called "Surrender" with the lyric "Rock and rolling, got my KISS records out"). Live records became mandatory for 1970s superstars, and we led the way.

+ + +

After the massive success of *Alive!,* we knew that we had to deliver a grand statement. We wanted a studio record that would top all our previous efforts. To achieve that, we brought in Bob Ezrin, who was already well known as a producer for his work with Alice Cooper and would later produce Pink Floyd's *The Wall.* We started recording in the Record Plant in New York in January 1976—only five months after the release of *Alive!*

Up until we met Bob Ezrin, we were leery of letting anybody else have a say as to what we should record. That included management, record companies, producers, anybody. Bob Ezrin was the first and continues to be the only producer who ever really had an effect on the band.

It's hard to say why we let Bob have so much control, yet it's also easy. It wasn't about his track record. It's never about a track record. It is more about the fact that when somebody has an idea and can communicate that idea as effectively as Bob, they automatically command a certain respect. Other bands have stories about meeting up with producers who teach them how to be professionals—before these producers came along, they were noble savages, beating on their guitars and just hoping for the best. It wasn't like that with KISS. We had known what we were doing since the beginning. Bob didn't make us go faster. In fact, if anything he slowed the process down considerably. But it was the way he slowed it down that was impressive. At one point I remember him stopping us in the middle of a rehearsal. "Okay," he said. "Do you guys know how to tune your instruments?"

We were all self-taught musicians. We said, "Of course—here's how you tune them."

He frowned. "No," he said. "There's another way to tune instruments, which is pitch-perfect. It's called harmonic tuning." And he showed us how to do it, which we had never seen in our lives. It was like going back to school, or to summer camp—he carried a whistle around, and whenever he wanted to get our attention, he would say, "Campers!" Every time we thought we had done enough to satisfy him, he would come at us with something else.

In some ways, he was quite a disciplinarian. When he didn't think we were getting a handle on something, he would send us outside the studio. Paul and I were excited, because we knew the experience was making the band better. We were rubbing our hands together, thinking *Oh, boy, this is going to a place we haven't been.* It was a really good adventure because we recognized that whatever we were doing, even though it was a step forward, it still sounded like KISS, but better than before. We literally heard the record coming together there in the studio, and it was the best version of the band to that point.

Much of the success of *Destroyer* had to do with Bob's bravery, particularly his interest in introducing new elements into our music. Bob's children would come in—he was going through a divorce at the time—and they actually wound up as the little voices in "God of Thunder." He was doing all kinds of things, like having symphony orchestras and choirs. What George Martin was to the Beatles, Bob Ezrin was to us. He had something that we had never seen before in a producer: a vision. He knew where he was going within the confines of what KISS was. And most important, he knew how to get there. While Paul and I had perspective and vision, we didn't quite know how to get there, because we were limited as musicians. There was one thing we did know, though—we wanted to create an experience that went beyond the experiences that other rock bands were creating.

Bob really listened to our songs and recognized that we were less about storytelling than about singing about our own feelings and perceptions: "I'm the king of the nighttime world." "I want to rock and roll all night." That was a quantum difference. "I am the God of Thunder." These were the kinds of statements we specialized in, and they differentiated us from other bands. When we spoke to Bob about this, he realized that the simplicity and self-absorption in the lyrics was purposeful, that we were a band with a distinct point of view rather than just a set of guys who didn't have a clue. We wanted to write anthems, songs that felt like the theme songs for a generation, songs that had a "you and me against the world" perspective.

◆ ◆ ◆

As much as Paul and I loved working with Bob, Ace and Peter hated it. For the first time, they couldn't take the easy way out. Ace was not about discipline—he wouldn't even show up on time. And nobody had ever sat Peter down and said, "Here is a two and a four." He has never been able to articulate his own playing: "Give me a one and a three on a kick, and a two and a four on the snare." He wouldn't have a clue what that meant, and to this day he doesn't know what a two or a four is. Peter has always played by feel and couldn't play the same thing twice.

As a result, Bob Ezrin's time with the band was very tough for Ace and Peter, or at least that's how they saw it. Peter in particular was devastated by it. He had never had any discipline; he was a street kid. Paul and I had always been critical of Ace and Peter because they didn't get the big picture. But here was this guy from the outside doing the same thing, only ten times more intensely.

Paul and I used to talk about who was taking the experience harder. In retrospect, I think both of them were feeling quite defeated, although their feelings manifested in different ways. Peter would come out furious that somebody was telling him what to play or how to sing. And that that's not rock and roll. It was the same personality that made him threaten to leave the band if we didn't include his "Strange Ways" solo, back in 1974.

Ace would simply leave. Sometimes he wouldn't show up at recording sessions. On one occasion he wanted to leave early because he had a card game at seven that evening. At some point Bob didn't worry about Ace or his excuses—he simply got another guitar player to come in to play Ace's parts. Mainly, it was a guy called Dick Wagner, who played with the Lou Reed Band. He was not credited, and to this day people think it's Ace on the album. Ace felt as if Paul and I especially were traitors, and that we told Bob Ezrin to get another guitar player because we never wanted him in the band anyway. Yet we were the ones who brought him into the band, pushed him to write his own songs, and asked him to be more than a guitar player and sing his own songs. He was oblivious to that, and continues to be.

+ + +

During the recording of *Destroyer* in 1975, I had another drug experience. Not an experience in which I took a drug, but the first time I ever saw cocaine cut up and ready to be snorted. A mirror was built into the control console at the recording studio, and I was clueless about its purpose. I kept on saying, "Look how stupid this is, you have to bend down to see your face. The least they could do is hang it up on the wall." And everybody would laugh. But nobody ever told me what it was for. At the time I was using Sweet 'N Low in my coffee, because I have always loved desserts but wanted to lose weight. One day I walked in, and there was powder on the mirror, and I was so oblivious to everything about drugs that I assumed it was Sweet 'N Low. I made myself some coffee and I brushed some of the stuff on the console into my cup. Then I thought twice about it and said to myself, *That's probably got dirt and stuff.* One of the engineers explained it to me: "No, that's cocaine. You cut it up, you snort it with a straw."

"That's stupid!" I said. It seemed so stupid to me, in fact, that I actually took Sweet 'N Low and spread it on the control console. I don't know if anybody took it or not. But I thought that was a funny thing at the time.

While we were recording *Destroyer,* we spent a lot of time in the studio, more than we ever had. During the course of those sessions, I'd be plugging one of the girls who worked there. I would say, "Excuse me, guys, I got to go pee," and slip away to fuck her pants off. On one occasion, I snuck her into a vocal booth and laid her down. I ravenously went at her and she at me until she stopped, patted me on the back, and pointed to the window portal: Ezrin and the band had seen the whole thing. Paul then got the message and started doing her. We were on swing shift.

♦ ♦ ♦

After KISS played a concert in Flint, Michigan, in 1975, Peter and I were in a limousine together, and he was trying to sing something he called "Beck," about a girl named Becky. I suggested that he change the name to Beth, both because it was a little easier to sing and because it would eliminate any misunderstanding that it was about Jeff Beck. Peter brought this nice little melody into the studio and sang it for Bob. Immediately Bob sat down and fleshed it out. He had a much wider musical library than any of us. He listened to jazz, to classical, to country. He stuck in a middle eight from a Mozart piano concerto, rewrote the lyric, and suddenly we had a song.

But we didn't really know what to do with it. Rock bands didn't do ballads, least of all in the midst of a concerted push for rock and roll credibility. The only way we validated the idea that there were strings on it was because of "Yesterday" by the Beatles. If it was cool for the Beatles, then we could do it. The first few singles from *Destroyer* hadn't done quite as well as we wanted. "Shout It Out Loud" was the first single, and it got into the Top 40. Then the label released "Flaming Youth," with a special picture disk, but that only got to number 74. The third single was "Detroit Rock City," with "Beth," this strange unclassifiable ballad, on the B-side. We had high hopes for "Detroit Rock City," but it didn't even chart, and the album—which had reached as high as number 11 and sold about 850,000—was beginning to taper off. That's when something strange started to happen. Radio stations turned over the record and started playing "Beth" instead of "Detroit Rock City," and it quickly became a huge hit.

"Beth" was a breakthrough single, establishing the record. Now, rather than having a hit with a live record and then sinking back down, we were riding the crest of two massive hit records. In pop music this has been the way to create superstars from stars, and sure enough, we were superstars. Soon after *Destroyer* came out, we played our first stadium, Anaheim Stadium in California, which held

This is me, without the makeup, and an editor of *Superteen* magazine, who interviewed me for an article in 1976.

55,000 fans. If it hadn't happened to us, we wouldn't have believed it: this was early 1976, only two years after we released our first record, and there we were playing stadiums before anyone other than the Beatles had. Bands that had been around for almost a decade, including Ted Nugent and Bob Seger, were opening for us. We knew something was going on. It was clear.

The first burst of fame coincided with the first wave of KISS merchandise. I had always seen the band as a means to an end—in my mind, making music was only part of the plan. The master plan was to create a cultural institution that was as iconic as Disney. From the very beginning, we were at the forefront of rock and roll merchandising: we had the usual products, like T-shirts and posters, but we also had an interest in expanding into other markets. We grew to the point that Bill Aucoin actually bought a share in a company called Boutwell, and we wound up in manufacturing. Warehouses in the southern California valley were manufacturing our own T-shirts, belt buckles, and stuff. Mail-order forms were enclosed inside the records. We did things other bands wouldn't have had the balls to do, the same things you see when you buy *Time* magazine—there's an order form inside. From the start, we didn't care that it invalidated what we did. We were not concerned with credibility. It just looked like a lot of fun.

As time went on, some bands took a stand against this kind of thing. Primarily they came from the big art rock movement in New York. We always thought they were geeks. It was as if all of a sudden the guys who never got laid in school put guitars around their necks. They didn't count for us. They didn't look like stars, they looked like students. And they always talked about stuff we couldn't care less about. Burning buildings? What are you talking about?

All of a sudden we were one of the biggest bands in the world. In the mid-1970s a lot of the bands we grew up with were not exactly at their peak. The Stones were not. The Who were not. And we were outselling them more than two to one. Bands like Queen were huge worldwide, but in America they didn't tour much. We didn't have many peers.

At that time misinformation about the band began to spread in the southern Bible Belt states, including a rumor that the name *KISS* stood for Knights In Satan's Service, and that the four of us were devil worshipers. Ironically, this rumor started as a result of an interview I gave in *Circus* magazine after our first album; in response to a question, I said that I sometimes wondered what human flesh tastes like. I never wanted to really find out, but I was curious intellectually. Later on, this comment seemed to ignite the whole idea that in some way KISS was aligned with devil worship. When I was asked whether I worshiped the devil, I simply refused to answer for a number of reasons: the first reason, of course, was that it was good press. Let people wonder. The other reason was my complete disregard for the people who were asking. The religious fanatics who were asking these questions didn't deserve the time of day. The uneducated always point to religious principles. Through the years, whenever religious fanatics accosted me, especially in the southern states, and quoted the Old Testament at me, I would quote them back chapter and verse. They didn't know that I had been a theology major in school. An idiot is an idiot . . . whether he quotes the Bible or not.

Fueling the fire for the Satan-worshiping nonsense was my hand signal, which involved the pinky, the thumb, and the index finger. This started innocently enough: during concerts, I'd hold the pick with my thumb and my two middle fingers. Some people mistakenly thought it was a gesture of some kind, so they started waving their index and pinky fingers toward me in return. The second part of the hand signal came from my love of Spider Man: in the comics, he sometimes had his middle finger pressed against the inside of his palm. I copied that in an early photo, and the fundamentalists seized on it. In point of fact, the hand signal actually means "I love you" in sign language, though I didn't know that at the time. This hand signal, ironically enough, became a standard gesture for other heavy metal bands and their fans, and it has been in constant circulation ever since.

I was getting the hang of handling magazine reporters. A *Rolling Stone* writer wanted to do a story on the band. He came up to a duplex I was renting on Riverside Drive in New York to interview me for what he said would be a cover story. When I met him, I was very careful to cultivate the Demon mystique. I wore all my spider and silver jewelry and my leather pants. I puffed up my hair as big as it would go. With my seven-inch platform boots with silver dollar signs on them, and black nail polish, I thought I was ready to project a perfect bad-ass rock and roll image. He was right there with me through this entire interview. Then at one point the door buzzer sounded. I answered it, and in the doorway was my mother with enough food to feed the world: fresh hot soups, veal cutlets, pancakes, jams, cake. She insisted that he and I—I think she called us "hungry boys"—stop what we were doing and eat. She kept calling me by my Hebrew name, Chaim, and told the writer I was a good boy. The big bad Demon was just a mama's boy.

Being a mama's boy, though, has never kept me from chasing the ladies. I bedded down one girl after another. There was no end to them—they were in every hotel room, every backstage area, every limousine. At one point I found out that the Carpenters were staying in the same hotel. I called Karen Carpenter, who was staying a few floors below me, and left my female guest in my room to go down there with the idea of seducing her. Karen was certainly playful enough on the phone with me: very giggly, very friendly, and very suggestive. But when I walked in on what I thought was going to be an evening of seduction, it became something else. Karen was a sweet, frail girl: she still looked fairly healthy, not as gaunt as she would later become from anorexia. I spent most of the early evening talking with her about all kinds of things. Mostly she was fascinated and curious about my bed-hopping lifestyle. She didn't understand it. Although she did admit that lust is a strong urge, and she agreed that men were susceptible to the powers of lust, she was nonetheless convinced that I didn't actually want to do what I wanted to do but was actually doing it to avoid intimacy. But she said all this in a very nonjudgmental way.

At the end of the conversation, I said, "Well, it was nice talking to you, I've gotta go." She wanted to know where I was going. I said I had left a girl upstairs and I would have to go and keep her company. Karen was flabbergasted that the girl would wait for me and simply not leave. I thought it was bizarre that she would even ask me that. Where I had initially walked down with seduction on my mind, the truth is, sex was the last thing that either one of us wanted from the other that night. Maybe because of that, the experience has remained in my mind all these years.

◆ ◆ ◆

Our lifestyle changed drastically after *Destroyer,* especially after the boost from "Beth." I bought houses for both my parents, even though I hadn't seen my father since he left me as a child in Israel. Paul did likewise for his folks.

But Ace and Peter lived at the edge: they bought many cars and lived in many houses. At one point Ace built a home recording studio with poured concrete, then found he couldn't use it because his neighborhood wasn't zoned for it. Between them they cracked up or crashed at least ten cars—Mercedeses, DeLoreans, you name it. The funniest one was Peter crashing in his garage. The fire department had to come in with the jaws of life to get him out of his car in his own garage.

Another part of our lifestyle changed too. As I have said, we always had plenty of women on the road, but now we had the means to treat them like queens, and that caused problems in our personal relationships. There are some hilarious stories about Peter. I had a liaison with a girl and then Peter fell for her. They saw each other for a little while, and then Peter brought her phone number back home. His wife was a jealous woman, and was brighter than Peter, so he hid the phone number under the stereo. His wife was cleaning one day, and she actually lifted up the stereo and found the number. So she called up this girl and said, "Hello? This is the Oregon Health Department. Are you so-and-so?"

The woman said, "Yes. Why are you calling me?"

"Well, we just need to find out if you are familiar with a Peter Criscuola, who is otherwise known as Peter Criss, drummer in KISS."

"Yes?"

"Well," Peter's wife said, "he may have the clap. We are trying to ascertain what period of time you may have had physical contact, because you may need to get a check-up. Can you tell us the specifics?"

At this the woman came clean with the specifics: it was this time of night, in this Holiday Inn. "Thank you very much," Peter's wife said, and hung up.

When he came home, she had him pinned. "Peter, where were you at seven-thirty at night on Monday . . . were you with so-and-so?" She had him dead to rights.

◆ ◆ ◆

In May 1976 we sold out Madison Square Garden for three nights in a row. This was a big deal for us; when we were starting out, the four of us used to sit in our loft at 10 East Twenty-third Street and say that we had only ten blocks to go to reach Madison Square Garden, which is on Thirty-third Street. And now we were there.

CBS News had a broadcaster named Kaity Tong—she was one of their big stars then. The cameras were all over us, and she kept asking me questions about the experience: less about rock and roll and more about the freak show aspect of our lives. "You guys look so weird. And you are the guy who sticks his tongue out—how long is it, anyway?" I was close to seven feet tall in the outfit, and she must have been about five-two. Her arm was stretched way up into the air to hold the microphone near my mouth. While she was interviewing me, with the cameras all around me, I felt something in back of me. I turned around, and my mom (all five-four of her) was trying to fix something, to make it look right. I was wearing a thin strip of leather with studs around it, and it ran right through the crack of my butt and connected to a codpiece covered with spikes, and my mother was trying to brush off a piece of lint, or clean a spot, or something. It was like trying to walk up in back of a tank and take off a piece of thread.

By this time my mother had remarried. Her new husband was a man named Eli, a Polish gentleman who had lost some family in the war. He worked in the clothing business, and he worshiped my mother. If they were walking down the street and she saw a piece of clothing she liked in a window, he would study it intently and then make an exact replica for her. The timing of the remarriage was good, because it allowed me to get on with my life. When I was younger, it was just the two of us, my mother and me, and at that time I probably would have had difficulty dealing with a remarriage. When Eli came along, though, I was already out of the house, at college, and ready to be on my own.

Eli and my mother didn't really understand the band project. I had this pact with my mother: if my music career didn't work out, I would fall back on teaching. That seemed to satisfy her, but beyond that, it was all a mystery to them. I don't remember talking to either of them very much at that time—I was so busy trying to build up the band—although I do recall having conversations with Eli about politics. I was a young man, more liberal and more accepting of difference. He was less liberal. One of the things I came to understand was that when you had seen what he had seen—when you had witnessed your family murdered by people supposedly representing your government—you didn't necessarily believe in liberal politics.

◆ ◆ ◆

In 1976 KISS went over to Europe for a major tour. We arrived at Heathrow Airport in London and came off the plane in full makeup. The press was all over us, and we drove around to all the sights and had pictures taken for the magazines. I was in awe, because it was England, the home of the Beatles. It was like a pilgrimage to Mecca.

One of our female aides in England was an attractive Indian woman. By the time we got to our hotel, I convinced her to be my guest in my room. It was a fine welcome to a new country. Our hotel overlooked Hyde Park. It was a medium-quality hotel, but it prided itself on archaic notions of proper behavior. For instance, when I had female visitors, they were not allowed to visit me in my room, so I had to sneak them in.

British nightlife was just as rewarding as American nightlife. One night we went to the Marquis Club, and it was packed. I roamed around the room looking for a new friend or two. I walked up to the bar and asked for a Coke. I never drank and have literally never been drunk in my life. Patti Smith was standing next to the bar. I don't recall saying a word to her. I was more preoccupied by two stunning girls standing at the far end of the room. All of a sudden Smith turned, slapped me across my face, slurred something, and walked off. To this day I am clueless as to what made her do that. But it didn't take me long to walk over to the two lovelies, start dancing with both of them on the dance floor, and in short order take them both back to the hotel. The ladies turned out to be two of the Coconuts from Kid Creole and the Coconuts, a band I later loved and would often go to see. The evening at the hotel began hot and heavy. We were apparently making quite a bit of noise, because there was a loud knock on my door. It was Paul. Didn't I realize, he said, that it was the middle of the night? Couldn't I keep the noise down? I apologized, came back in, and the girls and I moved the bed away from the wall, put the mattress on the floor, and continued on with our business. It was probably five in the morning when we all became ravenously hungry. I ordered a feast. It came up in a surprisingly short time, but I had inadvertently given the wrong room number, and the hotel delivered all the food to Paul's room. He was, by that time, in no mood to joke. From then on, Paul insisted he never wanted the room next to mine.

The rest of Europe wasn't quite as fulfilling as England. For starters, the accommodations were different from what we had come to expect. European hotels weren't like American hotels; they were smaller, and the plumbing didn't always work the way it was supposed to work. Also, *Alive!* wasn't selling well everywhere, so in some countries we felt like we were almost starting over. In some places we packed arenas, and in some places we played to mostly empty houses. France didn't have a strong rock and roll tradition— even to this day, it hasn't produced rock stars of any consequence. At times it was extremely frustrating. But for every France, there were places like the Scandinavian countries, which were wonderful. Wonderful crowds, wonderful fans, wonderful girls.

✦ ✦ ✦

We were thrilled with our new-found fame; it was what we had spent years working toward. Our families were thrilled for us. But even at the peak of our fame, we were isolated from the rest of the rock and roll world. We never appeared on other people's records. We never hung out. There was something solitary about us. This, too, was taken from the Beatles. When the Beatles played, nobody else belonged on that stage. If you were in the Stones, Tina Turner and whoever else could jump up onstage. But if you were in the Beatles, it was only the Beatles. That was how I felt about my band. If I went to see my band live, I didn't want to see anybody else step up. So we were like that. And through the years everybody said, "Hey, let's go jam." We didn't jam. We didn't hang out before or after the show. For me, at least, it was always about chasing skirt. I couldn't have cared less about another guy playing guitar. I wanted to know who would share my bed that night.

Also, at a time when movie stars often sat in the front row of rock shows, we never attracted any other celebrities. I have since learned that almost everyone in the world was a closet KISS fan. Jimmy Buffett wrote a song called "Mañana," for example, where he said, "You have never seen anything till you've seen a sunset / You have never seen a rock show until you've seen KISS." Cheap Trick wrote "Surrender," about Mom and Dad rolling around on the couch with the kid's KISS records. Every day of the week I meet someone who's a fan, whether it's Garth Brooks or Lenny Kravitz.

I have created a character named the Demon who is a WCW wrestler and uses the Gene Simmons makeup. Last year I got a request for an autograph from a five-year-old kid named David. His father requested it, actually, and asked if I would please make it out to David, from the Demon. "Do you want me to write Gene Simmons?" I asked.

"No," the father said. "He doesn't know who Gene Simmons or KISS is. He only knows about the Demon," the wrestler. The monster had become the star!

When it came time to go back into the studio to make our next album, we had to decide whether to work with Bob Ezrin again. Ace and Peter were pressing us to get back to basics, to being a four-piece rock and roll band without arrangements, ballads, or someone else telling us how to play. At the time a certain segment of our fan base felt that *Destroyer* was a very plush record. If you listen to it today, it's one of our most consistent rock records, and it probably stands the test of time as well as any, but there were violins, so for some people that was a problem. Change is always difficult for the hard and heavy.

i'm a legend

So Ace and Peter wanted to get back to doing straight-ahead rock and roll, and we were sensitive to that. We rented out the Star Theater, a theater in upstate New York that Frank Sinatra actually had a stake in. (Later on it went out of business mysteriously after a fire.) There was a center stage and seats all around it. We brought in Eddie Kramer and started work on the next album, *Rock and Roll Over*. We recorded the songs that Paul and I had written on tour. Ace and Peter also submitted songs, most of which were, at least in our estimation, not up to par. The ones that survived wound up being on the record but rearranged and rewritten. There were

tonight: LOVE GUN
1976~1977

From our 1977 tour at Budokan, Japan. We broke the record for live attendance held by the Beatles.

plenty of things that Paul and I did without taking credit for, because we knew that the fans preferred to think that everybody in the band wrote and was as creative as everybody else.

It was a relatively stable time for the band. We were fairly happy. Still, talking about stability in KISS is like talking about freedom in a prison. It's all relative. Ace and Peter continued to do the most bizarre things. Ace had a fascination with Nazi memorabilia, and in his drunken stupors he and his best friend would make videotapes of themselves dressed up as Nazis. At the time the mayor of New York was Ed Koch, who was Jewish, and Ace showed me a piece of tape where he and his best friend were making verbal threats against "the Jew in New York," saying, "We'll cook him up." Of course, he was drunk out of his mind. Paul and I weren't thrilled about that. But Ace laughed at how funny he was when he saw the tape.

Peter, too, was drinking heavily and using drugs. At one point he went into a club and allegedly demanded that a certain substance be put in front of him in a bowl. The owner of the club refused. So Peter tried to intimidate him, but nothing happened. Again, he was all bark and no bite. This was how he liked to do business—with intimidation and bluster.

◆ ◆ ◆

Despite all this hassle, Paul and I stayed loyal to the band. No matter what the lunacy was, the band was together. In retrospect, it might have been a mistake. We would have saved ourselves a ton of headaches if, at the first sign of trouble, we had made changes in the band. Throughout this time Ace and Peter were begging us to do exactly that. Later, when Ace made his solo album, he went on record and said that if he hadn't left the band, he would have killed himself, because he said he wasn't allowed creative freedom within KISS. But once he left the band, he went bankrupt, filed Chapter 11, and became a bigger drug addict than he ever had been, I'm sorry to say.

Ace, God bless him, has told me he believes in extraterrestrials, ghosts, karma, and other bizarre things. He has a lucky number, which is 27. If he gets change from a cashier, and he's got two pennies and a quarter, he'll stare at them until you ask him what he's doing, and then he'll say, "Look: if you add up these coins, they become 27." Or if you're in a restaurant, and the prices of the specials are on the board, he'll add up those numbers to figure out what to order. If a number there interferes with his lucky-number theory, he'll just discount it. At one point I told him, "Ace, I think you'd better pick another lucky number. You haven't been so lucky." But he doesn't understand. He's the kind of guy who will come back from Las Vegas and tell you about how much money he's won, without saying a word about how much he's lost.

Fame creates monsters, and I'm not just talking about Ace and Peter. I'm also talking about myself. At around this time, in 1977, we hired a new road manager, Frankie Scinlaro. He was on the shorter side and round, and we loved him. He missed his calling in life, because he constantly kept all of us laughing. Frankie had also been through the rock wars with other bands. He had heard all the drug and booze stories, and he was wise to Ace and Peter. He was also wise to Gene and Paul.

He gave all of us nicknames, once he got to know us. These names reached right down to the core of who we were and what each of our personal agendas was. One of Peter's nicknames, for example, was Peter Long, because he was always complaining. He was also called the Ayatollah Criscuola and Mr. Misery. Ace was High Octane, because he was frequently tanked. Paul was the He-She, because of his androgynous appeal. I was Gene the Nazarene. Frankie thought, rightfully so, that I had an inflated sense of myself and that I thought everyone else was an idiot. He would often say, "Oh, thank you so much for talking to me. I feel so honored. I want to grow up to be exactly like you." He kept bowing to me and scraping. It was humiliating, but I deserved it.

◆ ◆ ◆

In the mid-1970s we were popular enough that teenagers and even younger kids were buying our records. And that meant lots of other KISS products were in demand—Halloween masks, lunchboxes, stickers for school notebooks, pencil erasers. Moving forward with the merchandising changed the complexion of the band. It changed the size of the vision, the shape of our projects, everything. And it wasn't greeted with universal support from the band. Ace and Peter didn't like it, because they didn't see the big picture. But even Paul was a little reluctant. Some things he saw as improper in a rock and roll context. Paul often would, and still does, shoot down ideas, because he's more cautious—he tries to contain what we've got. Though I'm supposed to pick up the phone at all times and discuss new ideas with him, I often don't. I just plow straight ahead and do it, whether it's KISS My Ass toilet paper or KISSTORY books or whatever, and later on Paul and I have words with each other. They're never fatal disputes, though. They're spirited disagreements.

I would sit up and do drawings. In fact, I came in with an idea called KISSWorld in 1976 that had our lawyer's trademark. I wanted ten flatbed trucks with everything inside them, designed so that when they pulled up to a state fair, the walls of the trucks would open up and flatten out so that all the trucks connected to each other. There would be stairs and in the middle a big tent. And all of a sudden you would have a facility. You wouldn't have to rent out a venue. Instead, you would go to an open field, where you would sponsor KISS wet T-shirt contests, run concert film, host KISS tribute bands, and most important, sell KISS merchandise. I had it all designed, but the band decided not to do it. It was too big, they said, and too commercial. To this day I stand by it. Initially everybody thought these ideas were cheesy. But now, no matter who you are, you remember your first KISS lunchbox. Many people still have theirs.

◆ ◆ ◆

Every once in a while I would see a band that I knew was going to be big. Van Halen was one of them. I saw them in a club, the Starwood, in 1977. I went with Bebe Buell, a model who was friendly with a number of rock stars. (She's perhaps better known today as the mother of the actress Liv Tyler.) Bebe and I were going to see a band called the Boyzz, and opening was a new band called Van

We played in Cadillac, Michigan, in 1976. The football coach at the high school used KISS music to motivate his players to a state championship that year. When we arrived in Cadillac, everyone in the town was dressed up in KISS makeup.

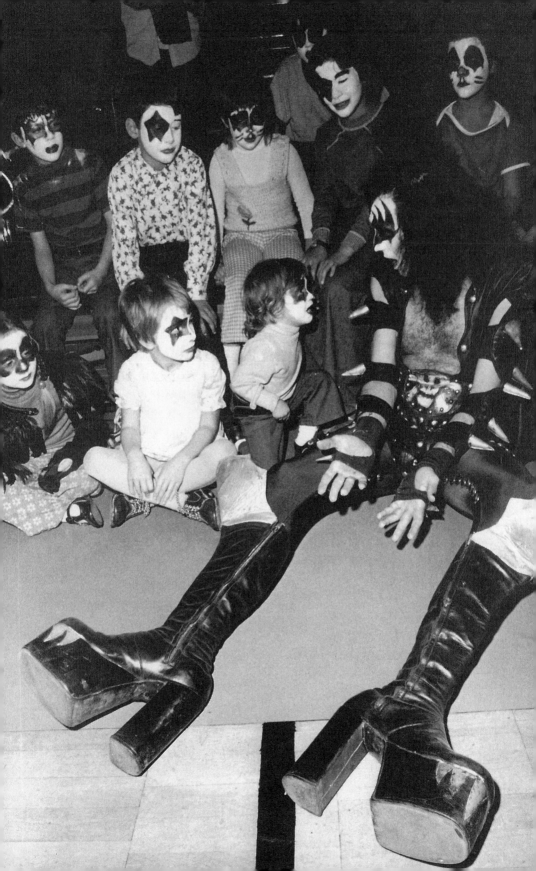

Halen. Within two songs I knew they were going to be huge. Strangely, they did only okay at the club. People liked them, but it wasn't a maniacal response. But I knew. I went backstage, went over to them, and introduced myself. I went right into business mode. I wanted to know their plans. They had a potential backer who was a yogurt manufacturer. I said, "Please do me a favor—don't do that. I'll fly you to New York, I'll produce your demo." I signed them to a contract.

Immediately I started to bring them around. In Los Angeles we went into Village Recorders, and in New York City I bought David Lee Roth some leather pants and belts and platform shoes. Then I produced their demo at Electric Lady studios—thirteen to fifteen songs, most of which wound up on the first and second albums. Some of those were my arrangements. The next step was to try to convince Bill Aucoin and the rest of KISS to sign them. But the rest of the guys in the band were angry that I was turning my attention to other acts, and Bill Aucoin thought Roth looked too much like Black Oak Arkansas. He didn't get it. I told Eddie Van Halen and the others that even though they were signed to me, I would try again after KISS toured. Within two or three months, Van Halen got interest from Warner Bros. I said, "You go for it. I'll tear up the contract, just go." Though this was the first time I got interested in a younger band, it was by no means the last—I would have plenty of other opportunities to work with groups starting their careers, or to help remake the careers of older artists. Working with bands other than KISS was liberating in some respects, because I could share every-

Relaxing in my hotel room during the Japanese tour.

thing I had learned about the record business. And often naïveté about the business is what does young bands in.

◆ ◆ ◆

KISS had conquered America. We had conquered Europe. And then in early 1977 we went to Japan to play a series of sold-out shows at Budokan in Tokyo. We learned later that we had broken the Beatles record there. We didn't know anything about Japan. When we landed there, we did the same thing that we did in England, which was to walk off the plane in full makeup and outfits in case there were any reporters. Well, that was a great plan, except that the Japanese customs officials didn't let us into the country, because they didn't believe that we were the same people as those pictured on our passports. So we had to take the makeup off, pass through, and then put it back on before we went outside.

When we finally emerged from the airport, there were about five thousand Japanese fans outside. The Japanese promoter, Mr. Udo, had arranged to have duplicate cars, and most of the fans ran after the duplicates while we snuck out the back and jumped into other cars. But enough of the fans figured it out and came after us. I really thought we were going to die. There were just so many people, crushing us. They were on top of the cars. They could physically lift up the car. It was major KISS mania, like what you see in the Beatles' *A Hard Day's Night,* but bigger because the cars were being rocked and rolled, and it wasn't just girls but guys as well. We later learned that the Japanese fans felt a great kinship with us because of our makeup, which looked like kabuki theater makeup, and also like the Japanese superhero shows. In the same way that some of our early American fans were black, because they didn't see us as either white or black, the Japanese took to us because they didn't see us as American or Asian.

The girls in Japan were also wonderful, very willing and very available. The interesting thing about Japanese women, in my experience, is that they have a little girl quality, a certain innocence about their sexuality. *Coquette* is a French word, and that concept just doesn't exist in Japan, at least as far as I saw. For instance, when

Japanese girls orgasm, a peculiar sound emanates from them that almost sounds like a baby crying.

Japan wasn't just another country; it was more like another world. Within the country, we traveled by the bullet train, the fastest train in the world. The Japanese fans, and especially the girls, would follow us everywhere we went. They would giggle, give us presents, and break into hysterical crying fits in front of us.

Peter brought Lydia, his wife, with him on the Japanese tour, so outside of work we didn't see much of him. Ace, on the other hand, was full of piss and vinegar. One night he knocked on my door and appeared in front of me drunk out of his mind in full Nazi uniform with his friend, saluting and yelling into my face, "Heil Hitler!" I have pictures. Ace knew how I felt about Nazi Germany. He knew that my mother had been in the concentration camps and that her whole family had been wiped out. But that didn't stop him. Many years later, during the 2001 KISS farewell tour in Japan, drummer Eric Singer (who had taken over for Peter Criss at the time) jokingly started calling Ace "Race Frehley."

During one of our off days in Japan, the band went to a night-club, where we were met by a gentleman who introduced himself as Gan. He was stout and powerful and could clearly take care of himself. We didn't speak Japanese, so we relied on translators. We went over to our VIP section, and within seconds girls started to line up and pass by us and giggle. The man next to me was of some importance, I could tell, because when he put a cigarette up to his mouth, two other men nearby immediately lit it for him. We exchanged pleasantries. I learned later that he might be from the *yakuza,* the Japanese mob.

One of the girls in the crowd reached out, and we shook hands. Gan broke off the contact, spit in her face, and raged at her in Japan-ese. She cried and ran off. The translator explained that Gan was merely doing what he thought was proper. He was there to protect us, and she was not "worthy" of touching me. This was clearly a completely different culture.

At one point I got up to go to the dance floor, and security men followed me. Most of the Japanese are smaller than Americans: a

Japanese girl might be five-two. One of the girls, a beauty about five-eight, made eye contact with me. I immediately went over and took her hand and pulled her toward the dance floor. She smiled. I told her I wanted to go back to the hotel, but the music was too loud. All she did was keep smiling. We got inside the hotel and I tried conversation, and then it dawned on me that she couldn't speak a word of English. It didn't seem to matter, though. We didn't need to talk. The next day one of our security guards told me she was a famous Japanese television star. Right before commercial breaks late at night, Japanese television would show a shot of a beautiful, naked girl smiling into the camera. When we got back to America, our KISS press office showed me a press clipping from Japan. There she was, smiling her smile in front of countless members of the Japanese press. The translator explained that the title of the article was "My Night of Passion with Gene Simmons." I didn't mind. I was actually quite flattered. She was gorgeous.

◆ ◆ ◆

Even though *Love Gun,* which was released in 1977, was our third album in a row to ship a million copies, the band came apart at the seams during that time. It wasn't that we were breaking up, but people were starting to need their own space again. We had been together for five years, which is coming up on the typical lifespan of a band. I always had the sense that the Beatles were around forever, but when you look at the number of years, it's astonishing how brief they were: only a decade of existence, and only seven years of recordings, from *Meet the Beatles* to *Let It Be.*

The strain was pulling us apart, but it was also pushing us forward, into new projects and uncharted waters. From the beginning I had been heavily indebted to comic books, and in 1978 we made good on that relationship by getting a comic book of our own. First a Marvel artist named Steve Gerber who was a big fan put us in the last two issues of *Howard the Duck.* We were demons who possessed Howard. Marvel noticed that those two *Howard the Duck* issues soared in sales even though we weren't on the cover. So they approached us about a KISS comic book.

Someone arranged for me to meet Stan Lee, the head of Marvel. He was a god to me. As a kid, I had sent a letter to Marvel critiquing something, and I actually got a postcard back, signed by Stan Lee, saying, "Never give up." It was signed, "Stan." And I thought, *That's it, I've made it.* Marvel comics were so important to me, because heroes like Spiderman had these screwed-up lives that contrasted with their superhero lives. *Superman,* which was a DC comic, was a classic concept, but I didn't read *Superman* as loyally. He wasn't a teenager. He didn't have problems.

When Stan Lee and I met, I told him his real name was Stanley Lieber, and that Larry Lieber, one of the inkers at Marvel, was his brother, and that Cadence Industries owned Marvel. I knew his secretary's name, which was Flo Steinberg. He was floored. We talked and found that we were kindred spirits. He had changed his name because he didn't want people to know he was Jewish, as had I. The wings on my outfit were influenced by a character called Black Bolt that Stan Lee had created.

As the KISS comic book project moved along, someone came up with the idea of putting real blood in the ink. It wasn't me—maybe it was Bill or Sean. We got into a DC3, one of those big prop planes, and flew up to Buffalo to Marvel's printing plant, where they pour the ink and make comic books. A notary public actually witnessed the blood being drawn. The comic book, which was published in 1978, became Marvel's biggest-selling comic book.

At around this time we decided to do another live album, a collection of material from *Destroyer, Rock and Roll Over,* and *Love Gun.* We did it partly at the insistence of the record company and partly to repay our fans for their loyal support: the first live album had helped to define our career, and a second would be a kind of bookend. In some ways we were crazy to even try, since 1977 was such an incredibly busy year—the Japanese tour took up most of March, *Love Gun* was released in June, and then *Alive II* followed in November. But we weren't ready to go into the studio. We were squabbling over material. And even if we had been ready, it would have taken time to get into the studio. Because we didn't want fans to feel cheated, we wrote new songs for one side of *Alive II.*

The band flew up to the Marvel comics printing plant in Buffalo to add our blood to the ink used in the KISS comic book. We are with Marvel head Stan Lee here.

When we finally went into the studio, Ace simply never showed up. We had to use other guitar players, like Bob Kulick and Rick Derringer. Ace was more furious than ever. "How could you do it without me?" he raged. How could we? Because these other guys showed up. This wasn't the first, nor would it be the last, of countless times Ace would turn his back on the band. Regardless, even without Ace, *Alive II* went on to be another multiplatinum double disc set.

✦ ✦ ✦

Midway through 1978 Hanna-Barbera, the famous cartoon producers, approached us about being in a movie. We had already been in *Howard the Duck* and in the Marvel comic book. We had an initial meeting, and they told us about the idea, and we shrugged our shoulders and said, "That sounds fine."

The movie was shot at an amusement park called Magic Mountain, which had the biggest roller coaster in the world. We were literally never on a soundstage. The entire story took place in the park. The story was, a mad scientist was terrorizing visitors to this haunted amusement park. KISS helped to unmask the scientist and solve the mystery.

The director of the movie was Gordon Hessler, a director of action and suspense movies. He was actually very sweet about it. He would do a shot and ask us how things went. What did we know? They basically shot around us, because we were the stars. We took two hours to put our makeup on.

By that time Ace and Peter were miserable. KISS was on the covers of all the magazines but it was often a solo shot only of me. Sometimes Paul got a cover, but it was hardly ever Ace, and it was never Peter. This wasn't anything I planned. The press picks up on whoever they pick up on. Ace and Peter thought I arranged and connived to keep them off the covers.

They still had their chance. We had two writers with us who were writing the script for *KISS Meets the Phantom of the Park,* and they wanted to get a sense of how everybody talked before they wrote the script. Ace in those days was noncommunicative. He didn't say much. No matter what you said to him, he would make this parrot sound, "Awk." Nobody understood it. And when he wasn't making the parrot noise, he would mumble nonsense to himself—"Thirteen for a dozen," or "I kills them all, one by one"—and then he would laugh. These phrases meant something only to Ace, and nobody had a clue what he was talking about.

When the script came in, Ace's character never spoke. He only said "Awk." Ace was furious. He wanted to know why they didn't give him any lines. To their credit, they turned around and said, "What are you, nuts? You have never said anything to us except 'Awk.' We thought that's the way you want to talk." Ace said he had a lot to say. Well, he should have said it.

When we did *KISS Meets the Phantom of the Park,* the rest of the band was incensed, because the newspaper ads usually showed a much larger photo of me. If they showed any other figures, they were all in the background, and my face was four times the size of everybody else's. Paul and I have always had a kind of brotherly competitive thing, and we had quite a bit of back-and-forth over the years. Paul would get slightly angry because he perceived that I was dominating the band too much, or vice versa. But the ads for the movie, and particularly those in *TV Guide,* really bothered Ace and Peter. They felt they weren't as involved in the film as Paul and I were. We didn't really have a choice. First of all, Peter had been involved in yet another car accident. He skidded four hundred feet before he crashed, and he wound up in the hospital. When he did speak in the movie, he was impossible to understand because of his thick Brooklyn accent. So his voice was dubbed by someone else. Even the simple matter of getting Peter and Ace in front of the camera didn't always work out. Sometimes they went missing. They just didn't come to the set. The only solution was to use doubles. For Peter, we had a fifty-five-year-old guy, and we put makeup on him. For Ace, an African American stunt double.

Making the movie wasn't smooth, it wasn't easy, and it wasn't particularly fun. But like almost everything else we did then, it was a success. *KISS Meets the Phantom* was eventually shown on NBC at Halloween. Because the television ratings were so strong, AVCO Embassy released it theatrically outside the United States. When we toured Canada, I saw it at a movie theater. When we toured Australia, I saw it at a drive-in. That was very bizarre, because I had grown up worshiping Bela Lugosi and Boris Karloff, and here we were running through a freak movie meeting Frankenstein and Dracula.

The problems kept surfacing, though. Most of them originated with Ace, who kept shooting himself in the foot, and Peter kept following right along. At one point Ace started saying, "That's it, I'm leaving. I'm going to do my own solo record." So Bill Aucoin said, "Look, don't leave the band. Let's all do solo records. Maybe what we need is time away from each other." Everybody agreed.

rst time I met Cher, it was 1978, at a party Neil Bog- throwing for Casablanca. I didn't really know any of the people there—I knew some by face and by reputation, but not personally. At some point in the evening, I found myself talking to Cher. I introduced myself, and she didn't believe that I was who I said I was. It turned out that her daughter, Chastity, was a KISS fan and had encouraged her mother to go to the party because she knew Gene Simmons would be there. But Cher apparently had it in her mind that she would be meeting Jean Simmons the movie actress. She didn't make the connection.

At that time I was starting to think of ideas for my solo album,

then she kissed

1978

There was a $25,000 reward for getting a picture of me without my makeup. *Creem* magazine did, but they didn't know it was me because we just denied it. Here I am with Cher.

which I envisioned as a big production, with tons of guest stars and a circus atmosphere. I thought it would be great if I could get Cher to sing on the record.

At the end of the night, I went over to her place. In the limo with us was *Welcome Back, Kotter*'s Marcia Strassman, who warned Cher about my wandering eyes. Normally this would have meant one thing and one thing only, but in this case it meant something else entirely. We were back at her place, and before I knew it we were talking about our lives, about where we had come from, about what we were like as children. All of a sudden I started to feel the presence of another person in the conversation. This was a strange feeling for me.

me: life with cher

Left to right: Bill Aucoin, Don Wasley, me, Cher, Billy Sameth, and Neil Bogart at the end of 1978.

She was smart, interesting, and funny. At that moment, at least, I set aside the thought of it turning into anything sexual.

The night went on, and Cher made some hot chocolate for the two of us, and we kept talking about things—her life, my life, my record. I remember the hot chocolate because she put marshmallows in it, which I had never seen done. She seemed interested in the fact that even though I was a rock and roller, I could put a sentence together, and also in the fact that I was straight and had never been drunk. Cher had just come out of a relationship with Gregg Allman, who had a reported serious substance abuse problem. Cher herself was always antidrug.

Early the next morning—five or six A.M.—she drove me back to L'Hermitage Hotel, where I was staying. We parted and agreed to talk more about my solo record. I felt there was something brewing. Meanwhile I wanted to see if she was interested in going out that evening. She said she was going to see the Tubes, the rock band, in concert. "Great," I said. "What time do you want me to pick you up?" She explained that she had already invited her friend Kate Jackson, who was in *Charlie's Angels* at the time. I didn't know Kate, but it was fine with me. We ate dinner, the three of us, and then afterward headed over to see the Tubes. Usually at a concert like this, I would arrive with the audience and leave with the audience. But this was different. When we went backstage, it was very awkward. Some of the Tubes were taken with Cher, so I sat in the corner and talked with Kate Jackson. Finally the backstage party was over, and we got in the car to go home. On the way back you could have heard a pin drop, and back in the house, when Cher finally spoke, she exploded. She told me that she didn't take very kindly to being ignored, especially when I was coming on to her girlfriend Kate. I was speechless. When I tried to talk to Cher about it, she told me that she never wanted to see me again.

In retrospect, I realize I should have been more aware. But I was oblivious to that kind of thing, because I hadn't had any real relationships, and because the whole jealousy thing was foreign to me. I wasn't accustomed to having conversations about how somebody else felt. I'm an only child. My mother came from incredible hardship; she was in the concentration camps, the worst tragedy of the twentieth century. I grew up relatively poor. I was happy if I had something to eat. For me, that was the beginning and the end of everything. If I wanted companionship, I'd get companionship. If I was tired, I went to sleep. Life was good, simple, and straightforward. Still, at first with Cher it was neither simple nor straightforward. I called her from the hotel and said that I was going to New York to work on a record, and that I would call her when I got there. "Fine," she said. "I can't talk to you now."

On my way to New York, and after I arrived, I was still thinking about her. There were other girls in my life, of course, girls I had seen before and would see after, but Cher was on my mind a tremendous amount. During the day I kept calling her, under the pretense that I wanted her to sing on my record. We would speak for hours on end and I found her fascinating. Our conversations usually got personal pretty fast, though. Early in our relationship she had me talking about this situation with Kate, and how she was angry that I had given attention to another woman. This seemed fair to me. It made sense. It was reasonable. And most of all it was compelling to me. There I was in New York with plenty of other women. My old life was back. Except that it wasn't back at all—part of me was thousands of miles away, with her.

One night while I was in the company of a beautiful young woman, the phone rang. It was Cher, and before I knew it, we were talking again. She wanted to know when I was coming back to California. She wanted to know when we could sit down and talk about the record. So then we started talking about us again—about Cher's feelings, about what she wanted from me. It was a strange situation made stranger by the fact that there was this beautiful girl in the other room waiting for me. I liked this girl. But there was something about the woman on the other end of the phone, this woman I hadn't been sexual with yet, that I couldn't ignore.

In New York we were working on a new greatest hits album, *Double Platinum*, and specifically on a new disco version of "Strutter." This was Neil Bogart's idea—he wanted to mix his two biggest properties, which were KISS and disco. It was pretty much the same song except for the drum track, which was added on later. I didn't care for the version and didn't really have much to do with it. At any rate, right when we finished recording the new version, I told the other guys that I had to leave. I was going out to California to see what was happening with the Cher situation. If you had known me at any time before that, you would have been sure that the guy standing in front of you in the studio was an impostor. Leaving without putting the final touches on a song and flying off to see a girl just wasn't something I did. But I was new to this relationship thing.

Cher met me at the Los Angeles airport in jeans and a T-shirt. At the time that was still one of the major differences between the coasts. California had already gone causal: it was all about dressing natural and looking natural. In New York, if you had money, you showed it on your back: silk shirts, leather pants, all those kinds of things. No one wore jeans and T-shirts except for bums. New York was the Dolls. L.A. was the Doobie Brothers.

From the airport we took a limousine back to her place. I must have expected things to accelerate immediately, must have expected there to be some activity in the car. But she threw me a curve: there was no sex in the car. Just cuddling and holding hands. There was just this kind of giddy sensation that wasn't like anything I had ever experienced before. When we got back to her house, it was more of the same—hot chocolate, giggling. I had my suitcase with me, and for all intents and purposes, and before I knew it, I moved in right then.

◆ ◆ ◆

Within the KISS world, the fact that I had gone to California was causing some ripples of discontent. For starters, Ace and Peter didn't like it. They thought it meant they were a secondary priority, that something else was more important to me, and they felt threatened by it. Interestingly, some of the fans felt the same way. It was similar in some regard to what happened with the early British bands: managers routinely suppressed information about the band members' steady girlfriends, and in some cases even wives, because those realities didn't harmonize with the way fans wanted to see their pop idols. This situation was roughly equivalent: KISS fans wanted to see us as hard-working, tough-living New York musicians, reviled by critics, aggressively outside the rock establishment. The idea that one of us was living in California with a huge pop star—a huge television star—wasn't immediately accepted.

The one person who understood my situation (even though, at first, he didn't approve) was Paul. He had gotten a taste of California over the years, whenever we had stopped there to record or tour, and when I went out west to live with Cher, he started to see Cher's sister, Georgeann. They got along so well that I thought they were going to get married. It didn't happen, but it wasn't because Paul was against marriage in principle. He had always wanted to get married, always wanted to have a monogamous relationship and children.

Life with Cher was a real adjustment. To start with, I had a whole new group of friends. Actually, that's not quite accurate. They were more like acquaintances—mostly people Cher was close to, from Dolly Parton to Kate Jackson to Jane Fonda. At first I felt quite awkward about that situation, because the idea of celebrities hanging out with celebrities always struck me as a bit odd.

Slowly, though, I got more comfortable. The fact that they were actors and not musicians helped. For one thing, actors could put a sentence together. That's a huge difference. That's their business. They communicate and look you in the eye. And they were able to appear in public without being seen as freaks. Being in KISS, by contrast, didn't prepare us for the social world. We didn't have very good people skills because we were so sheltered. Nobody even knew what we looked like without makeup. And we hardly ever saw people except in hotel rooms because we were always hiding from the paparazzi.

Still, when I first arrived in California, I was walking around on shaky legs. With groupies I didn't have to explain who and what I was. Suddenly I'm going around with Cher and being somewhat of a father to Chastity and Elijah, going on walks, having conversations. I remember once Cher woke me up early in the morning. We had moved to her Malibu home. I said, "What, what?" It must have been six in the morning.

"Let's go running," she said. I said, "Where to?" I put on my leather pants and silk shirt and snakeskin boots. "You can't dress like that," she said.

"Why not?" I said.

"Well, you've got to put on these sneakers and shorts. Because we're going to go run on the beach."

"Why?" I said. I was dumbfounded. I mean, you didn't do that in New York. Not in 1978. *Jog* was not even a word I knew. In New York it was always too cold to run, and where were you going to run, anyway? It was something you did when somebody was chasing you.

So we went. There I was, running alongside Cher in my snakeskin boots, and I could barely stand up because my boots were sinking into the sand. And out on the beach suddenly I saw Neil Diamond and then Barbra Streisand. It was like I was on another planet.

The bizarre thing about it is, they didn't act the way you thought they were going to act. They were just regular people. On the other hand, KISS fans may be struck similarly when they meet me. You know, I'm the guy that spits blood and then it's "Hello, nice to meet you." They're thinking, *Wait a minute, how come he didn't drool blood?*

I met Jane Fonda through Cher. Our interaction was brief. I was at the studio, and she came over to have dinner with me. In person she was more attractive than in her photographs or movies. She was bright and didn't chitchat very much. She seemed interested in the whole KISS thing and kept asking questions about it. She also asked my opinion about a movie she had been working on and what I thought about the title, *The China Syndrome*. She told me what it was about. I told her I didn't think much of the title. I said I preferred something like *What If* . . . The three dots following the *If* . . . would light up one at a time and start to cycle faster and faster with a beep being heard for each visual flash. The movie came out. It was called *The China Syndrome*.

◆ ◆ ◆

After a little while in California, I got distracted a bit from the rock and roll world. Even though I had always loved movies and wanted to explore that field, I was still a guy in a band. I didn't have a clue how to get into it, who the studio executives were, or what the structure was. But I started to get immersed in that world, mostly through Cher, who wasn't yet a movie star but was trying to break into film. She had her TV show, first with Sonny and then on her own, and she had done huge shows in Las Vegas. She was at that point probably the biggest star in the country, or certainly one who could be counted on to sell magazines.

When we went to parties, I watched how people interacted with each other. I noticed how Cher was to certain people—very cordial, even though afterward she would tell me that she didn't know who the person was. I thought that was bizarre, because in my experience, within the confines of a band, if someone came up to me and said, "Hi, it's so nice to see you again," I would say, honestly and straightforwardly, "I'm sorry, I don't remember ever meeting you. Who are you?"

It took me a while to get accustomed to Los Angeles, not just because of the surreal fact of all these celebrities milling around, treating each other like ordinary people, but because there were new rules. The same kind of thing that had happened after the Tubes concert happened again and again. We had conversations about her feelings, about how she wasn't sure how she felt, and so on. It was like a foreign language to me. I had never watched soap operas, partly because I never understood what everybody was so miserable about. In those shows everybody was good-looking. Everybody was rich. Everybody was healthy and young. And everybody was miserable. The promiscuous characters were berated and tortured for being alive and for not curtailing their natural lusts. The others were talking about their innermost emotions and needs and priorities. And eventually, everyone became promiscuous. It seemed absurd in every way. And then all of a sudden here it was in my own life: Cher telling me, "Here's how I feel, and here's what it means," and asking me, "What did you mean by that?" and "How do you feel?" I had absolutely no expertise in communicating on that level. The first question I kept thinking of, over and over again, was *Why are we even talking about this?* If you want to be with me, you are. And if you don't want to be with me, you're not. It's simple, nothing you have to verbalize.

I was being related to in a different way, for the first time in my life. Mostly the girls I'd met didn't have a lot of conversational skills, or they weren't really interested in flexing those muscles. They were just excited to be there with me, whether we were backstage or in a hotel room. Granted, I'd see some of them more than once, but by and large, our relationships were purely sexual. With Cher, though, I had met somebody who could hold her own in conversation, who had her own feelings and her own points of view about everything.

For example, Cher had her own opinions about the women I had been with. I wouldn't say that she was jealous, not exactly. I was a rock star and had been a rock star for quite some time, with a reputation for chasing skirt. As I have said, it was the only thing I could do on the road, since I didn't drink or take drugs. The thing that threw Cher a little bit was the photography. Since 1976 or so, I had been taking pictures of the girls I had been with, sometimes film footage. I didn't do it without their knowledge or compliance. In fact, most of the girls were thrilled about it. It was a hobby of mine, partly to keep things exciting and partly as a kind of documentary. There were so many girls—by the time I met Cher, somewhere in the neighborhood of a few thousand. At one point I told Cher about the photographs. It wasn't to confess, because I didn't feel guilty. I just wanted to share everything with her. She was shocked. She didn't understand why I would want to do that. As far as I was concerned, it wasn't any stranger than any other road behaviors—drinking, drugs, and that kind of thing. In fact, it was quite a bit less strange, and it didn't hurt anyone.

Politics also came up often, although it was celebrity-style politics. Once, I remember, I was in a room with a bunch of other people, friends of Cher's, and we were watching television commercials with footage of poor African children. People got sadder and sadder, and finally someone said, "That's it, I'm adopting that child." Then another one chimed in: "Yeah, me too." It was almost like the Home Shopping Network of kids. I didn't know what to make of it. At the core of it was an admirable impulse: you want to do something good for somebody. And these people weren't holding press conferences and saying, "Ladies and gentlemen, I just gave to charity." But it was strange to think that this was how people were finding out about the world—that they became aware of the existence of the poor because they were pictured on the television set. And it's strange that they decided to help out by picking up the phone and making a pledge.

There were lots of things like that in California. Therapy, for example, was something that had never appealed to me. Paul was big into therapy, and he used to tell me that my attitudes toward women, and my reluctance to commit to a marriage, would eventually create a huge conflict in my psyche, and then my world would crack, and I would have to go into analysis to figure out why I was doing what I was doing. Again, I thought this was bizarre. I was doing something I enjoyed, and it wasn't hurting me. It made life worth living, and I liked it. Ironically, much later, Paul's therapist actually ended up working for KISS, in a completely different capacity, a business capacity. And then he flipped out in front of me and Paul. So much for therapy.

California was also awash in est, and in meditation, and in Eastern mysticism. I didn't have much use for any of them. Even when the Beatles were going through their Maharishi phase, I felt betrayed. *You idiots,* I thought. While India may be a spiritually brilliant country, spirituality meant nothing to me. Children are dying there every day of starvation. I'd rather be unspiritual and fed than spiritual and starving. Sorry. This was always my philosophy—pragmatism. Let other people go into trances and think about spirituality or Werner Erhardt. I'd rather concentrate on having something to eat. The here and now. Be glad you can get a good night's sleep and eat a good meal and, if you're lucky enough, have somebody attractive sharing your bed with you. That's about all there is to life.

People magazine did a couple of cover stories about Cher's and my relationship, and although I was used to the idea that photographers tried to capture me without my KISS makeup, this kicked it up tremendously. We were constantly hounded by paparazzi, night and day. I started covering my face with handkerchiefs, like a bandit.

♦ ♦ ♦

I liked how Cher dealt with the other men who had been in her life, particularly Sonny Bono. I liked Sonny a lot. With Sonny and Cher, it was up and down. They were comfortable enough with each other, but they had their issues, she told me. They had been married, and things hadn't worked out. That's always complicated. Still, on one or two occasions we'd go shopping together, Sonny and his then-wife, Susie, and Cher and myself. When I told him what a big fan of his songwriting I was, he was shocked that I knew the history of what he had done: his production work with Phil Spector, that he had written "The Beat Goes On," "I Got You Babe," and many more songs.

Most of the time my life with Cher was great. Everything was hilarious. Everything was funny. I'd run down the street with her on my back. It was like we were two young kids. Once we went into a Westwood bookstore, and Cher and her sister Georgeann decided to walk down the street for a second. I said, "I'll just look around the bookstore." I was wearing samoans and very short shorts for the first time—standard-issue California dress—and I saw a couple pointing toward me, and I'm going, "Yeah, what are you looking at? Okay, so I'm in KISS and I'm dressed this way, and I'm browsing in a bookstore. Big deal." It's a New York thing—you're confrontational. So they turned around and walked away. When I walked over to Cher, I told her about it. "Can you imagine these people were staring at me? So what, so I'm in KISS."

"They weren't looking at you. Your balls are hanging out from your shorts."

I looked down, and sure enough there they were. They might as well have had a neon sign around them.

Likewise, when I took Cher to the Tavern on the Green in New York City, and we were having dinner, I saw flashbulbs going off at my back. "Look," I said to Cher. "This is so rude. I'll take care of it."

"No, it's okay," she said. "I'm used to this."

"It's my job," I said. I was insistent. "I'm the man. I'll take care of this." I got up and walked over to this midwestern family, maybe eight of them with Dad and Mom and the kids. He had his camera up, and I pointed at it and went into a long speech: "Sir, don't you realize, just because you're from Oshkosh and we're in New

York . . . okay, so Cher and I . . . okay, so I'm in KISS and I'm the guy with the long tongue." I'm like, "There is no reason why you have to take photos of us, because it's embarrassing. I mean, how would you like it if I took photos of you?" And he's going, "What are you talking about? I'm just taking photos of my family."

Our life together had comedy far more often than tragedy. Once we had an argument about something. But I don't argue. There is no argument with me. I don't even remember what it was about, but it was something that made Cher angry. I said, "Look, it's not worth it. I'll see you later," and I packed up my trunk and moved to Westwood. She then came in the Jeep with Chastity and said, "Okay, we won't argue, come on back." There is nothing worth fighting about except health and money, and the rest is okay.

By and large I had a monogamous relationship. By and large. Monogamy is not an issue for me. If somebody who is with me decides she wants to have a liaison, she will anyway, so I might as well just relax about it. And if you are going to break up, you are going to break up. The idea of "owning" somebody has never been part of it for me. I want to know that you are with me because you want to be, not because you have to be. If you *have* to be with somebody, then you become like every other wife and husband: you torture each other. There is the classic joke: Why do husbands die younger than their wives? Because they want to.

I don't want to do that. Every day has got to be fun. Hey, if we're not having fun together, whether you've been with ten sailors or I've been with ten nurses, if we are not enjoying it, why don't we just split and stop torturing each other? If we can't be lovers, why can't we at least be friends?

Cher brought out my playful side. On her birthday she awoke to the sound of a plane circling right above the Beverly Hills Hotel, where we were staying. It seemed dangerously close to us. When we ran out, she could clearly see a plane pulling a sign wishing her a happy birthday. I had gotten special clearance from the airport to fly in circles above the hotel. Later, she heard singing outside the bungalow. She opened the door to the sight of thirty-four college students, the Azusa Citrus Choir, singing beautiful songs. Later still, a full marching band came marching right into the bungalow, through and around us. And then two little people knocked on the door, presented Cher with frozen Snickers (her favorites), and escorted us out the door to a waiting tank, which took us down Sunset Boulevard to the Le Dome restaurant. Cars gave us the right of way when they saw the tank's gun turret in their rearview mirrors. At the restaurant I had a virtual Fellini's *Satyricon* full of people—guys on stilts, magicians, and belly dancers.

All of Cher's friends were there and the night was a huge success, until the belly dancer started to dance suggestively in front of me. At that point Cher became furious and stormed out. Her former manager stopped her and talked sense into her, and we drove back to the hotel together in silence.

Again, this was all new to me. I was standing on shaky emotional ground. I didn't really know what I was feeling. On one side I felt that nothing had happened, and on the other I felt indignant. Why should I have to feel guilty about anything? When we got back to the hotel, I had bought a giant television set, the best of its day, and had rented a soft-porn film. I had never watched one, and in retrospect I was only trying to make myself more interesting to Cher. We didn't watch it.

Once Cher bought a little black dog, and I named him Louie. I loved him. As a little boy, I had a dog who was everything to me. I never had many friends, and being an only child, I poured my love into my first dog. My mother worked all day, and all I had was that dog. He used to lick my face. At one point I became very ill, and my father blamed it on the dog. He took the dog into the city and let him go. I was heartbroken and never forgot him. When I set eyes on Louie, it was almost as if that first dog, that childhood dog, had finally come back home. I know it sounds melodramatic: the demon who throws up blood onstage cries when a little black dog looks at him. Go figure.

When Cher and I were back in New York, the relationship continued. She came over to my mom's house in Queens, and all my uncles and cousins were there. She was as sweet as could be, and Elijah Blue, her son by Gregg Allman, was very small at the time. At one point he climbed onto one of my cousin's laps and spit right in her face. He didn't know what he was doing. He was just a baby. In one way it was shocking, but it was also hilarious.

With Cher in New York, I was introduced to an entire other world, to which I had never thought I belonged. I went to Halston's house and anybody who was anybody was there, from Andy Warhol to Liza Minnelli. The few conversations I had focused mainly on the fact that I was a curiosity, the guy who sticks his tongue out and spits fire. At these events people would always be disappearing into bathrooms. I never understood what that was about; I was that naïve about drugs, even at that late date. And the conversations weren't particularly interesting for me, because I wasn't very interested in other people's lifestyles, even for the length of a brief conversation. "Did you hear that so-and-so just bought a new house?" someone would say. "And that they were thinking of designing it with a Mediterranean, but not a southern Californian, accent?" To me, it was chitchat. I've always been about the facts—give me the information. And then it's off to the pleasure zones. But sitting around playing mah-jongg and sipping tea is such an empty idea to me. I just don't understand. Whiling away the hours is a bore.

As a result, when I met other celebrities, I wasn't too interested. Many of them were great, though. Steve Rubell always treated me terrifically. Warhol was always very cordial. "I like your art," he would say. (I always thought that was a strange notion, but coming from a guy who made a Campbell's Soup can into pop art, I guess I understand it.) All in all the pretentiousness of the scene seemed silly to me. I always thought Art should be the name of a guy, and then the rest of it should be up to the public. I believe in the American ideal—of the people, by the people, for the people. You get to do stuff, whether it's a painting or a book, and then it's up to us, the people, to decide if it's art, not the person who creates it. So the idea of some artist saying "I am an artist" seems a bit full of oneself. I'd like to think that you wouldn't have the right to say that unless the people agreed. I have always believed in "the great unwashed masses."

Still, however idyllic life with Cher was, I had to get back to work.

◆ ◆ ◆

Since Ace had broached the subject of solo albums during the filming of *KISS Meets the Phantom of the Park,* I had my own solo album on my mind. I had begun working on new songs. In KISS we all worked differently. Usually I would walk in and present the band with anywhere from twenty to thirty new songs. Out of my batch, we would whittle them down to four or six for an album. Peter would get a songwriting credit when and if someone brought in a song mostly finished and he contributed a part. Ace, on the rare occasion he actually got up to work, might come in with a few songs. Paul would usually wait until the last minute, but somehow he would always come up with the goods.

I wanted my solo album to be the greatest show on earth, with choirs and tons of special guest stars. My initial vision included everyone from Lassie to Jerry Lee Lewis to Lennon (who was still alive then) and McCartney. These weren't all possible, of course. Jerry Lee Lewis couldn't make it as a result of a scheduling conflict. Lassie too had a scheduling conflict. As for Lennon and McCartney, I called up their management and made an offer for them to appear on the album. When they said no, I hired two guys from *Beatlemania,* the Beatles tribute stage show, to do the singing.

I didn't replace Jerry Lee and Lassie, but the final record included many, many guest appearances. Early on, I took over Cherokee Studios in Los Angeles and called on musicians from other bands to come and help me do the demos of the new songs. Joe Perry from Aerosmith came down and played a killer solo on one of the new songs. Katey Sagal, who I saw for a short time around the same time I was seeing Cher, and two other girls from The Group With No Name sang on a few others. I excitedly played Cher the new songs I had been working on, but usually a blank look came over her face. She never really understood our music. While I was telling her about my new songs, she would be telling me about her dreams to remake *The Enchanted Cottage,* a movie she loved. We were both dreamers.

As I went on with the solo project, I wanted to pursue my Beatles obsession, so I rented a recording studio in Oxford, England, down the road from where George Harrison lived. Anytime I wanted another star to appear on the record, I flew them in and treated them like royalty.

I tried to make a point—a showy point, granted—that I was capable of playing guitar. So on the album I didn't play bass at all, I only played guitar. Cher and Chastity appeared on one song called "Living in Sin at the Holiday Inn."

Sean Delaney produced my solo record, and he brought in Michael Kamen to arrange and conduct about thirty of the finest string players in Los Angeles. One morning they had arrived and were seated inside the recording studio ready to do their parts on a song I had written called "Man of 1,000 Faces." Sean had arranged to have them all wear Gene Simmons face masks, the ones that were for sale in stores. It was certainly one of the most bizarre moments in my life: to open the door to see a roomful of violin players all looking like me.

On another occasion I had Janis Ian at the studio at the same time Grace Slick came down to record with me. I had met Grace on tour, because she was seeing our lighting director and would visit him on the road. Janis, Sean, and I were discussing some ideas, when suddenly all hell broke loose. Grace had apparently ingested some chemical that didn't agree with her constitution. She flipped out, and studio staff helped her out of the studio.

Other pairings were just as exciting. Helen Reddy came down to sing on a song called "True Confessions." I had Ping-Pong tables set up inside the recording studio, and Helen and I played Ping-Pong. Donna Summer did me the favor of singing with me on "Burning Up with Fever." She blew the roof right off. We got along well. By that time she had become our record company's next big thing. KISS was the first act to sign with Casablanca, and Donna was up-and-coming at the label. And Bob Seger, another hard-driving rock and roll vocalist, sang with me on "Radioactive," which became the single off the record. We had known Bob for many years—earlier, he had opened for us on a tour.

At one of the shows, while Seger and his band were getting

ready to go onstage, I stood alongside Alto Reed, his horn/sax guy. Alto mentioned that he needed something to drink—he said his mouth was dry. I offered him a piece of gum, which he said he would start chewing right away. That night was a strange one for the Seger show. You see, at that point in my life, I loved pranks and would often buy whoopee cushions and the like. I also bought Onion Gum, which looks like gum and tastes like gum initially— until about the tenth chew, when a horrid onion taste explodes in your mouth.

◆ ◆ ◆

The solo project was unprecedented. No other group in history had ever released four solo albums simultaneously. Even though the solo albums were a way for Ace and Peter to feel they had a bit more creative control, we were intent on controlling the project. Both our management and our record company—Casablanca released all four solo records on the same day in 1978—insisted that each album have the same kind of artwork. We all used the same artist, Eraldo Carugati, so the entire project felt like a coordinated band solo release, something that has never been done before or since.

All the albums did well: they sold strong initially and have continued to perform. After twenty-plus years of sales figures, I'm at the top, slightly ahead of Ace, who is slightly ahead of Paul. Peter's sold the least well of the four. None of the albums really yielded hits. The song that got the farthest was Ace's cover of a song called "New York Groove," which went to number 14. Peter didn't chart. "Radioactive," my single, stopped in the twenties, and Paul's "Hold Me, Touch Me" was a little lower than that.

The solo album was a big boost for Ace. For the first time he was thrilled, because he could walk into a room and be the only star, the guy who had his own thing going on, his own album with his own face on the cover. The irony was that when he first joined the band, he didn't want to sing or write songs. He just wanted to be the guitar player. We had forced him to start writing songs. Once he found out he could do it, he actually delivered the goods. He was able to put out an album that in a lot of ways was probably the most cohesive of the four.

In the late 1970s, the Bee Gees were arguably the biggest band in the world, but Barry Gibb's son Steve just wanted to dress like me!

The solo albums sold about a million each. But Casablanca was accustomed to having two albums a year from us as a band, and they didn't count the solo ones. So just after that, Neil Bogart put out a greatest hits record, *Double Platinum*.

◆ ◆ ◆

I had to go back to New York and start getting ready for the next KISS tour, and I wanted Cher and the kids to come live with me. I went to F.A.O. Schwarz and bought a six-foot-long bed shaped like a sneaker for Chastity. They all came with a nanny, and when Cher saw my condo, she said it wasn't big enough and moved into the Pierre Hotel.

It soon became clear that if I wanted Cher to be with me in New York, I would have to finally buy a home that would suit her. So I went shopping for a larger place. Cher and I were refused at the Dakota, where John Lennon lived. We were deemed to be too much trouble, because the press was on our tail night and day. I finally found a space I thought she would like: the top floor of the former Heart Fund building, on the corner of Fifth Avenue and Sixty-fourth Street, across from the children's zoo at Central Park. There was nothing on the top floor then, so I bought "air rights," which meant that I could build a dwelling on the entire top floor of the existing building. I hired Cher's architect from California and flew him to New York. While the penthouse was being built, KISS went out on tour. When we came back home, I took the elevator up to the penthouse. It opened up into my floor. There were Romanesque columns and a giant bathtub in the middle of the larger bedroom, with marble all over the place. It was a showpiece. Cher loved it, and so did I. The problem was that by the time it was finished, Cher and I had stopped being lovers and were back to being friends.

◆ ◆ ◆

The headaches with the other two guys in the band continued. Peter was depressed, Ace was as infuriating as ever, and both of them were increasingly being controlled by substances. Ace's behavior was probably more interesting, although no less maddening. Ace has always struck me as never living up to his potential. He could play guitar, write songs, and do any number of other things. But he's never applied himself. He's admitted to being chronically lazy and a flake. He can put an idea together that has a spark of brilliance. But he won't go that extra mile to get trademarks and copyrights. You can see hundreds of guitar straps today, for example, with big lightning bolt designs on them, straps that are used by everyone, from country acts to rap bands—that's Ace's design. He walked in one day with this strap, and I said, "That's great. Let's trademark that. It'll sell like hotcakes." I had a heart-to-heart talk with him. He just wouldn't do it. After the fact I said, "You really missed out on a big one."

"Ah," he said, "I'll think of another one." He never did.

With these kinds of headaches in the band, there were plenty of times I would have preferred to stay with Cher. But whenever I sat down and thought seriously about things, I realized that, at least at that point, I would never risk breaking the band up or leaving. It was all-inclusive and invasive. So in one way I sort of forgot that I had any options; I gave myself completely to the band and defined myself that way. I was Gene Simmons from KISS; *from KISS* might as well have been my last name. Soon enough the four of us were in contact again. We didn't tour in back of the solo albums. We were talking about meeting in New York to record a new album. This one we decided to call *Dynasty*.

DYNASTY was recorded in New York City with Vinnie Poncia, who had been Peter's producer for his solo album. Paul and I had met with Vinnie at Bill Aucoin's suggestion, in part to show Peter that we thought well of his record and to bring him back into the fold. By that time Peter was our biggest liability, because he had become dependent on chemicals. Ironically, Vinnie decided that even though he produced Peter's record, he didn't think Peter was good enough to drum on a KISS record. Peter was not qualified to

dirty livin': DYNASTY and UNMASKED 1979~1980

make any judgments about material or arrangements, he said. In Vinnie Poncia's estimation, Peter was close to tone deaf and didn't play drums well enough.

At times I have reassessed my criticisms of Ace and Peter. Sometimes I have to remind myself that everybody has their cross to bear. If I were Ace or Peter, I would find Gene Simmons very difficult to take. I've never been high, except in a dentist's chair and that one incident with the brownies, and I don't have much use for small talk. Whenever I spoke to Ace and Peter, it was to get information: who, what, why, when, where, and how. They just didn't deal well with that. We would have numerous meetings before a tour or recording session, and they just couldn't sit still. They'd be cracking jokes and throwing food at each other, and every time, at the end of the meeting, they would ask me, "What was that about? What were you saying?" Or a day later they would ask, "Okay, when are we going to talk about the album?" And I would have to explain that we had talked about it, and that they had agreed to certain terms. Nothing would stick. Ace and Peter didn't take notes, didn't read

Ah, it's good to be king.

memos. It was a bull-in-a-china-shop situation: they would come into a room not knowing where anything was and figuring that whatever was going to happen was going to happen.

This was always a problem, but in 1979 the stakes were much higher. By that time KISS was a big fat bloated beast. We each had our own security guard. Culturally the band reached its peak around 1979. We topped the Gallup poll as top rock band three years in a row, from 1977 to 1979. Number two was the Beatles, then the Bee Gees, then Led Zeppelin. We were so much a part of the cultural landscape, so much a part of what people thought of when they thought about rock and roll, it was hard to imagine being any bigger.

The bodyguards served us all in different ways. I liked it because I could get twice as many phone numbers from girls, and they were certainly handy during a concert, when I would say, "Fourteen-three," which meant "After the show bring me the girl in the fourteenth seat, third row." For me, it was all about skirt chasing. I didn't need them as actual security: I'm six foot two.

For the Dynasty tour in 1979, I wanted to make up with bombast what we had clearly started lacking in musical precision. We made the stage much bigger, with a design Paul brought in. We had elevator lifts that brought us up from under the stage, which everyone from Michael Jackson to Jon Bon Jovi to Garth Brooks would do later. We also had a lighting system that looked like it came out of *Close Encounters of the Third Kind*. It could move up and down. The drums levitated higher than they ever had. We even had the front of the stage disconnect and lift the band over the heads of the people in the front rows.

To up the stakes even more, I got the bright idea of having a rig built to fly me up to the light system fifty-five feet above the ground. Every night, I would throw up the blood that had been hidden in my mouth during the previous blackout, stand there erect and proud, and wait for the audience to give me my due. I would demand it. And although at that point I felt powerful, the feeling would quickly dissipate as I was flying straight up through the air at six feet a second. I was scared stiff every night and I kept thinking to myself every time I flew up there in the dark, *What an idiot I was to have gotten myself into this mess.*

♦ ♦ ♦

My relationship with Cher had changed my romantic life. It made me reconsider some of the basic things I had assumed about women. It also changed my financial life. In some ways, I guess, it forced me to grow up. Before Cher I had never lived with anyone. Even in 1979, when we were on top of the world, I was paying two hundred dollars a month rent in New York City, and that was my full exposure financially. I didn't have a car. I didn't know how to drive and didn't want to learn. I was completely happy and was amassing a nice fortune, because I wasn't spending any money. I hardly ever went shopping and had no real girlfriends to throw money at. Every once in a while I'd splurge and ask Tavern on the Green to send food up to my apartment, but that was it.

While I was with Cher, though, I got used to spending more money. In fact, all of us had more expenses, whether they were real expenses, like families or girlfriends, or childish expenses, like cars. So for creative and financial reasons alike, we needed a hit.

KISS was everywhere in the 1970s.

By the time of the *Dynasty* recording sessions, Paul was specifically trying to write a hit single—and he did. He came up with one with a guy named Desmond Child. Paul's song, "I Was Made for Lovin' You," dovetailed nicely with what Casablanca wanted; they were hinting more strongly than ever that they wanted to have a single from KISS. Paul embraced this idea, and I fought it slightly, although not out of any sense of grand principle. I would sit down and try to work with Vinnie Poncia, who had come from a different school of thought, but who I liked. He had produced Ringo Starr, and he was a pop singles guy. "I Was Made for Lovin' You" had a certain driving force and a catchy melody. I didn't really see it. Paul knew it was a hit song, but it was Vinnie Poncia who pushed for us to record it.

At the same time, the whole band was being pulled apart. The biggest problem was Peter, who was by this point becoming unhealthy, in part because of the chemicals, and certainly because he wasn't allowed to play drums. We had always been able to placate him before, but this time, under even more pressure, he became harder to control. We hadn't been away very long, only a year really, and fans had gotten plenty of music in that stretch—*Alive II, Double Platinum,* and all four solo albums, all of them selling platinum—but the record label was accustomed to having two KISS records each and every year, because of the blistering pace that we had set through the mid-1970s.

As we got ready to finish *Dynasty,* Bill Aucoin alerted us to the idea of a "Return of KISS" campaign and told us that we were going in for a cover photo shoot with Scavullo, the big fashion photographer. He put us in straitjackets; we got the photos done, and they looked great. A few days later we did a video session for a series of television commercials keyed to the same theme. That session went less smoothly. The director insisted on take after take, and the day was getting longer. Peter was especially unhappy with the way it was going, so he ran into the bathroom and started to complain. Bill Aucoin tried to calm Peter down. Peter then got so upset, either with himself or with the way things were going—and I assume that the chemicals in his system had something to do with it—that he took his fist and smashed it into a glass case so hard that a shard went right through his hand. He had to be taken to a hospital and stitched up. Now there was a question of whether there was even going to be a tour, whether Peter's damaged tendons would allow him to use his right hand at all.

We were horrified. Our initial thought right away was for Peter's safety, because we lived with him and cared about him, no matter the consistent torture he put us through. But afterward, when the shock of the accident wore off, Paul and I got angry. "Oh, my God," we would say, "what an idiot." Can you imagine being so upset at anything that you'd drive your fist through a glass case? The whole James Dean lifestyle had never appealed to me. Because after that guy dies in a car crash, I'm going to sleep with his girl-friend.

✦ ✦ ✦

Dynasty was released, and immediately "I Was Made for Lovin' You" went to the top of the charts. It was huge, the biggest single we'd ever had worldwide. To this day it is one of only two gold singles released by KISS. (The other one is "Beth.") But when you have a hit single, you also have pressure to follow it up with more singles and even more aggressive touring. A year before, the four of us had been feeling our way through our own lives, getting a little breathing room. Now here we were, right back in the thick of things.

The tour was huge, and both Ace and Peter were so miserable they turned on each other and, for a moment, actually swung at each other. They both cried and fell into each other's arms afterward.

It was 1980—time for another album. Once we started working on *Unmasked*, it was clear that Peter's chemical problems had become major and that he needed some serious help. But he couldn't get that help within the context of the band. There was too much temptation, too many distractions, and he was causing all of us too much stress.

We had a discussion with Vinnie Poncia, and he said, "Look, I don't want to use Peter on *Unmasked*. I want to use Anton Fig." Anton, who later became the drummer for David Letterman's late-night band, was a friend of Ace's, and he had appeared on Ace's solo album. He was also in a band called Spider that was managed by Bill Aucoin. Using Anton instead of Peter played into Ace's hands, because it made him feel more in control. This was the kind of balancing act that Paul and I were used to—one year making Peter feel better about himself, the next year doing the same for Ace.

The decision to use a different drummer on the album was just the first step in dealing with Peter. We honestly weren't sure what to do with him. He had been with the band since we started, and KISS was an extremely loyal organization. Toward the end of the recording sessions, Poncia asked him to come in and add some harmonies on selected songs. That didn't go very well either. After the album came out, we were getting ready to go on tour, and Bill Aucoin came by to talk. "Look," he said, "you guys have a tour to do. I don't want to get another drummer. Give Peter another chance." Peter had talked with Bill and Ace, and they agreed that he needed another chance. He wanted to come in and show how different he was.

So we set up a meeting at SIR Rehearsal Studios in New York, and at the appointed time Peter appeared, carrying a music stand—the kind that symphony orchestra players have, with a clip for the sheet music. He looked very serious and intense. Peter couldn't read or write music, not then and not now. None of us could. We were a self-taught rock band. But by that time he was so delusional that he thought if he had a music stand, he could convince us that he had changed. I'm surprised he didn't bring a baton. "You guys," he said, "I've completely changed my life around. I've been studying drums and music for the past six months, and I can read music. I'm completely better."

I looked at the music sheets incredulously and then at him. "Can you read and write music, Peter?"

"Sure," he said, then mumbled something, but I couldn't make head or tail of it. Then we started playing, and he was worse than ever. So we had a meeting afterward, and we said, "Peter is unhealthy. He's going to kill himself. He's got to leave the band and get some help." So, after much deliberation, everybody, including Ace, voted him out of the band. To the press we used the traditional rock-band excuses: creative differences, desire to begin a solo career, and so on. We never said that Peter was thrown out of the band because he was a drug addict. We wouldn't have done that to him, to the fans, or to ourselves.

◆ ◆ ◆

By 1981 my relationship with Cher had changed. We were still seeing each other, but we had moved on.

Even though its shape had shifted, the relationship had changed me permanently. Up through my late twenties, I had been dead set against anything and anyone getting in my way. As much as I loved women, the idea of a relationship struck me as impossibly confining. When you have a serious girlfriend or a wife, life is full of commands: sit, stay, roll over. I didn't want to learn new tricks. I wanted to grow to be an old dog and lift my leg and pee anywhere I chose. I thought I knew myself well enough to say that I would never "give in," or be in a relationship that limited my happiness, or never have children. I wanted to be completely selfish because, in some ways, I wanted to be fair and not start something I wouldn't finish. A lot of men get in relationships, have children, and then walk out. Like my father. I didn't want to become my father.

Then came the relationship with Cher, and it hit me like a truck. I was so taken off guard that I started doing everything I thought I wouldn't normally do. I wore shorts. I pulled my hair back. I allowed myself to be happy in simpler ways, with simpler things. When Cher and I decided to change things there was no pain or anguish, because neither of us had tortured the other. From what I have seen, so many relationships are based on intense extremes of love or hate. The first phase is all about love and devotion, this feeling that you would do anything for the other person. Then things go wrong, and couples become venomously vengeful, and anything and everything is fair game. That wasn't the way Cher and I were, ever. When it began to end, I reminded myself how wonderful she was and how lucky I had been to have known her, and prepared to go back to my whoring ways. The last thing I expected was to meet another woman and start another serious relationship.

It was Christmastime, and I had to return to New York from California to audition new drummers to replace Peter. I was talking to Cher, because we were still close, and she asked me to get her a Christmas present.

"I don't know what to buy you for Christmas," I said.

"Go and talk to my friend Diana. She'll show you what I like. We shop at the same places." This was Diana Ross, who had begun her career with the Supremes, become not only Motown's biggest star but one of the biggest stars in the world, and then had gone on to an immensely successful solo career, both in music and in movies. She was more than a singer. She was an icon.

When I came into New York, I tracked down Diana on the phone, and she invited me over to her place. I remember coming in and immediately thinking two things about her: first, that she was very sensual, and second, that she was in firm control of her career. At that point she was taking steps to leave Motown, and she seemed to know a lot about her career. I sat there and we talked. She wanted to know how KISS worked since our success didn't rely on hit singles. I tried to explain our philosophy, of playing concerts and creating a fan base that was founded on loyalty, not on hit songs. This was the polar opposite to the kind of career Diana had built, but I could tell that it interested her, and she wanted to understand it better. While we were talking, she made coffee, and then she offered me a piece of chocolate cake. This isn't a euphemism. I inhaled it so quickly that she offered me a second piece, and that one went away too.

Over the next few weeks, Diana and I became friends. We talked and I took her to dinner a few times. We even played racquetball. I was a pretty good player, and Diana had never played before, so we spent most of our time on the floor of the court laughing about how fast the ball was going. We didn't think much of it, and I'm not sure that either of us had any hidden agenda, but pretty quickly it became apparent something was happening between us.

Diana was a strong woman and there wasn't any real pressure on me to be the centerpiece of her life. I admired how she conducted her personal life. She had been married to Bob Silverstein, and I was struck by the fact that she was still close to him. He was a good guy and we got along.

Being with Diana was a combination of joys. That is, I'd like to think, everyone's hope—that a relationship can exist on more than sexual energy, like the ability to sit and actually like being with each other. Diana and I would talk about lots of things. I confided in her early on how I was scared of having kids and that I thought I would never get married. She seemed to know something I didn't but never preached to me. She clearly loved her children and, I would like to think, wanted the same joy for me, but she never pushed the idea that I should become a father.

In the back of my mind, perhaps to justify my fear of commitment, was the notion that men don't seem to go through their lives agonizing over when it is time to have children. We don't have a biological clock. If we have any kind of clock, it probably goes off within a day or two if we don't have some kind of "companionship." Women, on the other hand, are reminded of wanting children all the time—culturally and, I think, biologically.

Being in KISS afforded me the opportunity of an inexhaustible supply of beautiful girls who simply wanted to be with me—perhaps only because I was in KISS. And the only thing they wanted was what I wanted too. Society's rules didn't apply in my hotel room, or on the bus, or wherever I would have liaisons. In another environment a girl might first want to get to know a prospective suitor and be taken out to dinner; inside my bedroom it was clearly "wham, bam, thank you, ma'am." No what-does-it-all-mean sermon. No dinner. Just dessert. And they didn't mind sharing. The more the merrier. If I took one of these ladies with me for a week, it would start beautifully, but within a few days it would become clear that lust is one thing, companionship another. I wanted not only to bed a beautiful girl, but I also wanted to talk to her. I wanted her to have something to say back to me. To disagree with me. To give me a run for my money. Well, let's not go that far.

If I was in the studio, she would wait for me. If I wanted to go someplace, she would want to go there too. Now, mind you, this sounds like the kind of situation any guy would dream of, but aside from the joys of having some young, lusty girl share my bed, the waking hours tended to grow stale with her.

There was a constant pull and tug inside of me. On the one hand, I craved and clearly loved being in bed in the arms of a beauty, but I also loved to cuddle. I always wanted to be with girls, but I didn't want them to want me—not too much, at least.

I had invented myself. I had come from another culture and had experienced a totally different reality than others I knew. Once I came to America, I soon discovered the secret of the great melting pot: I had been born in Israel, spoke a gutteral language, wore a yarmulke, and was of the "chosen" persuasion. If I was to get everything I ever wanted out of life, I would have to "dress British, think Yiddish."

Gene Simmons was *my* name. I gave myself that name, I wasn't given the name. There are many things in life that we don't have control over. We are born into a race and nationality. We are raised to follow a certain religion. We are raised to speak a certain language. We are given a first and last name by our parents. We don't have any choice in the matter. And then we are expected to marry and have children, within our religion and our race.

I would have none of it. I would decide how I would live my life. Who I would share my bed with. And I damn well couldn't care less what anyone else thought. At the end of my life, I will have done or attempted anything I ever wanted to do. I will have no regrets. I will not think "I woulda, coulda, shoulda . . ."

Life should be about choices, and only I was going to choose what was right for me. The only problem was that by the time I met and fell for Diana Ross, I had started to like the idea of having children. I didn't admit it to myself. Not then. But I remember walking into Diana's home in Connecticut and feeling the love she and her three girls shared. I liked being there.

It felt safe. I was surrounded by children. I was living with a woman I loved being with, day and night. But they weren't my children and we weren't married. Being with Diana was liberating. She didn't need me to fulfill her life. She was a mother and a superstar. We were together because we wanted to be.

I brought Diana and the kids over to my mother's house for Passover dinner. We spent one summer together at Martha's Vineyard. It was the first time I didn't think about work. Not all the time, anyway.

The guys in the band thought I was completely insane by now. I was. I was the guy in the band who was constantly on the hunt for skirt, but here I was settling into domestic life. For the second time!

After UNMASKED came out in 1980, we started to look for a new drummer. Auditions were held in downtown New York City. Hundreds of people auditioned. Finally we got in this guy who was a stove cleaner in White Plains, New York, whose name was Paul Caravello.

Paul answered one of the ads, and I'll never forget his audition. He came in and he had the biggest head of hair I'd ever seen. He almost looked like a Muppet. And he was shorter than any of us. Peter had been the shortest too, but Paul was even shorter, maybe five-five. Still, he was great from the start, cute as a button, with a

just a boy:
meets the elders

I found it more interesting talking to John Reid, who was Elton John's manager in 1980, than to anyone else. As a performer I knew one side of the music industry, but I wanted to learn more about the business side as well.

heart of gold. At the end of the audition, he actually got up and thanked us and said, "Before I leave, can I have your autograph?" It struck us all, even Ace, as being a sweet thing. He wanted this break so badly, in such a pure way. While working as a stove cleaner, he'd been in bands on and off and was actually a much better drummer than Peter and sang with good pitch. He was an all-around better thing for KISS than Peter was at that point.

Once he left the audition, we immediately decided he should be in the band. We called him up and offered him the job, and he couldn't believe it. We changed his name from Paul Caravello to Eric

a new member
1980~1982

On the Australia tour in 1980 we took over a restaurant. I really wasn't as sad as I looked, sitting there next to that lovely lady.

Carr, and we even went out and bought him a Porsche so he wouldn't feel substandard. We wanted him to know that he was in the fold, that he was one of us.

Bringing Eric into the band the way we did—just before a tour, with very little preparation and tons of enthusiasm—was like living the beginning of our careers all over again. It was an astonishing thing to watch him take on his new role, and to watch ourselves try to integrate him. First, there was the matter of his personality within the band: What was his character going to be? What was his makeup going to be? Was he going to be an elephant or a giraffe? For an ordinary band his personality might have been an issue; for KISS it was an issue times ten. For a while we decided that Eric would look like a hawk, but later he came up with a fox persona. We introduced him by playing at the Palladium in New York City, to a crowd of about three thousand people. That was the trial by fire, and he passed with flying colors. Then we went off to Europe, taking Bon Jovi on their first European tour.

Everything was brand-new for Eric. He was wide-eyed as we started our European tour and not used to the kind of fame we were experiencing. One night we were in a hotel in England, and he was downstairs in the bar. There were girls there, as always. One of them introduced herself as a photographer for *Melody Maker,* a British music industry paper. Eric talked to her for a while and gave her the complete new-rock-star rap. At one point he asked her if she wanted to come up and take nude pictures of him. She said, "Sure." So they went up, and apparently he had told her, "Look, these pictures are just for you." She said that she understood completely. Eric got into a bathtub nude, holding a champagne glass with shades on and this big mop-top head of hair. Apparently they didn't spend the night together—after she took the pictures, she took off. The next day Eric related the story to us. We doubled over laughing. It was like Trust on the Road 101. "Are you out of your mind?" we said. "This girl is going to print those photos." Eric protested for a second, but then the truth dawned on him. "Oh, my God!" he said. "You think she will?" Of course she did.

Everywhere we went with Eric, he was just like that. He was

never malicious. He worked hard. He showed up on time. He was a complete professional. But there was constant comedy, because he was so inexperienced and trusting. At one of the airports in Europe, he showed up in a camouflage outfit with an ammunition belt around him. All the bullets were hollow, but it wasn't immediately apparent, and at any rate it wasn't the kind of thing you brought to an airport. So of course some of the machine-gun-toting security guards at the airport took him off to the side. That's how much they didn't trust him. They thought he was wearing a wig because his hair was so big. "What's under there?" they asked. I mean they really went from top to bottom. He even had an anal inspection. He was protesting all the way: "What are you talking about? I'm from White Plains." While Peter had complained constantly, Eric was more than fun to have around. He was terrific.

After Europe we went to Australia. At that point we were the biggest thing the Australians had ever seen. One in every fourteen people in that country had bought a KISS record. We played multiple dates in soccer stadiums when nobody else had ever played stadiums there. The first band to ever play stadiums anywhere in the world was the Beatles, at Shea Stadium. People don't realize that before then bands just didn't get to be that big. But when we played Down Under, we were on the cover of every newspaper. On one cover the headline even said, KISS BOOTS. This was the most trivial story imaginable: we had sent out our platform heels to get fixed at a boot store. Well, somehow the proprietor wound up being on the cover of the newspaper. There were terrorist attacks and wars were being fought, but on the cover there was nothing but the band: KISS ARMY INVADES AUSTRALIA. We couldn't go anywhere. We were trapped on the top floor of our hotel. Helicopters with zoom lenses were trying to get photos of us without makeup, because there was a price on our heads. America had gone nuts for KISS in 1974. Japan had taken it to the next level in 1977. But Australia in 1981 was like nothing we had ever seen. Anything we wanted was ours.

The effect of all this hysteria was that we couldn't go anywhere. This might have been torture, but the Australian promoter, bless him, rented out entire clubs and filled them with girls. They were the top-notch models in the country, and they kept us busy.

At these parties Ace would get blitzed. An Aussie press man became one of Ace's drinking buddies, and at one of the parties, while everyone was sitting around talking, Ace and the gentleman started making out. I don't really believe that Ace pitched for the other team, but it wouldn't matter if he did. It was clear, however, after he got enough alcohol into his system, all bets were off. He would lose his inhibitions and think nothing of kissing and making out with men. Ace and Peter would think nothing of kissing each other. I think this was an infatuation, on both their parts, with the *Godfather* culture that had become very popular with them, a sort of "we know the right people" attitude, proof that they shared a bond, with Peter being Italian and Ace always threatening to call the right people to do his dirty work if he wasn't treated well.

During one of those lavish private parties on the Australian tour, Eric became fascinated by one girl in the club. He was wearing a camouflage outfit again, and everyone else was dressed for nightlife—the guys in leather jackets and frilly shirts, and the girls in very little—except for this one girl, who looked like a female version of Eric in a women's camouflage outfit. She was very beautiful, and very shapely, but Eric didn't want to go over, so I arranged for the girl to come over and talk to him, and the two of them really hit it off. He was in the process of convincing her to come back to the hotel, and she kind of laughed and said, "Look, I can't go back with you. I'm married." Eric backed off immediately. I was amazed. "What's the problem?" I said. "If you want her to come, just invite her, and then it's up to her. Whether she's married or not, it's her choice." So he told her where we were going to be next: Melbourne, I think. And wouldn't you know it—she decided to come to see him. She got on a plane and flew to meet us.

Most guys would have been thrilled, but Eric was so nervous that by the end of the day he had horrible gas pains. He had to go to the bathroom every five minutes. And it wasn't the kind of gas you could get rid of silently. They were all of the *1812 Overture* variety. Needless to say, the girl didn't hang out for long. It was always like that with Eric. Something would always happen to him. On another tour a few years later, when we were on the road in America touring for *Creatures of the Night,* Eric wrote a long letter in response to a girl who had written him. Eric was always very emotional, and it wasn't unusual for him to reply to a fan letter with a five-or-ten-page handwritten answer. After he replied to one letter, he ended up having something of a friendship with this girl from Phoenix.

When we got to Phoenix on the tour, Eric told me me about the girl. He couldn't wait to see her. After our sound check Eric left, and I noticed a stunning girl in a red dress standing at the back of the empty hall. She had on makeup, perfume, the whole thing. As was my custom, I brought her into my office, which was the backstage bathroom, and threw her on the floor. We had an exchange, shall we say. We became very close friends in a number of positions, and there was a photo session afterward. There always was. Then she happily left.

Later that evening, as we were putting on our makeup, I told Eric about my liaison. He wasn't really listening; he was still preoccupied with his Phoenix girl. So we started talking about that, and I

I'm sure when Ace woke up the next day he didn't remember any of this.

happened to ask him how he would know her, since they had never met. "Well," he said, "she told me she'd be wearing a red dress." As he was telling me what she looked like, the horror of it dawned on me. I showed him the photos from that afternoon's meet-and-greet and asked, "Is this her?" Well, he was devastated. I apologized. I told him I didn't know. And that wasn't even the end of it. That night back at the hotel the two of them met, and he was very upset with her. They fought, and he threw her out, and she came down the hall for a second visit with me.

I didn't want Eric to be upset with me—not over this or over anything else. I tried to give him the lay of the land and told him that he couldn't take any of this seriously. For me, it was about fun and games: if you go to a beauty pageant and there are four girls there, do you really care who you wind up with? But since it was all so new to him it really affected him.

The Unmasked tour had been a turbulent one for the band. Diana had decided to fly over so we could spend some time together during the first part of the tour, when we were in London. It became very difficult even to go to a restaurant. There were paparazzi constantly prowling around, trying to get photos of us together and me

Bill Aucoin with Elton John.

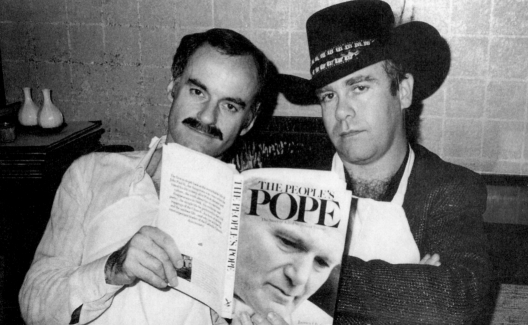

without my makeup. To make matters worse, the band and Bill Aucoin had a meeting and decided to confront me about "going Hollywood." They said, and rightfully so, that because my relationship with Diana and, before that, with Cher were so public, it changed the fans' perspective of KISS. We had always been outsiders who never fraternized with other celebrities, and now there I was actually having relationships with these women. It just wasn't rock and roll, I was told.

All this inner turmoil in the band wasn't helping Ace's mental well-being. Aucoin no longer seemed to have the spark of leadership. Eric was simply happy to be there and hardly ever voiced an opinion. I was not the favorite guy in the band at that time. After the tour, we retreated to our separate homes and spent time away from each other. I came back to New York to a new dynamic that would unfold before my eyes.

Diana and I were not together most of the time. And one day Cher called and told me she had been offered an acting part in a Broadway play called *Come Back to the Five and Dime, Jimmy Dean, Jimmy Dean,* to be directed by Robert Altman, and could she stay at my place. I said yes without hesitation. If we were no longer lovers, we were certainly still friends.

In hindsight, this was probably unfair to Diana. Although we each had condos on Fifth Avenue only five blocks from each other, I'd be with Diana in the daytime and sometimes keep Cher company at night. She was venturing into a new area in her life as an actress and felt unsure of herself. She needed me and I was happy to be there for her. Though Diana and Cher had been friends before, it was clear that their friendship could no longer continue.

But this too would pass, and Diana and I grew closer. She was recording new material for what would become her first non-Motown record, and KISS was about to enter the studio to record a kind of record we had never done before: a concept album called *The Elder.*

♦ ♦ ♦

While Eric was such a positive force Ace was going deeper and deeper into seclusion. Although he liked Eric very much, he couldn't really hang out with him because Eric wouldn't get high. So more and more Ace went off to Las Vegas with his friends and gambled and drank and drove his fast cars too fast.

We decided we needed Bob Ezrin back in our lives, because he was the guy who had delivered *Destroyer,* probably our best studio album. We contacted him, and he decided he wanted to work on a new record with us. Bob decided that we should move up to Toronto and cut the record there. We started rehearsing in Ace's home studio in Connecticut, but almost immediately there were problems, the first being that Ace had no intention of leaving Connecticut for Toronto. Also, Ezrin made it clear to Ace that his material was not going to wind up on the album, or at least not very much of it, because it wasn't impressing him. And Bob himself was having some substance problems. It was a very unhealthy situation for all of us, and it was unfortunate, because this was the first record that Eric Carr was going to play on.

Initially at least, the material for this new album, which ended up being called *The Elder,* was promising. Eric showed us that he was leagues beyond Peter by teaching himself how to play guitar and cowriting a song I helped him with called "Under the Rose." He became a real contributing member of the band, even to the point of dealing with the facts of KISS life. For example, I had written a song called "I"—one of whose lines was "I don't need to get wasted; it only holds me down / 'Cause I got a will of my own and the guts to stand alone." The chorus went, "Because I believe in me." That had always been my philosophy, so I decided to write a song about it. I was excited about recording "I," but Ezrin didn't feel that Eric's drumming was cutting it on that song, and he brought in a session player. With Peter, that would have resulted in major drama. Eric, though he wasn't happy about it, dealt with it.

◆ ◆ ◆

The Elder came at a strange time in the band's history. For starters, we were no longer with Casablanca Records. Neil Bogart had been bought out by Polygram, and we went from recording for a label where we had a personal relationship with the president to record-

Beauty and the Beast:
The media was fascinated by
my relationship with Cher.

Me and Cher with Richard T.
Bear, center. Bear played piano
on my solo record. This was
taken in Oxford, England,
where I recorded.

During the *KISS Meets the Phantom* shoot, I went out into the crowd to greet my bosses. KISS has always had a peculiar notion in our heads. The KISS Army who come to see us are the bosses. They can always fire us. So it is up to us to make sure we never disappoint them. We just work here.

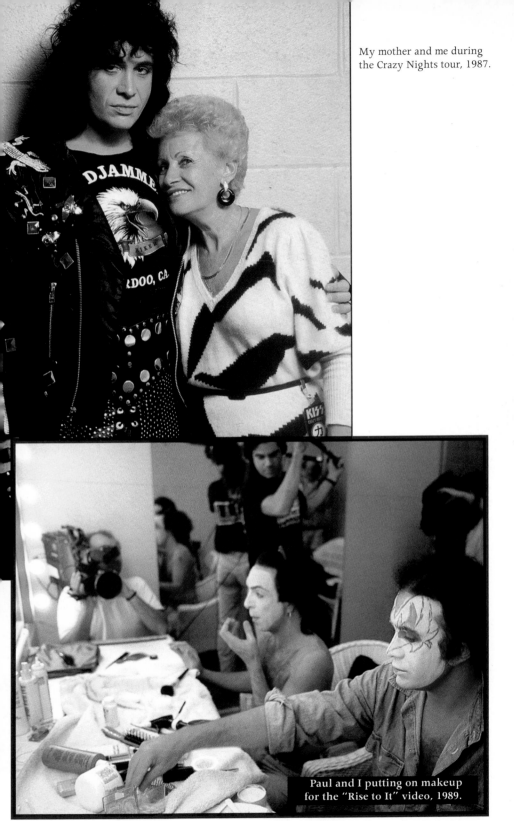

My mother and me during the Crazy Nights tour, 1987.

Paul and I putting on makeup for the "Rise to It" video, 1989.

Shannon, Nick, and me with
Siegfried and Roy in 1993.

Jay Leno did a number of KISS-related skits. One of them was about a new machine the Post Office had for licking stamps: my head with the tongue sticking out. In 1997 Jay asked us to be on the show, but we were playing four sold-out nights in Los Angeles and couldn't come. He was kind enough to bring his entire crew out to the Forum to film the KISS skits.

Opposite: One of my youngest obsessed fans. I met this guy when we played Alberta, Canada, on the Psycho Circus tour in 1998. He was five years old. I told him that I was Gene Simmons and he shot right back that *he* was the real Gene Simmons.

PLAYBOY

ENTERTAINMENT FOR MEN

MARCH 1999 • $4.9

SEX & MUSIC ISSUE

THE GIRLS OF KISS

**LAURYN HILL
BEASTIE BOYS
MUSIC POLL
WINNERS**

**INTERVIEW
WITH HORNY
DREW CAREY**

**SEDUCTIVE
RUDOLPH GIULIANI
IRRESISTIBLE
KEITH OLBERMANN**

**EXCLUSIV
FICTION
PREVIEW
THE RETURN
OF LITTLE
BIG MAN**

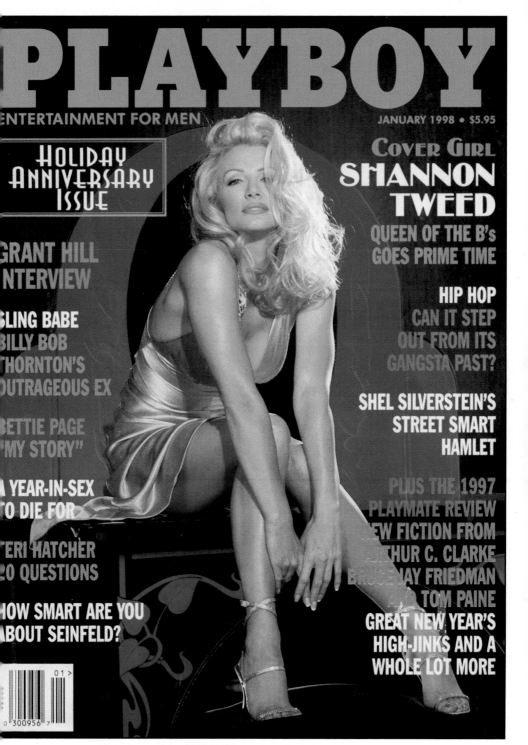

PLAYBOY

ENTERTAINMENT FOR MEN

JANUARY 1998 • $5.95

HOLIDAY ANNIVERSARY ISSUE

COVER GIRL
SHANNON TWEED
QUEEN OF THE B's GOES PRIME TIME

HIP HOP
CAN IT STEP OUT FROM ITS GANGSTA PAST?

SHEL SILVERSTEIN'S STREET SMART HAMLET

PLUS THE 1997 PLAYMATE REVIEW
NEW FICTION FROM ARTHUR C. CLARKE BRUCE JAY FRIEDMAN AND TOM PAINE
GREAT NEW YEAR'S HIGH-JINKS AND A WHOLE LOT MORE

GRANT HILL INTERVIEW

SLING BABE BILLY BOB THORNTON'S OUTRAGEOUS EX

BETTIE PAGE "MY STORY"

A YEAR-IN-SEX TO DIE FOR

TERI HATCHER 20 QUESTIONS

HOW SMART ARE YOU ABOUT SEINFELD?

0 300956 7

01 >

How many kids do you know whose parents have both been on the cover of *Playboy*?

Sophie and Shannon on the set of a video Shannon was shooting in 1996.

Sophie at her first ballet lesson at age four, and Nick in his karate outfit at age five. I have the most beautiful kids in the world.

ing for a large entity called Polygram with an enormous staff. We felt lost.

Also I was starting to knock on Hollywood's doors whenever I was in California. I had some ideas for movies and television shows. One was about a black cowboy called Gabriel who lived just before the Civil War. I came up with the idea that he was the bastard son of a plantation owner who had been forced to join the Union Army as a buffalo soldier. In the end he has to go down to the South and confront his plantation master, who was his father but also the man who raped his mother. I thought this might make a good movie, so I took it to Paramount Pictures.

When I say I took it to Paramount, I mean that I went to see Sherry Lansing, the head of the studio. I was never the kind of person to wait for managers and agents to arrange a meeting. I told Sherry the Gabriel story, and she said she would think about it. We became friendly. We found out that we'd both taught sixth grade and that we had similar ideas about things. I was attracted to her from the start, but although we went out from time to time, I never did anything about it.

From those initial meetings in Hollywood, I came up with the idea for *The Elder*. I wasn't sure whether it would be a record or a movie. All I knew, at first, was a line that stuck in my mind: "When the earth was young they were already old." I conceived of a race of immortal beings, energy-based beings, a take-off of Marvel's Watcher. These beings were more observers than participants. They didn't interfere with human choice, and as a result people were ultimately responsible for their own deeds, good and bad. The more I worked on it, the more I thought this would be a strong movie pitch.

When Bob Ezrin read my short story, he said, "Well, this is great. We should do a concept record about your short story." Ezrin made this announcement to the band and said we were going to try to make all of our songs fit around this one central idea. We put all the songs in the pot and got busy rewriting some lyrics, and soon enough we had a rough story line. The work went quickly because we knew what we wanted: our own *Tommy*. This was the first KISS project where someone—in this case, Bob Ezrin—talked the band members into the notion that credibility and respect from critics are as important as the love of the fans. As a result, it was a very serious record for us.

It was a bit surprising for Eric, I'm sure. When he first joined, the band was expecting to do a straight rock and roll record, so he was a little caught off-guard. He was not necessarily a big fan of the idea. Also, as much as Paul and I trusted Bob's instincts and supported his idea, Ace opposed it. He was completely against it, to the point that he refused to show up yet again. He wouldn't go up to Toronto and said he would phone in his solo. As it turned out, whenever Ace appears on that record, it's as a result of that process. Copies of the twenty-four-track masters were flown to his home studio in Connecticut from Toronto. At home he put down a number of different solos, and then it was up to Bob, when it was flown back to Toronto, to figure out which solos to use—or whether, as happened in some cases, another guitar player should be brought in. A number of other guitar players played because Ace just didn't show up.

Unfortunately all the work that went into *The Elder* seemed to be for nothing. We had a record that, for the first time, bombed so badly it didn't even go gold. We truly were at a crossroads. We had cut our hair, though we still wore makeup. We had a new member in the band, Eric. And we were trying to figure out what to do in the wake of *The Elder*'s disappointing performance.

We weren't going to tour with a record that didn't sell, so we turned our attention to television and videos. We shot "A World Without Heroes," which was cowritten by myself, Lou Reed, Paul, and Bob Ezrin and would later be covered on one of Cher's records. We also shot a video of "I," which would have the dubious distinction of charting in the top ten only in Italy. We did a whirlwind promo tour of Europe and made television appearances. We then went to Mexico City, where KISS was huge. On the way into the city, the limo was playing one of four different radio stations that had KISS radio programs, programs that did nothing but play KISS songs and interviews for four hours.

At the Mexico City hotel, we were feted by the Mexican record company. We were given gold record awards and hosted the press in full KISS makeup. Ace took the opportunity to piss into a large bottle and put it next to other bottles of champagne. But, though it was a funny moment, it signaled what was about to happen.

When we returned to America, Ace wouldn't return phone calls. We had arranged to be on the Eurovision television show shown throughout Europe to millions of people. Here was an opportunity to reach a lot of people and perhaps resurrect a dying record. We scheduled a live broadcast feed of us lip-synching to "I" from the stage of Studio 54 in New York. When the clock hit ten, we would be on. Live.

Ace never showed up. We sent limos and George Sewitt, our security guard, to Ace's home. But on returning, he said Ace was close to comatose. The show had to go on. We performed without Ace and, for the first and last time, as a trio.

Polygram decided to release a greatest hits record in Europe only that was to be called *Killers*. We needed four new songs for it. So we got together with a producer named Michael Jackson whom Paul and I liked very much. He came from a different musical background but had some good ideas. He had produced Jesse Colin Young from the Youngbloods, one of my favorite bands. On meeting him, I strongly urged him to do something about his name. I mean, two Michael Jacksons just wouldn't fly—I suggested Michael James Jackson, and he did change it to that.

The writing process started. It was clear things would be different. Ace was nowhere to be found. We would deal with that issue when and if we had to, but for now we had work to do.

KISS moved to Los Angeles, where Jackson was based. Paul and Eric rented places and I moved into Diana's Beverly Hills home. I was completely distracted by Hollywood and movies, and my songwriting, as a consequence, suffered greatly. The four new songs were all written by Paul and cowriters. One of Paul's songs needed a bridge, so I suggested a melody line he didn't care for. I saved the melody and would later reuse it as the centerpiece of a song called "I Love It Loud."

By 1981, I was spending more and more time in Hollywood. I

was approached by Marcy Carsey, a producer of shows like *The Cosby Show* and *Roseanne,* to try out for a show to be called *Grotus.* I would be the star. I shot a short pilot and everyone seemed to like it enough to get me in front of the ABC staff. There were ten people around a table and we chatted for five minutes. Then they offered me my own TV series. I was stunned.

I went outside with my business guy, who explained the deal to me. I would get $60,000 an episode. He told me if I left KISS, where I was making substantially more, I would in essence be paying for the privilege of being on television.

Aucoin and the band were not happy with me being on TV. This confirmed for them what they told me earlier—that I had gone Hollywood, the worst thing you could do back then. The band was in turmoil: Ace was miserable, Aucoin was slacking, Eric was disillusioned, and Paul felt betrayed by my interest in television. And my fans weren't happy either. The press was having a field day talking about the Beast from KISS who was dating the Motown diva. The fans turned on me because of it. I had wanted to live my own life, and if this was the price I had to pay, so be it. But in the end I didn't do the TV show; I stayed with the band.

Ace looking at the papers on tour.

✦ ✦ ✦

Killers went out in Europe, and the record company was happy that we were going to make some money for them. At the same time that *Killers* was being done, we started writing seriously for a new album that we imagined as a heavy record, a big guitar record, to get back to who we were. We knew that Eric was talented enough to be a kind of John Bonham figure and that in addition he could actually sing. As this heavy record got off the ground—we titled it *Creatures of the Night*—Michael James Jackson called in a guy from Canada who had had a disco hit. It was Bryan Adams and his partner Jim Vallence, and the three of us wrote "War Machine" and then "Rock and Roll Hell." The material was strong. We were excited, the three of us. I say "the three of us" because Ace, once again, was nowhere to be found. He refused to come out to California. He never showed up, never played a single note on the record. When we spoke to him, he told us that he was working on his solo material. This was a clear signal that he wanted to leave the band; still, for some crazy reason, we worked hard to keep him within the band. At one point Paul drove up to Ace's house to find out what was wrong. Ace launched into a long speech about how he needed a solo career. Paul, very reasonably, told him he could have both. Ace rejected the idea out of hand, and it became patently obvious that he was going to leave KISS.

In the face of his inevitable departure, we tried to move things along as smoothly as possible. We put his face on the cover and pretended that he played on the album, although he never appeared once. We were concerned that our fans wouldn't be able to deal with the departures of two members in two records. It would be devastating to them and to their idea of us.

The search for a new guitarist started almost immediately. We used five or six different guitar players on *Creatures of the Night,* everybody from Rick Derringer to Vinnie Cusano, who would later become Vinnie Vincent and have a temporary place in the band. His performance should have been a shot across the bow for us—it was torture working with him. He didn't like to be told what or how to play. And from the outset, he did things like inviting us out to dinner and then, when the check came, announcing that he had forgotten his wallet. I didn't mind paying, but why would you go and invite me to dinner and then make believe you don't have your wallet? We thought he was wrong for the band. I kept telling him, "Look, you can't be the guitar player. You're too thin, you're too small, and you just don't look like you're part of the band." And he kept saying saying, "No, no, I belong, I belong."

By 1982 things weren't going well between the band and Bill Aucoin either. At the end of the day, the numbers we expected weren't there. Bill, as it turned out, was a terrific idea guy, but he didn't seem to know how to make the best use of the money. When you plan a tour, maybe you don't need four security guards for the band. Maybe you just need two. And if every security guy is getting $1,500 a week, then if you cut out two guys, you're saving $3,000 a week for, say, twenty weeks. Every dollar saved could be a dollar in our pockets. But these kinds of cost-cutting measures were not really his strong suit.

We weren't the only unhappy band on earth. During that time Eddie Van Halen came down to the studio and played the beginnings of what would become "Jump" for us. I took him to lunch, and he told me how unhappy he was in Van Halen, how David Lee Roth was driving him nuts. He wanted to know whether I would consider taking him into KISS because he had heard we were looking for a lead guitarist. I didn't think he was serious. We had lunch across from the Record Plant recording studios and I listened to him tell me his troubles. Vinnie Vincent was with us—Vinnie, at this point, was a contributing songwriter and lead guitarist on the *Creatures* record only.

We thought KISS with Eddie Van Halen on lead guitar was certainly an exciting idea, but if it came to pass, what would his makeup character be? We thought it better for KISS to find an unknown and for Eddie to go back to Van Halen. I tried to assure him it would work out. It did, for a time.

We eventually caved in and accepted Vinnie. If we had hoped that taking him into the fold might lessen the headache of dealing with him, those hopes were not fulfilled. First of all, he wanted to hold on to his name, Vinnie Cusano. I told him at the outset that it was not a good idea: it sounded like a fruit vendor, and fairly or unfairly, rock and roll is about image. Everybody else had a nondescript name where you couldn't figure out their ethnicity or anything else about them. I had changed my name and he would have to do the same. He finally agreed that his name was problematic, but then he had his own ideas about what the new one should be. He wanted to be called Mick Fury. I didn't have the heart to tell him that he wasn't qualified to do this kind of stuff, that he should just show up on time and make lots of money.

Vinnie worsened. He didn't sign his contract, ever. Finally we told him he had to sign. It was an offer of employment. He could be in the band or not, but we didn't want to discuss it. It was nonnegotiable. There was a calendar too: with *Creatures* done, we either had to lose the window of a tour or go off on tour with this guy. We decided, rightly or wrongly, to go on the tour with him. Paul designed Vinnie's ankh makeup and his Wiz character.

Paul and Eric Carr on the way to Brazil in 1981 to play an outdoor concert.

KISS was now made up of Eric Carr, Vinnie Vincent, Paul, and me. We liked *Creatures of the Night* and hoped for the best. But the album did poorly. We booked an American tour, and it was the least successful tour we'd ever done. The music scene was changing: acts like Michael Jackson and the Clash were in ascent, and no one showed up to hear us play. In North America, that is; abroad, especially in South America, we played to the biggest audiences we'd ever played, stadiums full of people. Even though the experience was depressing in some respects, it opened our eyes to the idea that no one city and no one marketplace is definitive. If you're not mak-

all hell's breakin'
and my stint as

1983~

ing it in the United States, go to Brazil. If you're not making it in Colombia, try Italy.

The biggest change at that time was the rise of MTV. Music was being overtaken by a certain visual style. We had been a visual band since the beginning, but oddly, our idea of visual panache didn't necessarily translate in the world of early 1980s rock and roll, which was dominated by hair-metal bands. Hair bands were dominant because they gave younger teenagers, and especially younger girls, access to a kind of rock music that had been considered too dangerous for them before. Girls who were only thirteen and four-

loose: LICK IT UP
a movie star

1984

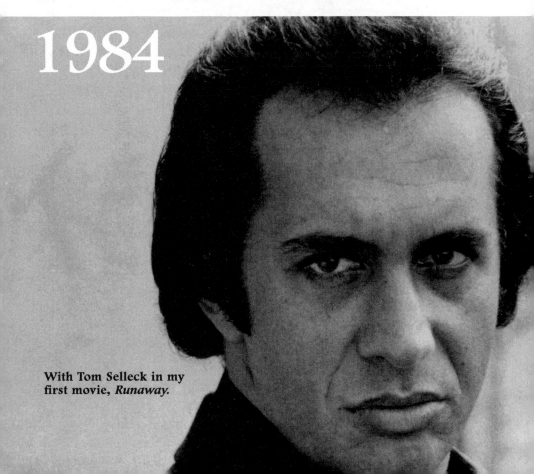

With Tom Selleck in my first movie, *Runaway*.

teen were having their first brushes with sexuality, and for their early crushes, they were turning to these hair-metal bands, to Bon Jovi, to Poison. As it turned out, we had one band member who was perfectly suited for this transition: Paul Stanley. He was at home being that kind of front man, dancing on the stage. So for the first time in our career, we did exactly what we saw happening with other bands. It's not worth debating the justification, worrying over originality and inspiration. We were a working band. Instead of being leaders, we decided basically to follow.

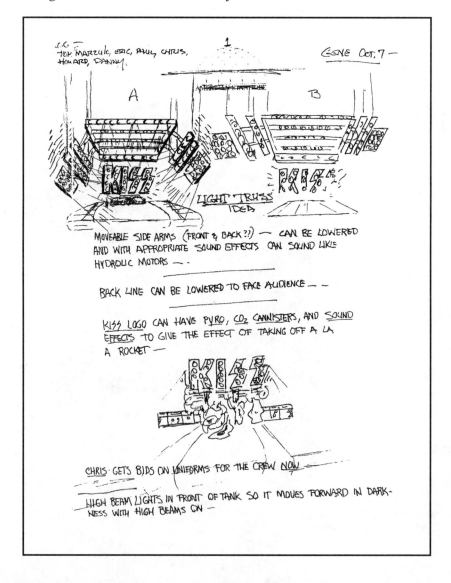

At around that same time, we decided to drop the one visual element that had been associated with KISS most strongly and from the very beginning: our makeup. When we started working on *Lick It Up,* it was a good time musically. We had Michael James Jackson producing once again, and Vinnie Vincent was our guitarist and a contributing songwriter. Vinnie and Paul were particularly successful during this period; the two of them wrote "Lick It Up," the title track from that album. In the middle of recording the album, more or less out of nowhere, Paul pulled me aside and said, "Gene, I think

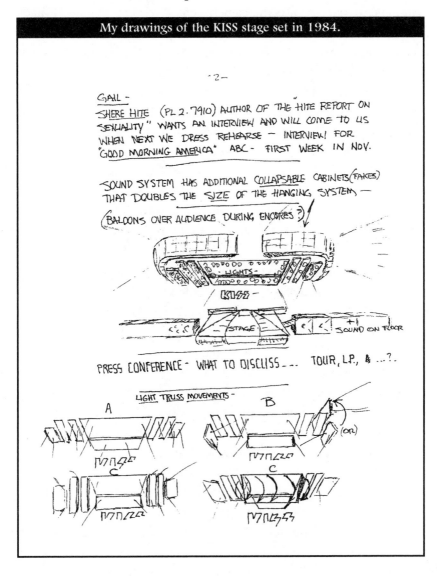

My drawings of the KISS stage set in 1984.

it's time to take our makeup off." His reasoning was sound—with all the personnel changes, we had moved farther and farther away from plausible characters. Vinnie Vincent's character, the Wizard, wasn't sticking with fans the way the Demon or the Starchild had. "Let's prove something to the fans," Paul said. "Let's go and be a real band without makeup."

I reluctantly agreed. I didn't know if it was going to work or not, but I heard what Paul was saying—there was nowhere else for us to go. We did a photo session just to see what it would look like. We looked straight into the camera lens. We were defiant. I made one small concession to the fans—I stuck out my tongue, to try to keep something that connected us with the past, to remind fans that we weren't a brand-new band.

We decided to unveil ourselves live on MTV. First, superimposed over our faces, were photos of us in full KISS makeup. As the veejay announced each of our names, the makeup photos dissolved to our bare faces. We made the best of it, but I was scared stiff.

Lick It Up was released and immediately tripled the sales of *Creatures of the Night*. It went platinum and we were soon filling up concert halls again. This was clearly a new lease on life.

◆ ◆ ◆

Eric Carr must have felt as if the ground were moving under him every time he took a step. He was thrilled to join the KISS he knew and loved, but the first record he played on was a concept album. The second was *Creatures of the Night*. Then, with the third record he played on, KISS took off the makeup.

After we took off our makeup and embraced the MTV age, the crowd changed dramatically. Back in the early days, we had started off with a bizarre crowd, opening for other bands, and KISS was perceived as a dangerous band of rock-metal rebels. When we became more mainstream, the toys and the games brought us a very young crowd. At some point Mom and Dad would show up with their three-year-old kids. It became like the circus. The 1980s brought yet another shift. Suddenly we were popular with teenage girls. They came to the show. They got in front. They screamed. And sometimes they seemed to want to do more than just scream; some of them were clearly groupies in training. For the record, I should say that I never went after the underage ones—enough legal-age girls were showing up. But these young girls would come backstage. They were always around. I would walk into my room, and usually there would be a girl there.

The early and mid-1980s were a troubling time for me in some respects. My connection to KISS, the dominant part of my life for a decade, began to change. Mainly what happened was that I started to get lost. I didn't know how I was supposed to act, because the no-makeup version of the band was an entirely new idea. Paul was in his prime. He was very comfortable being who he was, because in some ways Paul is the same offstage as onstage. For those couple of years it became more his band. Paul was always the guy who spoke in the interviews. When you saw photos of KISS, they tended more and more to be photos of Paul. Still, if I stuck my tongue out enough times, I would eventually get in the frame.

It's important to be clear about what happened. Paul didn't push me out of the spotlight. He would never do that to me. It's just that his ability to capture the public's attention increased as the music scene changed. My reaction was to try to muscle my way back into the spotlight by buying some truly outlandish androgynous clothing. It didn't work, not the way I wanted it to. It just made me look like a football player in a tutu.

This period also gave me an opportunity to watch Paul at work, and it was an interesting process. Paul's sense of things is what you'd more traditionally think of as the female perspective. Call me simplistic, but I think women are less interested in the endgame, in winding up in bed with somebody, than in just being recognized for being attractive. Paul is more like that. Paul is less interested in whether the girl winds up in bed with him than in whether she finds him good-looking. I'm not interested in whether she finds me attractive; I'm only interested in whether she winds up in bed with me. Paul and I both like chocolate cake, so you would think we're alike, but we're completely different. He only likes the frosting. I hate the frosting—I only like the stuff you can chew, the devil's food. So if you walk by a cake and see the devil's food missing, you know I've been there. If you walk by and see the frosting missing, Paul's been there. Between the two of us, we can split a whole cake. So in a very real way, we are opposite pieces of the same puzzle. Somehow it worked.

◆ ◆ ◆

One of the funniest incidents in my life happened not onstage but in the audience. It was in the mid-1980s, and I had gone to La Cage aux Folles, a drag nightclub in Los Angeles. It was a real show-business crowd—Milton Berle was on my left, with his wife, and other celebrities were there as well. The lights went down, and the music started for the pageant of drag queens. The first one to come out was dressed as Cher. The drag Cher paraded around and finally went off-stage right. The next drag queen was dressed as Diana Ross. And right after that was a drag Liza Minnelli. That's the trinity for gay men, the ultimate divas, and all three of them were important in my life.

I had first met Liza when I went with Cher to a party at Halston's. In 1979 I met her again. She was playing a few nights at Radio City Music Hall. I had no romantic aspirations, and I certainly didn't think of getting into the Liza Minnelli business. We became friends and would go to dinner occasionally. Liza, Judy Garland's daughter, had been a star of stage and screen for decades.

Whenever we got together, our conversation would turn to music. Liza would ask about KISS. She wanted me to explain to her how it had all happened, how we had gone from obscurity to world-wide fame. I explained that it wasn't just one person—it was a huge confluence of record labels and management. She said there was nothing Madonna had that she didn't have, except for the right songs. I basically told her the lay of the land as I saw it. The Ethel Merman style of singing, with a wide vibrato, was a thing of the past. It wasn't going to fly. The average teenage girl didn't know a thing about that world. If she was interested in letting go of her past and recreating Liza Minnelli, then I could help her out. I became her music business manager.

I took her up to Columbia Records and introduced her to Walter Yetnikoff. He gave us the green light right away. He didn't waste time looking at bottom lines or consulting with vice presidents. He was a classic mogul. A young A&R guy named Michael Goldstone came up with an idea to put Liza with the Pet Shop Boys and do a modern Euro-disco album. I explained this to Liza and told her what it would require.

As I got more and more involved in Liza's recording career, we were seen together. Some of the gossip magazines started reporting "KISS star captures Liza's heart," which wasn't the case at all. Liza and I had a totally professional relationship. I would meet with her at her apartment and then we would meet at the Fifth Avenue penthouse where I lived. We talked endlessly about movies, music, and her aspirations to break into the pop field. I enjoyed her company. I enjoyed going to events with her, like the grand opening of the first Hard Rock Café. I respected her as an artist, and I wanted to help her with her career. But that was all I wanted.

The single she cut with the Pet Shop Boys was a huge international record. In America it didn't sell, but it gave her something more important: momentum. At that time Dean Martin had fallen out of a tour he had undertaken with Sammy Davis Jr. and Frank Sinatra. Liza joined that show, and in the middle of it she played twenty-three shows at Radio City Music Hall straight. That must be some kind of record: 6,500 people for three weeks straight.

I wasn't the only one who liked Frank Sinatra. When I started working with Liza, Peter Criss kept telling me how much he loved him. I contacted his road manager, who got me front-row tickets to see Sinatra in Los Angeles. Sinatra looked at us and winked. Peter was in heaven. He had just gotten the *Good Housekeeping* seal of approval from the Chairman of the Board.

Liza had her ups and downs in life. Just as I was starting my own record company, Simmons Records, she and I decided to part ways. She wanted to go back full into the high-stepping-and-belting tradition of singing. I wasn't in favor of it; I thought people would think she was just putting on a mask as a modern pop singer. She couldn't break free of Broadway. To some people, that may have been important stuff. To the record-buying public, it meant nothing. In the end we couldn't make it work. I met with Mickey Rudin, one of the top lawyers in the entertainment business, and we dissolved our agreement.

Around the same time Liza left my life, Neil Bogart, the president of our label and the man who had helped us so much in our early years, who had supported us as we rocketed to fame, was stricken with cancer. One night I went to a music industry charity event at the Hilton in New York City. I was sitting with Neil, who had become very puffy, and I was joking with him, telling him, "I love pastries too." I didn't realize he was sick. My heart sank when I realized later on that the physical changes had to do with the illness.

A few years later our business manager called and said, "Would you like to go to the funeral?" What funeral? "Well," he said, "Neil Bogart just passed away." We flew out to Los Angeles and stood there, numb, while everyone from Neil Diamond to Donna Summer delivered eulogies. He was clearly well loved by lots of people. Astonishingly, his son, Timothy Bogart, wrote a script I'm now producing for a movie. Life seems to go in circles.

◆ ◆ ◆

By 1983, KISS had dropped Ace Frehley and then Vinnie Vincent. We had gone from the biggest band in the world to a band seemingly on its last legs. We ultimately brought in another guitarist, Mark St. John, for *Animalize,* but he lasted for only one record. He developed something called Reiter's syndrome, a hardening of the muscles in the hands. They blew up to the size of balloons, so obviously he couldn't play. The Reiter's syndrome had started to accelerate during the making of the record and we were worried, but Mark insisted that it wouldn't affect him. We actually started a tour with him and played a smaller hall in Poughkeepsie, New York. It was clear from that show that his medical problem was significant, and that he wasn't the right guitarist for KISS.

Paul and I had decided to produce *Animalize* ourselves. After we finished the basic tracks and I finished my vocals, I told Paul that

I would trust him to finish the album. He wasn't pleased, but I had a film opportunity I didn't want to pass up, so Paul ended up doing the work.

I had wanted to act in movies for a long time. It dated back to my earliest interests, which were oriented more toward science fiction and fantasy films than to music. Whenever I saw movies, I read the credits. On one film it said that the casting directors were a firm named Fenton and Feinberg. I called the operator and found out where Fenton and Feinberg were. I didn't even know their first names. I called them up and said, "Hi, I'm Gene Simmons from KISS. Can I come in and talk with you?"

"Sure," Mike Fenton said.

We set a time, and I showed up for my appointment and immediately announced, "I'd like to be in movies." Just like that. I didn't see the point in wasting time with a big wind-up. Mike Fenton called Michael Crichton, the director, who was a novelist and a screenwriter—and who would go on to write *Jurassic Park* and *Twister* and to create *E.R.*—and within thirty seconds they had offered me a job.

Actually, I had to pass one small screen test. Michael Crichton turned to me and asked me to do something strange. "Look me in the eyes," he said, "and don't make any expression. Don't grimace. Don't contort your face. And without saying anything, convey with your look that you're going to tear our hearts out." I stared at him with murder in my heart, and it seemed to work. I got a costarring part in *Runaway,* starring Tom Selleck. I hadn't even read the script. I was told that I would be playing the villain.

On the first day of the shoot, in Vancouver, the part called for me to walk up and ring a doorbell and say a line. I was supposed to pretend I was a repairman coming to fix something. I was supposed to communicate a certain untrustworthiness and threat. I read my line, and then afterward Michael Crichton yelled, "Cut!" I walked over to Crichton and said, "Look, I really apologize. I'll do anything you want me to do. I'm so sorry I messed it up. What did I do wrong?"

"No, no, no," he said. "Let me explain something to you. In

With Cynthia Rhodes, my costar in *Runaway.*

movies, if the director says 'Cut' and you move on to another scene, that means good. If I say, 'Let's do it again,' that's bad."

Movies had a completely different dynamic than rock and roll. It was like pulling teeth. You sit around for sixteen hours a day. The only thing I could do was try to figure out which of the female extras I'd like to take home that night. There were always interesting-looking girls on the side. And I'd be flying in girls left and right from California. It was a busy time and also an interesting time, because I met a whole new group of people and tried many new things. Kirstie Alley played my girlfriend. I got to stick a knife through her neck in the movie. That made me a real likable fellow. I tried coming on to the actress Cynthia Rhodes. That didn't work out, so I tried her sister. That didn't work either, so I went for one of the extras on the set, a real knockout of a Canadian girl. That worked. If at first you don't succeed . . .

When I was in Los Angeles on one occasion, I hooked up with Stan Brooks, who was working with the Guber/Peters film company. I had first met him in 1981 during the *Grotus* experience. He introduced me to Jeff Loeb and Matt Weissman, and at the Beverly Hills Hotel we came up with an idea that would eventually become *Commando*, a breakout film for Arnold Schwarzenegger. It was going to be a starring role for me, but when I showed the script to Michael Rachmill, who was the producer of *Runaway*, he dissuaded me. I believed him and let it go. I later revisited the script with the intention of trying to have someone else take a look at it, but it was too late. Producer Joel Silver had bought it, and it was being made. That was the last time I would let someone else decide for me what worked and what didn't.

◆ ◆ ◆

In 1984, during the making of *Runaway*, I would have enough time off during weekends that I could fly into Los Angeles and run around to the parties. The best parties were at the Playboy Mansion, especially the Midsummer Night's Dream parties, which were big summer bashes with hundreds of girls in corsets and underwear and a select group of eligible bachelors. Guys were not allowed in unless they were dressed in pajamas, and girls had to wear as little as possible. The ratio was something like four hundred girls to one hundred guys. That's how Hugh Hefner liked his parties. At this point Diana and I had adjusted our relationship—we were still together, but we had our freedom. Before the party I told her that I was going up to the Playboy Mansion and that I was planning on flirting and having a good time.

At the party I spent some time—and made some time—with a few gorgeous women, and then I ran into Richard Perry, a record producer I knew who had produced everybody from Rod Stewart to the Pointer Sisters. Perry introduced me to a girl named Shannon Tweed and her sister, Tracy Tweed. Both of them wore stiletto heels and corsets, and both of them were formidable—well over six feet tall. You can imagine the effect. I was devastated by Shannon in particular and did everything to try to woo her. We talked for a while. At first she wasn't interested, but after a while she came back around to talk with me. Then she took me to the library, where a secret door behind a bookcase opened into a passage that led to a wine cellar below. She sat down on a table in there, and I remembered thinking this was clearly an invitation.

But five minutes went by without any sex, and then ten minutes. I remember just being lost in conversation with her. She came from Newfoundland in Canada, and I came from Israel, and we started talking about the strangeness of America, and how we both felt like fish out of water. After that we went upstairs, not having fully consummated our first meeting. On the way out she gave me her number and said, "Call me."

After meeting Shannon, I lost interest in the other new friends I had made that night, including Miss February.

I went back to the Beverly Hills Hotel, and all that night and the next morning I tried calling the number. She had given me a wrong number. A guy answered. He'd never heard of Shannon Tweed. I couldn't figure it out. Eventually I decided that I had been taken for a ride. Then as I was watching television in my single room at the hotel, I saw a photo being pushed under my door. I got up and looked at the photo. It was a black-and-white headshot of Shannon. Then I looked on the back, and there was a handwritten note—"I've never been so insulted," it said. "If you took my number, why didn't you call me? Next time be a man and don't start anything you're not going to finish." It was that kind of letter. And on the bottom it said, "If you still have the guts, here's the phone number." The number was different from the number she had given me the day before—only one digit different, but that's enough. I called her up immediately and said, "I say what I mean and mean what I say, and you gave me the wrong number."

"The wrong number?" she said. "Don't you think I know my own phone number?"

"I'm just saying that the last number is different," I said. She was angry at first, but eventually she relented. I went over to see her and was overtaken with passion and lust. I thrust my hand under her sweater and then kissed her deeply. She didn't seem to mind, and we became acquainted very quickly.

Soon after that I called up Diana to tell her about Shannon. I didn't want her to hear about it from the tabloids. I explained to her that I had met this girl and wanted to spend some time with her and see how that relationship went. She wished me the best and told me she hoped I was happy. Diana has always had the grace and class that I wish all women had.

About three weeks later, Diana and I spoke again. Right off she asked, "Are you still with Shannon Tweed?" I said yes. I wasn't sure where the conversation was going. Then Diana dropped a bombshell. "You know," she said, "she's my sister-in-law." Unbeknownst to me, Shannon's sister, Tracy, had secretly married Diana Ross's brother, Chico.

◆ ◆ ◆

Soon enough, I moved into Shannon's Los Angeles apartment. She was everything I never knew I wanted in a girl. She had her own career. She had acted on television shows and starred in dozens of movies. She didn't seem to want anything from me, and she was drop-dead gorgeous.

Although I didn't know it at the time, Shannon had just come out of a relationship with Hugh Hefner and had lived at the Playboy Mansion with him. She'd wanted a career and he'd wanted her there, so she moved out. She had also graced the covers of *Playboy* a number of times, and her portrait hung, I'm sure, on many walls around the country.

As soon as we met, I told her everything. I told her I never wanted to get married, to her or anyone else, ever. I told her I never wanted to have children. I told her I was afraid of commitments of any kind and that I wanted to be free to pursue my ambitions, whatever they may be, without having to check in with someone. She was okay with all of it.

In fact, she said, she wanted the same thing for herself. I was hooked.

I told her my philosophy, that I'd found the whole idea of marriage and commitment to be faulty at best and, in my opinion, obsolete and impractical. A major thing wrong with marriage is that traditionally one of the two getting married is a man, and men aren't cut out for marriage. A second problem is that someone other than the one who gave birth to you, your mother, is going to dominate you. My mother stopped asking me where I was going, who I was seeing, and when I was coming home decades ago; I would be damned if I let anyone else ever have that right.

Despite my posturings, I was scared. Shannon disarmed me because everything about her was so honest. There were no games, no hidden agendas. If that isn't enough, Shannon was and continues to be the most striking woman I have ever seen in my life.

I wanted us to work. I also wanted to feel safe. I wanted everything. I wanted the goddess and I didn't want to have to grow up just yet. So at first I lived with her in her apartment. I didn't want to plant any roots too deeply. But by the end of the first year I learned how to drive, at the age of thirty-four. I bought my first car, a Rolls-Royce, and decided to buy a place to live with Shannon. I bought a home on two acres in Beverly Hills, and paid cash.

Though I was falling for Shannon more deeply every day, I was still cautious. I had read too many horror stories of relationships turning ugly—lawyers, alimony, lawsuits. I wanted no part of it. I would rather live alone for the rest of my life than have anyone dominate me or in any way expect payment for having shared my bed. That seemed to be the way everyone else lived their lives. People got married, then they got divorced and hated each other.

Statistically, marriage doesn't work. Divorce often happens within a few years of marriage—at a rate as high as 75 percent in some parts of the country. Men are miserable, women are miserable, and both are trapped. When a couple splits up, often the man has to pay his ex-wife 50 percent of what he makes—before taxes, which is lunacy. The highest tax rate around is 48 percent, and in return the government gives you the armed forces, free schools, social security, and nationwide infrastructure. Your ex-wife gives you a few years of companionship for her 50 percent. My mother gave me life, and she's not getting 50 percent!

It seems to me to be a lose-lose proposition. When a man marries a woman he promises to stay with her and support her until he's six feet under. And he's not supposed to be attracted to or be with another woman for the rest of his life, from his twenties, say, until his death. He takes this oath in front of God, his wife, and all assembled. Everyone lies about their ability to fulfill these promises, but

A picture of the woman I met at the Playboy Mansion in 1984—Shannon Tweed.

they go through with it anyway. And when the marriage is over, a man had better be able to reach deep in his pockets. Who invented this system? The devil?

Despite my strong feelings about marriage, I still wanted to make a relationship with Shannon work. To say my life changed drastically when I bought that Beverly Hills house is to put it mildly. I had never had a driver's license before—you don't need one in New York. Taxis are everywhere and if you have a car, you need a lot of luck finding a space to park it in. And you never know if the car will be there the next morning.

I had a tennis court in California but I'd never played tennis. I had a swimming pool, and, although I could swim, I never went swimming. Between tours, my sleeping habits changed. Where once I had a lot more in common with nocturnal creatures, now I had a beautiful six-foot Playmate to wake up next to. Someone I wanted to bring breakfast in bed to. Someone I cared about.

My neighbor next door was Donna Mills; on the other side, Kate Jackson. A few doors down lived Cher. Later on everyone sold and moved away. I stayed. I liked it. I felt I was home, for the first time.

This level of intimacy made me want to share everything with Shannon. I started talking about everything, about how I was straight, had never been drunk, but that I had chased a skirt or two in my day. I even told her about the photographs. I had always felt, if I had been with a girl, I wanted a picture of the experience. I had had literally a few thousand liaisons and had taken photos of almost all the ladies. I told her she needed to know about me. No secrets. I remember putting all the pictures on the table and letting her go through them. She couldn't believe it. She didn't understand it. But, most important, she wasn't judgmental. She has always been like that, as long as I can remember. I didn't know much about Shannon's life until we started living together. I didn't read *Playboy*, although I had obviously seen the magazine at friends' homes. I wasn't aware, until she showed me, how many times she had been on the cover and inside. Perhaps some men would have a problem with millions of others looking at nude photographs of the woman they are with, but I was actually proud of the fact. Nudity to me isn't an issue. Violence and drugs are. As far as I am concerned, if everyone had more sex there would be less violence.

Shannon was the girl of my dreams. She kept getting more and more beautiful. She never asked me where I was going. She never asked me when I was coming back. When we were away from each other I would call every day without fail. Not because I had to or because it was expected—that would never have worked for me. I did it because I wanted to.

The year 1985 saw us solidify KISS, with a lineup consisting of Bruce Kulick, Eric Carr, Paul, and myself. We had another platinum seller with *Asylum,* and we were doing it all without makeup and without the original lineup. We'd had new business management who had taken over Bill Aucoin's duties from 1982 on, and that relationship had run its course as well. We let them go and hired Larry Mazur as a consultant. We were hesitant to employ new managers—they wanted too much money—so for all intents and purposes we were self-managed.

At this time *Runaway* came out—to generally favorable reviews—and I immediately got another movie offer. *Wanted: Dead*

trial by fire: the KISS family

or *Alive* was to be directed by Gary Sherman and would star Rutger Hauer. I was slated to play the villain. When I arrived on the set the first day of shooting, I was introduced to the crew and to Rutger. He came over, shook my hand, and right there in front of everyone took my face in his hands and kissed me full on the mouth. The crew laughed their heads off. I was stunned.

I enjoyed working on the movie, but my film career was really starting to irritate Paul and management. They wondered if I wanted to stay in the band or go for an acting career. The answer was that I wanted it all. But that wasn't entirely fair to Paul, who was committed to KISS full time.

a death in 1985~1993

I acted in another movie called *Never Too Young to Die*. This time I played two roles, one as a CIA agent, and the other as his alter ego, a transvestite rock star named Ragnar. I wore stiletto heels and a bra with a corset attached. I wore women's makeup. I wore fishnet stockings. I looked like an evil painted woman.

One day after I had gotten into my full getup, I started to teeter my way onto the set. Along the way I passed the trucking crew, who promptly ripped me a new asshole: "Hey Gene, lookin' good." "Hey, what are you doin' later, baby?" I hated it. During one of the scenes, I had to mouth an old Wayne County line: "It takes a man like me to be a woman like me." My backup band were real transvestites who gave me tips on how to be convincing. The movie also starred John Stamos and Vanity, who enjoyed flirting with me almost as much as I enjoyed flirting back.

Then in 1986 I was offered a film called *Red Surf*. The cast included Dedee Pfeiffer, Michelle's sister, and George Clooney. I played a Vietnam vet who has had his fill of killing. At the end of the

The band without the makeup in 1988—me, Paul, Eric Carr, and Bruce Kulick.

movie I had to come and save everyone from certain death. I was getting accustomed to the movie business.

I was living in California with Shannon while the rest of the band was in New York. Eric was working out just great on drums, and the whole touring environment was stressfree for the first time, now that Ace and Peter were no longer in the band.

◆ ◆ ◆

By 1987 KISS had gone through a series of guitarists. We had brought in Bruce Kulick in 1984. In an odd coincidence, Bruce was the brother of Bob Kulick, who had auditioned for KISS at its inception. While Bruce lacked a personal style, he was quite accomplished and was willing to reproduce Ace's solos from the records. Bruce has always been a professional, and being in the band with him was a joy. Initially he lacked a certain stage presence, but though he was sensitive about his shortcomings, he was willing to work to become a better stage performer.

Paul was looking for other ways to express himself, including acting. He would later go on to star in the stage version of *Phantom of the Opera* and closed the show after 150 performances in Toronto. Then he decided to put together a solo band, the Paul Stanley Band, and go out on his own tour. His band consisted of Bob Kulick on guitar and a drummer named Eric Singer. I went to see Paul perform and sat up in the balcony with Eric Carr. It was interesting, actually, watching Paul from the audience instead of standing next to him onstage. Eric Carr was concerned he would be replaced by Eric Singer, who was a terrific drummer and singer. At the end of Paul's tour, the two of us turned our attention back to KISS.

We were now making more money than we had even in the glory days of the 1970s. Gone were the excesses of management perks, inefficient stage designs, and expensive recording sessions. In 1989 I found an inexpensive demo studio, and we recorded our next album, *Hot in the Shade,* there. It was done for a fraction of our usual costs, with no producer fees involved. We produced it ourselves.

Paul wrote a song with Michael Bolton called "Forever" that

It takes a man like me to be a woman like me: dressed up as a transvestite for my role in *Never Too Young to Die* in 1985.

made it into the Top 10, and the ensuing tour was a big success. We had a forty-foot-high sphinx in the center of the stage, and we appeared in the mouth as the eyes were shooting flames and fog came out of the nose. With or without makeup, KISS was selling out concerts again.

Life has given me the opportunity to take advantage of my whims, at least to the point where I can get doors opened. One day I was sitting around thinking of other projects that interested me, and it suddenly occurred to me that I would like to have a record label. I had always taken an interest in younger bands. If there was a Geffen Records, I thought, why couldn't there be a Simmons Records? At the time the RCA label didn't really have a strong rock and roll presence, which seemed unfortunate to me—it had been the home of Elvis Presley. RCA seemed like a promise unfulfilled. As usual, I didn't bother with lawyers or complicated proposal letters. I just got on the telephone and called Bob Buziak, the president of RCA. I didn't get him; instead I got Heinz Henn, the European head, who had seen KISS in several German shows. Henn, Buziak, and I met, exchanged views and philosophies, and before I knew it, I had a record label: Simmons Records.

The first album my label released was a self-titled debut by a band named House of Lords, which featured a guy named Greg Guiffria. He had been in a band named Angel that had signed to Casablanca Records on my recommendation, and then after that he had a band named Guiffria that had a big hit in the mid-1980s, a song named "Call to the Heart." I signed Greg only on the condition that I would executive-produce his record—I would have full control over the name, the look, everything. I didn't want the name to be Guiffria. I wanted them to be House of Lords, which was a name I owned and had trademarked. I wanted to direct their image. That record went to number one on the U.K. import chart before it was ever released in the United States.

Other bands followed, including a California rock band called Silent Rage. But the original concept got a bit blurred over time. For example, a band called Gypsy Rose was an act that RCA found. I didn't have anything to do with it, but they wanted me to put it out on my label for credibility purposes. I also courted Joe Walsh for a solo record and was managing, producing, and writing for many artists. I was still in KISS, and even if I wasn't devoting my full attention to the band, I knew it had to remain a top priority. Pretty soon it became clear to me that there just were not enough hours in the day for me to manage my own label. When the time came, RCA didn't pick up the option, and Simmons Records disappeared. As I write this book, though, I am talking to several major labels about reviving Simmons Records.

The joint venture I had with RCA, Simmons Records, promised to be the beginning of a brand new career for me. At this point I was relatively unhappy with KISS and was looking for other ways to creatively express myself.

♦ ♦ ♦

During the summer break from the *Hot in the Shade* tour, I came back to L.A. and to Shannon. I had it all. KISS was doing well; I was living with a queen. What else could I want? I was about to find out. One evening Shannon and I went to a Neil Bogart Memorial Cancer Fund event, which was being held at the Santa Monica racetrack. I was talking to Sherry Lansing and Joyce Bogart, and the conversation turned toward marriage. I mentioned how scared I was of marriage. Well, Joyce said, "What about kids?" Before I could utter a word, Shannon said, in a voice just above a whisper, "I'm pregnant."

I didn't hear her say it, not consciously. I heard the words, but they never connected with my brain. I never thought I would ever hear those words from anyone. I remember feeling dizzy as the blood rushed to my head. Before I knew it, Shannon and I were alone and facing each other. Everyone else had left us. I didn't say anything—I was holding my breath.

So here it was, finally: the day I never thought would happen. What was I going to do? Would I accept my responsibility? More important, was this something that I might have wanted all along but never had the courage to admit to myself?

I looked into Shannon's eyes and saw that this was something she really wanted. I can't tell you why, but at that instant I knew I wanted the same thing. I wanted to be a father. It wasn't the notion "Well, this is supposed to happen." I just knew it deep inside.

Over the course of her pregnancy, Shannon became quite voluptuous and even more desirable. She was sexy and curvaceous. I couldn't keep my hands off her. As the pregnancy went along, we joked that she needed a suit of armor to protect her from me.

I had become something of an expert at keeping my emotions under control. Suddenly, pure white fear started to creep in. *Oh, my God,* I thought, *there's gonna be a baby. Is it going to be a boy or a girl?* And, *Oh, my God—what if it's a girl? How do I talk to a girl?* All these things that I never verbalized, that I never even dared think of, were suddenly upon me. I was a wreck, I have to say. Shannon had a little morning sickness—it was nothing out of the ordinary for a pregnant woman. But for me it was all out of the ordinary, and I was very concerned about her and the baby.

KISS went on tour to Europe and I took Shannon along. It was the first time I had taken a girl on tour with me. I tried to explain what touring was about. She saw girls lifting their tops during the shows. She answered the phones when the girls would call. She was a good sport about it.

When we were in London to play Wembley Stadium, I saw a girl I may have had a liaison with, I can't recall. I mentioned this to Shannon, who was now visibly pregnant. The girl followed me around, and one day I answered the front door to find her standing there. With Shannon in the background, she offered to kick Shannon's stomach to kill the baby. She ran off when she heard Shannon coming.

When we came back to America, we went to see a doctor. At one point he asked if we wanted to know the sex of the baby. We did, so they set up an ultrasound machine to look into Shannon to actually see the outline of the baby. This was about a month before the birth. I thought I was watching a science fiction movie, with the baby inside, moving. "So," the doctor said, "I suppose you'd want to know that you're going to have a boy."

"Well, yeah, sure," I said. "I can tell." I thought that he was going to be the most well-endowed son on the face of the planet. But it turns out that what I was looking at was the umbilical cord. The thing looked longer than his leg, which, in fact, it was. But what did I know about umbilical cords? I just wanted the best for my son.

Finally, Shannon went into labor in the middle of the night. We got into the car, and I drove her to the hospital. It was all very calm. We had taken Lamaze classes and knew that we were supposed to control labor with breathing, not rush to the hospital in a panic, but take it slow and easy. When she went into the delivery room, it was for a labor that lasted about twenty-three hours. Every once in a while I'd go into the room and feed Shannon some ice cubes. We have always joked around a lot, so while she was in pain, she'd say, "Don't ever touch me again. Don't you ever put your hands on me again. Look what you've done!" The jokes would soon die away because the pain would come back. I was there for every second of that birth. I watched the birth happen. I was the first person to see the crown of my son's head appear. I was the first person who held my son. When my son first opened his eyes, he saw me. I was the first thing he saw. I cut the umbilical cord—you have to cut it twice, once in the middle and once up close. Nicholas Adam Tweed Simmons was born at eight pounds eleven ounces.

Aside from a man's own birth and death, I would have to say the birth of his child is probably the pivotal point in his life. Emotions were running like crazy. I felt like I was on a roller-coaster ride. I don't know if I ever blinked my eyes, but I have the sense that I didn't. I wanted to keep all my senses wide open, so I could record this moment, which I never imagined would ever happen. There I was, holding in my arms a real live human being who was looking at me—and who was going to be looking to me for everything: for life, for sustenance, for knowledge. I was going to have to be there. They talk about the maternal instinct, but there's a paternal instinct too, I'm sure.

A man came toward me, and I heard these soothing words: "All right, Gene, that's the doctor. He's going to take the baby and clean him up." While I understood the words intellectually, I emotionally didn't want to let my baby go. I kept repeating this to my son, to Shannon, to the doctor. I didn't want to let him go. I remember resolving that, if it came to it, I would fight to the death. It was like when guys fight on the street. When you're fighting to the death, when an animal's cornered, fists aren't even an issue. I had a picture in my mind of completely enveloping the doctor with my legs and arms and sinking my teeth into his neck. I would cut his jugular and kill him where he stood because he was taking my son. To this day I have a mental picture of that poor innocent doctor in his death throes—he is drowning in his own blood with his jugular completely torn apart, and my face is covered with his blood. I had never felt anything like that before in my life. I didn't understand that kind of rage. I remember Shannon saying something like, "Gene, it's okay." I must have had my eyes wide open and my nostrils flaring.

I gave up my son to the doctor. But what they did next seemed like torture. They took Nicholas's finger and stuck it with something sharp so it bled. I wanted to kill the nurse, even after she explained to me that they were testing for clotting factors. Then they stuck a tube down his nose and his throat to get out all the liquids. They put things in his eyes. They circumcised him. Then it was all over.

I don't know that I slept at all for two or three days. I must have stayed awake around the clock just watching Nicholas. He kept looking at me. I felt a little inadequate. As a man, all I knew how to do was make money and chase skirt, and all of a sudden here was a baby who was now depending on me for everything. Was I doing it right? Who knew? What do you do when a baby poops in your hand as you're holding him? Do you put him down? Do you wipe? *Help!* That's all I remember saying for many weeks. And then the months went by, and the first word he said was "Daddy." I remember my knees buckling. I thought about taking all my credit cards and saying, "Here. It's all yours. Just keep saying 'Daddy.'" I never thought I'd ever hear those words from anybody. It's true that I lived with Cher's children and Diana's children, but they were at ages where they could take care of themselves. Here, instead, were the challenges of real fatherhood, and for me there was an additional challenge: would I be like my own father, or would I stick around and do what I was supposed to do? In my mind—but more important in my heart—there was never any question.

Nicholas was a dream baby. When he'd cry in the middle of the night I would jump up and run to him, not that I would necessarily know what the hell to do when I got there.

One afternoon, between tours, Shannon was changing his diaper, and she called to me to come in and help. I rushed in and she asked me to take over. I grabbed both sides of the diaper as if I were a skilled surgeon and was admiring the fact that my son was defying gravity with his appendage even at such an early age. I remember smiling as I leaned over to close the diaper, when Nick let me have it straight in the face. I caught Shannon laughing in the other room. She had timed it just right.

When he turned two, I arranged for a full petting zoo to be brought over and set up on the tennis court. There were more kids and parents there than I had ever seen assembled in one place.

Nicholas, age one and a half, in Beverly Hills.

Besides all the ducks, rabbits, and rams there was a miniature horse. Nick was helped on and took his first ride. I had to wait until I was about seven to get dressed up as a cowboy back in Israel; I never got a chance then to ride a horse. My son would beat me to it by the time he was two.

I was reliving my childhood through my son.

I was able to speak English, Hungarian, and Hebrew, as well as some German and a few Japanese phrases. I had a B.A. in education and had taught sixth grade. I was a self-made man, and yet I found Shannon had a sort of life wisdom I never even contemplated. For one thing, prior to becoming a father, I never really imagined wanting children. After becoming a father, I couldn't imagine not wanting children. Shannon seemed to know this about me. She never questioned my decisions about not wanting marriage or children, but she didn't seem as shocked as I was at how much I loved being a father.

At an early age my mother used to tell me, "I would throw

myself in front of that truck for you." I never knew what she meant by that. Why would she want to do that? Later I found myself telling Nicholas the same phrase. I'm sure he thought the same thing I had.

By Nick's second year, he slept with us in a six-and-a-half-foot-wide, seven-foot-long gigantic bed. The accepted wisdom was to let your child sleep alone. We didn't care. We wanted to be together twenty-four hours a day.

California was everything New York wasn't. The weather was paradise and people seemed nicer. I am reminded of the New York joke that goes "A man from California visits New York and asks the first gentleman he meets, 'Excuse me sir. Is this the way to the Empire State Building or should I just go fuck myself?'"

I was to find out that paradise had its problems as well. Late one night, the silence was shattered by a 6.7 earthquake that shook Los Angeles within a 150-mile radius. It literally shook like a carnival ride. I immediately jumped up and grabbed Nicholas and, with Shannon running behind, we first stood in the doorway of the bed-

Nicholas at age five.

room and then ran down the stairs that were shaking and swinging. Luckily the house was not damaged much, but when we watched the news it looked as if Los Angles had been in a war zone.

I wasn't the only one who was feeling the pull of domesticity. A few years later Paul met Pam Bowen and soon decided to marry her. The wedding was to be held at the Bel-Air Hotel. Before the event, I racked my brain for a present—I just couldn't figure out what to get Paul to show him how much he meant to me.

I was the best man, and at the wedding I was scared stiff. It wasn't my wedding, but it was close enough. Afterward we went inside for food and music. Guests got up and wished Paul and Pam all the best. At one point I grabbed the microphone and asked Paul for his permission to do something out of the ordinary. Then I parted the curtain and gave the stagehands a nod. They brought out a large television set. I stuck a cassette into the video machine, and there was Tony Bennett, holding a champagne glass in his hand. He toasted the couple, sang "To the Good Life," and wished Paul and Pam all the happiness in the world. I had called Tony Bennett, and he was kind enough to make all this happen. A kinder and classier guy doesn't exist.

✦ ✦ ✦

It was an era of good feeling, a time when emotional bonds were solidifying and new life seemed to be blooming everywhere. Maybe it was inevitable, then, that the happiness would be counterbalanced by some sadness. When we got off tour, Eric Carr called me and told me that he had woken up one morning coughing blood. The very thought sent a chill up my spine. He was immediately placed in the hospital, where doctors found a growth on his heart. They told him that he would need emergency open-heart surgery.

Paul and I immediately flew to New York to be with Eric the night before the operation. When I walked into his room, he was in great spirits, alert and joking. We offered to get him anything he wanted. He asked for a McDonald's hamburger and fries, which was what he practically lived on while we were touring. We brought back the food, and we all joked together before we left. A few days later we visited Eric in the hospital again. All had gone well, he said. The doctors were happy with the results. Paul and I felt relieved. What we didn't know—what Eric wasn't telling us—was that he had cancer. Fairly quickly he became very ill. He lost all his hair, his huge Italian afro, and it broke our hearts. We were getting ready to record an album that we planned to call *Revenge,* and Paul and I decided that although we would pay for all of Eric's medical expenses and do whatever we could to help him fight his illness, we needed to start our album. At least for a time, that meant replacing him with a studio drummer. We tried our best to explain, but I'm sure it still hurt him.

By early 1991 we had decided to give Bob Ezrin another shot at producing. We still felt that *Destroyer* was one of the strongest albums we had ever made. And while we weren't sure Bob was up to it—especially after the bad experience of *The Elder*—we were interested enough to do one song with him as a kind of test. The producers of the film *Bill and Ted's Excellent Adventure* needed a song for their soundtrack, and they wanted us to record "God Gave Rock and Roll to You." Bob, Paul, and I rewrote the lyrics and rerecorded the song, which went into the Top 10 in England. That was reason enough to stick with Bob for a full record.

Since Eric Carr was still sick, we went through another round of drum auditions. After we failed to find the right drummer, Paul suggested Eric Singer for the album and brought him on for a few months. Eric Singer was a very funny guy, completely professional. We were not planning to bring him into the band, since we were hoping for Eric Carr's recovery. When it came time to shoot the video for "God Gave Rock and Roll to You," Eric Carr begged to be in the video, even though he hadn't played on the recording. We were concerned about whether he was healthy enough or strong enough to do it. But we agreed.

Eric showed up and stayed until the very end of the video shoot, which lasted until three in the morning. He never complained, not once. I believed that he could somehow turn things around.

It was not to be. During the recording of *Revenge* in 1991, Eric Carr passed away. We were devastated and flew to New York for the funeral. Ace showed up as well to pay his respects. We said hello to each other but sat in different parts of the church. The fans lined the driveway leading up to the church, and everyone was in tears. The fans had loved Eric, and they weren't the only ones. It devastated everybody. Whether Ace cared for Paul or myself at that point nobody can say, but he always felt very close to Eric. The biggest concern that Eric Carr ever had was that Peter Criss might have hated him for taking his place in the band. He didn't want Peter to think that he usurped him on purpose, or that he didn't respect what Peter had contributed to the band. When he first met Peter, he said, "I'm so sorry." It stopped Peter in his tracks. I think he had expected to be defensive around Eric, to try to size him up and convince himself that Eric wasn't as good a drummer as he was. But he was completely taken aback by Eric's kindness. Peter speaks fondly of him even today.

◆ ◆ ◆

Saddened, sobered, we resumed work on *Revenge*. One evening I went to see a group I had produced, EZO, perform in a club. Vinnie Vincent came up to me and apologized for causing the band so much grief while he was a member. He wanted to patch things up and wondered if I would consider writing some songs with him.

Sure, I said. I wanted to let bygones be bygones. I called Paul and told him that Vinnie had apparently changed. Paul wrote songs with him as well. But before the album was released, Vinnie was up to his old tricks again. He reneged on a signed deal we had made and decided that he wanted to renegotiate. He eventually sued us and lost. As far as I was concerned, he was persona non grata forever.

Away from us, he didn't exactly thrive. He formed a band called the Vinnie Vincent Invasion and signed to Chrysalis Records, but he managed only a couple of records before he was dropped. Actually, the band as a whole wasn't dropped—Chrysalis re-signed everyone else and renamed the band Slaughter, who then went on to achieve platinum sales. Vinnie then signed a deal with Enigma, but no record was ever released. People at the label told me that he had erased his own master tapes because he didn't think the material was good enough. He may have been right.

In 1992 *Revenge* came out and did well, going gold. We wanted to go back on tour with Eric Singer and did a series of club dates to introduce him to the faithful fans. Then, we went out on a very successful arena tour—the stage show featured a Statue of Liberty motif. We felt as if Seattle and the grunge bands had killed rock and roll; there was so much bad press for any band that got up onstage to put up a straight show. Grunge killed off the marketplace entirely—there were no lights, no costumes—and by the millions white kids went over to rap, because bands looked like bums. At least rappers were talking about girls and money. A decade later the grunge bands are dead, and the hair bands that they knocked off the map are back with successful summer package tours.

◆ ◆ ◆

Shannon got pregnant again, and this time it was a girl. By then I had become a full-time father. I had bought roller skates, taken my son for ice cream, and passed on my knowledge. I have pictures of myself as a baby and Nicholas as a baby, and we look like twins. He was a miniature version of me, and in many ways that made the experience easier to handle psychologically. But how would I handle a little girl? How did little girls think? I had so many worries, but all of them evaporated the minute I saw Sophie. I was smitten immediately. She tilted her head to one side, and I was gone.

One of Sophie's first sentences was, "Daddy, it doesn't suck." She was pointing to her bottle. At the age of three she said, "Daddy, can I have a Porsche?" Yes, sweetheart, I'll buy you a whole fleet of them.

Being a father the second time was just as wonderful, if not more so. The last thing on my mind had been kids—I thought I would die with my freedom. Underneath that, of course, it was all about fear. I didn't want to run out on my kids when they were six or seven the way my father had run out on me. I wanted to be there. I wanted my kids to know I would always be there for them, and I wanted them to respect me.

Sophie and me.

Part of gaining that respect was explaining to them how Shannon and I had chosen to live and conduct ourselves as parents. My philosophy was simple: I always felt that in this predetermined world, you should take every opportunity to change things to suit you. If you don't like your name, pick another. If you want to straighten your hair, straighten it. If you can't stand where you're living, move. My kids have both Tweed and Simmons as their last names, but when they get older they will have the chance to keep or change their names.

Shannon and I also tried to clarify our arrangement. As soon as our children were old enough to understand, we explained that we weren't married, that we were together because we wanted to be. They accepted this, more or less, and where it confused them, we took pains to discuss it at great length. Both Nicholas and Sophie have had classmates and friends whose parents were separated or divorced, and Shannon pointed out to them that this was a painful situation, especially because it required breaking an oath. All in all, I have encouraged them to think of themselves as individuals. When you create a painting, it has to be original. Don't paint by numbers. All these metaphors are long-winded ways of saying something very simple: trust yourself to be your own guide.

As I write this book, Nicholas is twelve. Sophie is nine. He didn't miss a day of school between first and fifth grade and is in advanced studies in sixth grade, as well as having another year of perfect attendance. She constantly earns best student awards. They are wonderful, loving children, and I would do anything for them. I don't know if life can get better, and they are a large part of why I feel this way. I can see the way they have changed my life every time I visit my mother's house. I am an only child, remember, and for many years my mother's house was a shrine to me. You couldn't find a spot on the wall without a picture of me: here's Gene eating in a high chair, there's Gene playing, there's Gene standing around doing nothing. Now I go over there, and if I'm lucky, I can find a few pictures of me pushed to the back of a table. The rest have been replaced by pictures of my kids. My mother has gone from being the world's most indulgent, wonderful, loving parent to being the world's most indulgent, wonderful, loving grandparent.

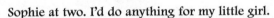

Sophie at two. I'd do anything for my little girl.

When all the planets line up, you have a chance either to take advantage of it or else miss the opportunity. I had always been aware of our passionate fans, and in the mid-1990s they started holding KISS conventions, in which they got together, dressed up in makeup, and celebrated the KISS experience: not only buying and trading memorabilia but having discussions, showing concert films, and so on. It was a real gathering of the tribe. I read about these conventions and wished I could be there. They had a sense of purpose and togetherness that seemed very genuine, especially in light of all the excess and artificiality we had endured. And then it hit me: we could just hold our own KISS conventions. KISS had

reason to live: with the KISS

Signing merchandise for fans.

always been about the fans, and we had always been the quintessential American band, of the people, by the people, and for the people. Yet we had grown to the point that we were surrounded by bodyguards and had a moat around the stage. Why didn't we make ourselves available? Why didn't we sit up on that stage, answer questions from the heart, and interact with the people who had made us who we were?

I needed to find someone who could help me make this convention idea into a reality. I had produced two albums by a band named Black 'N Blue, and I went to their guitar player, Tommy Thayer, and sat him down for a heart-to-heart conversation. I told him that

face to face
army   1993~1995

KISS float in the Pasadena Parade, 1994.

his band was not going to make it. I told him that, in my estimation, he had come to a crossroads in his life, and that soon he was going to have to make a choice: he could go into the real world and get a real job, or else he could come work with me. He wanted to know what kind of job I was offering him. I said, "I don't know. Every day I'll get up, and I'll let you know what your job is going to be. And if you're going to say, 'I don't do windows,' you'd better tell me no now. Because whatever has to be done, including getting the coffee, is what you'll do. Or else don't do it."

Tommy didn't even blink. He just rolled up his sleeves and said, "Okay, what do you want to do?" Without any experience, Tommy and I started to research the possibility of hosting these conventions.

The first thing that struck me was the problem of our liability. If we hosted a KISS convention, and we had parking, and a guy cracked up his car, he might sue us. If we served food, and somebody got food poisoning, she might sue us. If we rented a concert hall, and it caught on fire or there was an accident, more lawsuits. So we needed a place where we could put on a suit-proof convention, a place where I didn't have to staff up and hire personnel to take care of parking, catering, and so forth. The answer seemed to be hotel ballrooms. I made an initial phone call or two just to see how it would work. It turned out that it was pretty reasonable to rent out a ballroom for twelve hours or so, assuming we let the hotel keep all the parking fees, the money from the food, and any receipts if the conventioneers decided to spend the night. I sent Tommy Thayer on a trip across the country, lining up the cities. At the same time I personally sent out mailings to fans, especially those within small communities so they could be part of the conventions.

When the conventions started, the crew was pretty small: me and Paul, Tommy Thayer, Eric Singer, and Bruce Kulick. Tommy arranged with some other guys locally to put together a lot of the memorabilia that I had saved, plus the KISS outfits, and to display it all in a kind of KISS Hall of Fame, with seven-foot-high Plexiglas enclosures.

At the conventions we had show-and-tell. We played an

acoustic set. We answered questions from fans, and we answered them truthfully, which means that the answers weren't always happy ones. If a fan asked, "Is it true that Ace drinks?" my answer would be "Yes." If a fan asked, "Did Ace play on 'Flaming Youth'?" my answer would be "No." This was long before that *Storytellers* series on VH1, but that was the sense of it, if you add in an extensive autograph session afterward. It was twelve hours solid with the fans.

We did twenty-three cities total, and the very first one was in Los Angeles at a Hilton hotel. By this point Peter Criss's daughter was in her teens. She had never seen KISS in makeup and had only heard about it from her father. She wanted to go to the L.A. convention. So Peter called a journalist and wanted to know if the journalist could arrange for him and his daughter to go to the convention. The journalist called me immediately, and I called Peter. "Peter," I said, "you don't have to ask somebody else. You are a part of the band's history. This should be your place too. We'll send a limo to pick you up. You'll be treated like a king, because you are. Whatever you want is yours." For a few years I hadn't seen much of either Ace or Peter. Through the mid-1990s I had worked on a number of side projects, producing acts like Black 'N Blue (Tommy Thayer's band), Wendy O. Williams (of the Plasmatics), Keel, and EZO, and sometimes I invited Peter and Ace on these projects. But I didn't have any real thoughts about bringing them back into KISS. Ace and Peter had become so crippled by their emotional problems and by various substances—they had become so diminished as human beings and as musicians—that they would have been an embarrassment. It's one thing to get together again in a room and trade old stories, but when you put the makeup back on and step up on that stage, how are you going to be convincing? Still, I thought Peter deserved his spot onstage at these conventions.

There's a funny side note to this story. About six months earlier Tom and Roseanne Arnold—they were together at that point—had called me to find out if I wanted to contribute to or somehow get involved in the Peter Criss Fund. They had read that Peter was down on his luck, that he was homeless and living under a bridge. I told them, "Don't pay attention to those stories, they're not true. It may be true that Peter is broke, but I don't think he's living under a bridge." They insisted that they had read this piece and heard the same news from others. Two or three months after that I was watching Phil Donahue's show, and the guest was none other than Peter Criss, talking about a guy who was living under a bridge and who bore a rough resemblance to Peter. One of the tabloids had either paid this guy or swallowed his story, and this trumped-up tale about Peter living under a bridge began to make the rounds. So that was how Peter reappeared on my radar. By this time both Ace and Peter were relegated to playing clubs, and at one point they decided to tour together as the Bad Boys of Rock. They were playing KISS songs, but they couldn't use the KISS logos or makeup. Peter would later tell me that being on tour with Ace was not easy, because Ace would continually be drunk or high, and because there was always a big discussion about who was going to headline. This was during their 1994 tour.

I invited Peter to come down to the convention. And Eric Singer, God bless him, said, "You know what? You should ask him if he wants to come up when we do our acoustic set. Maybe he'll want to sing a song or two. I'm sure the fans would love it." When Eric said that, we all looked at each other and said, "Sure, why not?"

Before the convention we got together and rehearsed with Peter. He tried playing drums, but it was substandard. So Eric Singer decided to play the drums behind Peter, while Peter just got up on a stool and sang. As it turned out, it was a heartwarming appearance. I looked across the stage and thought that it was a real shame that Peter's other problems had prevented him from doing his best for the band, and for himself. Because the fans loved it. They were having so much fun. And so was I, to be honest. I wish we could have isolated the moment in time when we sang those two songs together. It was magic.

It wasn't just seeing Peter that made those KISS conventions magic, as we learned from the other ones. The experience of doing them really opened up our eyes to the living, breathing thing that we had created above and beyond the records and songs. There it was: the KISS Army, the KISS nation, alive and well. Clearly, what was running through their veins was belief in this bizarre thing that we had created. Children were named after our songs. We would meet them. "Hi, I'm Christine. I can't wait to turn sixteen so I can become Christine Sixteen." And they'd giggle. "Meet my daughter Beth." On and on and on. "What's your name?" "I'm Doctor Love." "Oh really! And what's your name?" "I'm Mister Speed." Sometimes there would even be weddings at the conventions, and the bride and groom would wear full KISS makeup.

One of the most gratifying parts of the shows was the fan testimonials. People would tell us that they had been outcasts, nobodies, until they heard KISS, and from then on they had a refuge. It almost sounded religious. Girls wanted to come up and kiss us, and that was funny, and everybody got a kick out of it. But sometimes we would all—Paul, me, Eric, and Bruce—get lumps in our throats. At one of the conventions, an attractive young woman got up and told us about her boyfriend. They had met, fallen in love, and gotten engaged. Then out of the blue, he had gotten cancer, and when it became clear he was going to die, he called off the wedding, because he didn't want to affect her life in this way, even though she was still willing to go through with it. Before he died, he asked her one thing: "Would you please bury my KISS records with me?" She explained to the rest of the people at the convention that the idea that someone could love a band so much had seemed strange to her. "Now I understand," she said. Then she collapsed, just burst into tears, and the whole place went silent out of respect and admiration for this woman. So often we'd get off that stage exhausted, not just because we were there for hours but because it was emotionally draining. The conventions reminded us how much the fans loved us and how much we loved the fans.

◆ ◆ ◆

When Peter left the convention in Los Angeles, he went home and picked up the phone and called Ace and told him what a rush it was and how great it felt. Ace expressed an interest in participating too.

As we went along on the convention trail, people started to

talk about them. The word of mouth was tremendous. At some point MTV sent crews out, and one of the people to take notice was a guy named Alex Coletti, the producer of MTV's *Unplugged* series. We had been filming every one of these conventions, because we wanted to put out a long-form video about them. Coletti saw the tape of fans getting up onstage and jamming with us, and people crying. "Why doesn't KISS bring its convention to the MTV studios and do an episode of *Unplugged*?" he said. Paul and I talked about it and decided to invite Peter and Ace to join us, not for the New York KISS convention, but for the *Unplugged* taping. We would have the entire KISS lineup: Eric, Bruce, Ace, Peter, Gene, and Paul. And when Ace and Peter went on, Eric and Bruce would be offstage, out of respect for them, so they could sing their songs. Then we'd all get together and do one or two together as a band.

When I called Peter to tell him about it, he jumped at the opportunity right away. When I called Ace, he said, "That sounds great. Thanks so much for calling me. My manager is George Sewitt."

George Sewitt was initially our security guy. He was very adept in martial arts. Then somehow he had expanded into management and started representing Ace and Vinnie Vincent. When Vinnie Vincent left, Sewitt took on another client: Peter Criss. As a result of Ace using Sewitt as a go-between, the negotiations for this one-off KISS reunion on *Unplugged* became all-consuming for me. I had daily discussions with Sewitt about the fact that there wouldn't be any pay, that we were just doing this for MTV, that we would play just two songs with the band, that we would retain the rights to release the performance as a long-form video, and so forth. Part of what took so long was my own meticulousness; I'm all about making a list and checking it twice. Other people let lawyers take over. I don't.

But another reason the negotiations became so protracted was Ace himself. Initially Ace said, "Sure, I'll show up with my guitar, and we'll do a couple of songs together. That's great, I look forward to it. Thanks so much." But then came a series of conversations where Ace wanted a suite, and then a pair of roadies, and then five thousand dollars for guitar strings and popcorn and peanuts. Then he wanted another suite for his daughter. At one point George Sewitt was calling MTV directly. I immediately cut him off at the pass. "You're not to call MTV," I said. "You don't represent KISS, and this is a KISS show. We will let you know where to go and what time to show up. You may be Ace's manager, but please don't get confused about what that means."

I had to be stern, because MTV would listen to anybody who represented themselves as being part of KISS. The left hand was the same as the right hand, in their estimation. Even though Paul and I were trying to keep on the best friendly face, dealing with Ace and George Sewitt was torture. The deal kept changing every single day. And with Peter it was always walking on thin ice because he was shaky emotionally. He was alone at that point, between marriages. His daughter was on the West Coast with his former wife, who didn't have the kindest things to say about Peter.

We had no problems with the rest of the guys. Through the entire reunion process, Bruce and Eric were terrific. They were the sweetest, most professional guys. They never said anything bad about anybody. They always did their job, always showed up on time. They were real gentlemen who put their egos aside for the good of the fans. In fact, they were so accommodating that they planted the seeds for what would become their worst nightmare. Their kindness enabled Ace and Peter to step in and, unfortunately, push them out of a job.

We rehearsed at Sir Studios in New York. Peter walked in with his head down, and we immediately hugged him and told him to have a good time. Then Ace walked in and we started working.

It became very clear immediately that Ace's guitar playing had sunk to a club level, and we made sure that Eric Singer played drums along with Peter just to keep him in time. But no matter what the problems were, whenever it was time for them to come on, Ace stepped up, and that magic thing happened. Despite all the problems, despite all the torture, when we played together it felt like 1974 again. We weren't as good as we were with Eric or Bruce, not as proficient or as tuneful. But we had a kind of a swagger, a loose rock

At our MTV *Unplugged* appearance. From left to right: Eric Singer, Peter Criss, me, Ace Frehley, Paul Stanley, Bruce Kulick.

and roll thing that perhaps the Stones have always been more about than the Beatles. The fans loved it. It looked great.

Afterward we shook hands and wished each other luck. We didn't think for a second about reforming the band, mainly because we had to fly to Los Angeles to mix our new album, *Carnival of Souls*.

✦ ✦ ✦

The conventions had reminded me that our fans were among the most passionate in the world. Plenty of other rock stars were KISS fans too, either openly or secretly, and one day I got an idea for a KISS tribute record. I wanted the top stars of the day to play their favorite KISS songs. Paul didn't get it and didn't think the record company would go for it. They did—Paul and I went to New York and sold it as a KISS record so that we could get our millions in advance, despite the fact that the band ended up appearing on only one song. Then on my own I started making all the calls. One of the first was to Neil Young, through his manager Elliott Roberts, who must have thought I was on crack. "Let me get this straight," he said. "You want Neil Young to appear on a KISS tribute album?" And I said, "That's right, why shouldn't he?" I made the same calls to Madonna's people, because I wanted her to cover "I Was Made for

Lovin' You," and on and on. I worked the phones for about ten hours a day for two months straight, calling everybody in the universe. I lined up Ozzy Osbourne to team up with Stone Temple Pilots on "War Machine." I got Nine Inch Nails to agree to a cover of "Love Gun." I had Sir Mix-a-Lot doing a rap version of "Rock and Roll All Nite." I didn't care if they were my taste or not, I wanted a stellar lineup, because at the end I'm all about winning the prize. How you get there doesn't matter.

The conception of the project was beautiful. The execution was trickier, mainly because the record companies got in the way. One of their complaints was that I wasn't paying the bands very much to do the tracks. My attitude was that it was just for fun, that they should go into the studio and knock something out and see if it worked. Many of the musicians agreed with me.

Lenny Kravitz, for example, did a cover of "Deuce," and after he sent the tape, he told me he had this fantasy of Stevie Wonder playing harmonica on the track. So I called Stevie. I had met him only once, when Diana Ross and I went to see him at Wembley in London. But he got on the telephone and immediately agreed. He and his assistant came down to Cherokee Studio, and I put on the Lenny Kravitz song, and he said, "Okay, what do you want me to play?" All of a sudden, this voice in my head said, *Oh my God. I am going to be telling Stevie Wonder what to play on his harp.* I improvised a little melody, and he played it back immediately. Finally I said, "You know what? I feel awkward telling Stevie Wonder to do anything. Why don't you just do what you do? Just let the song go by. I'll play it twice. Then just put down what you feel." Within two or three takes, he did it and thank you very much. He is a genius.

The other big coup was getting Garth Brooks. Garth came through Paul, who had met him, and when I first spoke with Garth, he agreed to contribute a song to the record on one condition—that KISS back him up on "Hard Luck Woman." We flew into Nashville at night, didn't tell anybody. We had no bodyguards. We carried our own guitars. Garth was a complete gentleman. The whole studio was opened up for us. The song went smoothly. As it turned out, Garth was a huge KISS fan; Queen and KISS were his main influences when he was growing up. I had never seen the connection before, but that's because I knew Garth only from his records. When I finally saw him in concert, I understood what he was talking about: he was flying through the air, levitating the drums, shooting off fireworks. It was country KISS.

Even during this project, which was a tremendous amount of fun, the old KISS problems cropped up again. Paul came up with an idea for the cover: a take-off on the cover of Led Zeppelin's *Presence*, which shows a family sitting together at a table. We wanted to do a similar cover but put the whole family in KISS makeup. So Paul went down to a photo house, and we found a picture of an American family and put everybody's face in makeup. Somehow word got out, and somebody from Ace's camp called and told us that we couldn't use Ace's makeup. We checked the contracts, and the truth was that we were well within our rights. We owned the Spaceman. But I didn't want to fight with Ace, so we decided to change the makeup.

We went out of our way to make Ace and Peter feel good about the project. On the inside cover art, a handwritten note to the two of them said, "Dear Ace and Peter, hope you are well. This whole thing couldn't have happened without you." It was a very friendly note, very honest. When the album, *KISS My Ass,* came out, it did very well and became another platinum record for us. We played with Garth on the *Tonight Show* and life continued to be stressfree without Ace and Peter.

◆ ◆ ◆

In the 1990s grunge music was the most popular style of rock and roll. Thanks to bands like Nirvana, Pearl Jam, and Soundgarden, it was dominant on the airwaves and on MTV. While we were making *Carnival of Souls,* we made a conscious effort to reinvent ourselves again, this time with swampy guitars and more alienation in the lyrics. The result wasn't very convincing. We enjoyed making it. We had plenty of interesting times. We learned more about this new style and about our own musical abilities. But as we mixed the record, we realized that that version of KISS had run its course. I called George Sewitt to explore whether Ace and Peter, both of whom were now chemical-free, I was told, were up for a reunion.

Direct communication with Ace and Peter was always difficult. Neither of them had people skills and they never answered their phones. Peter always had a roadie who would be his mouthpiece, and Ace always liked to have a manager or a keeper around him. I told George that I would fly to New York to meet him at our lawyer's office, although the lawyer wouldn't be present, just George and me. At that meeting I told him what KISS would be willing to offer Ace for rejoining the band for a tour. I showed him how much ticket prices would run, how many people I thought would show up at the concerts, what the capacity of the concert halls would be, and so on. George studied the figure and then said, "Well, that's an offer, but how come it's not bigger?"

"Because," I said, "this is not a negotiation. This is an offer of employment." For fifteen years, I explained, we had gotten along fine. We had made KISS into a very big international band, without makeup, without Ace, and without Peter. The only way we would even think about letting the two of them back in was under an

Garth Brooks is a huge KISS fan. We backed him up on "Hard Luck Woman" and he contributed a song to our tribute album.

employee agreement. We weren't interested in being partners. If Ace wanted to come on board and become a multimillionaire yet again, we'd be happy to have him. We offered the same to Peter. This was a guaranteed number, I explained. If the tour bombed, Paul and I would be on the hook. If it worked out, we might win big. Either way Ace was guaranteed to be a multimillionaire. George and I parted cordially. I told him he had two or three days to decide. To George's credit, he saw the big picture and shortly thereafter called me to say, "It's a deal."

Ace and Peter both flew out to Los Angeles and came to my guest house for a band meeting. I told everyone how happy I was to do this, how thrilled I was that we had come to an agreement. Then Ace turned around and reneged. "I don't care what you give Peter," he said. "I want more." Peter was beside himself, because it was the same old stuff again, the two weaker members of the band playing off each other. Our instinct was to flatly say no to this demand, but we didn't want the deal to dissipate, so we agreed. The next day Ace changed the deal again. "I want an equal split," he said.

We said, "That's the end of the deal. Thank you very much, good-bye. It's been nice knowing you, God bless." Ace then back-pedaled, explained that he had to have more than Peter, even if it was only slightly more. He kept insisting, and still does, that he was much more important than Peter. This was all about his self-esteem.

This was classic Ace. We always wondered whether he would do the work he said he would do and stand by the agreements he entered. We probably had legal standing to sue Ace, but despite all the dysfunctional elements, we have always looked at KISS as a family. We had once sued Polygram records and won. We had sued Howard Marks, our former business manager, and won. We have yet to lose a suit. But we didn't want to resort to that with either Ace or Peter.

Once the band did finally get together, once the numbers were set, I personally typed up a list of conditions. First, whether the tour was doing well or miserably, we could pull the plug at any time. Period. Also, all band members were to show up on time. They were to do interviews when asked. There were going to be strenuous rehearsals. Peter's drumming had deteriorated to an unacceptable level, and he could not remember his parts. Likewise, Ace's guitar playing had become a shadow of its former self. Ace's memory did not serve him well either. Decades of self-abuse had, in my opinion, taken their toll. Tommy Thayer, who had been in a KISS tribute band after Black 'N Blue, knew all of Ace's solos inside out, and he had to teach them back to Ace. We insisted that there would be a workout regimen with personal trainers every morning, and then arduous rehearsals, with no drugs and no booze. If anyone used, they were gone.

Right away Ace broke almost every rule. Peter, to his credit, showed up on time and worked hard. But Ace didn't show up on time. He didn't talk to the press. By the second or third week of rehearsals, I faxed George Sewitt saying, "We are ready to pull the plug. Ace Frehley is not a team player." George Sewitt suggested we have a heart-to-heart with Ace. So Paul, Ace, and I met at the Sunset Marquis, about a month into rehearsals. Ace was full of excuses: his dog was sick, he was having trouble with his family, the government was hassling him about taxes. But he agreed to settle down.

We were without a manager at that point, but we needed one: it became clear that this tour was going to be much bigger in scope than we had expected. I called up ICM, CAA, and the major booking agencies to test the waters, to see what percentage we could get from a booking agency. I explained that KISS was reuniting and that we were interested in having a manager come on board, but that we were not interested in paying a percentage of gross, only net. We had come too far along in this business. We knew too much. Nobody was going to get a percentage of the gross before we paid expenses. They could participate after we paid all the expenses, but there was no way they would make more money than we would.

At some point in the search for a manager, I suggested Doc McGee. We had given Mötley Crüe and Bon Jovi their first tours, and Doc had managed them both. We made him an offer, stressing that the terms weren't really flexible. He accepted.

Right away Doc's involvement paid dividends. While talking to an agent at CAA, he came up with this idea that we should appear on the Grammy Awards: not perform, not even say a word, just appear in full makeup and costumes next to Tupac Shakur. "If you do that," Doc said, "then people will know the band is back together." That's exactly what we did. There was no press, no noth-

Shannon and me on New Year's Eve in the mid-1990s.

ing. We sidled right up to Tupac, who was going to present an award. By that point the word had leaked. A few minutes before, we had passed by the backstage green room, where all the stars hang out and wait for their turn to get up in front of the microphone. Everyone was there, from Gloria Estefan to Luther Vandross. As we passed by the green room, all the stars went into shock. "Hey, look!" someone said. Then the whole green room erupted with applause. Once we saw how these celebrities reacted, without any prompting, then we knew this was real. Before a single ticket was sold, before a single review was written, we knew it was the right time. The planets had lined up.

Tupac announced to the audience that he had a surprise, and we walked out onto the stage. The first guy who jumped up was Eddie Vedder. Then the whole crowd jumped to its feet. We were back.

The Grammy Awards ceremony was the beginning of our comeback trail. Within about a month Doc decided to book Detroit's Tiger Stadium as the first show. It sounded like the height of lunacy to us. The safe way would have been to test our act in a smaller market, someplace like Dothan, Alabama, where we could sharpen our act and the problems in the show wouldn't be scrutinized quite so intensely. But Doc booked a baseball stadium in Detroit. To be honest, we weren't even sure we would sell out the show. Tickets went on sale one Friday night. At six in the morning on Saturday, Doc called me at home to tell me that he had some good

forever: reunions and farewells
1996~2001

news and some bad news. I asked for the bad news first. "Well," he said, "we don't have any more tickets to sell." We had sold out the whole stadium—about fifty thousand seats—out in under an hour.

I immediately called Peter and told him. He said, "Yeah, yeah," in a voice that made me believe he was still half-asleep or didn't understand what I was telling him. But by the end of the conversation, he was hooting and hollering.

◆ ◆ ◆

Peter was so jubilant that for a minute I thought this tour might go smoothly. But it wasn't to be. We had a photo session with Barry Levine, who had worked with us back in 1976, and Ace complained that it was taking too long. Though we had intense personal training sessions with weights and aerobics to prepare us for the concerts, halfway through his sessions Ace would stop. Peter didn't stop, but every step of the way he complained that the guy who was

For the First Time in 17 Years, the Original Members!

KISS

ALIVE/WORLDWIDE 96-97

Gene Simmons ✶ Ace Frehley ✶ Paul Stanley ✶ Peter Criss

14. a 15.12. 96 20.00 hod.

SPORTOVNÍ HALA VÝSTAVIŠTĚ PRAHA

PŘEDPRODEJ VSTUPENEK FAN - PASÁŽ JALTA, VÁCL. NÁM. 43, TICKETPRO, TEL.:02/24 81 40 20
HROMADNÉ OBJEDNÁVKY: INTERKONCERTS, TEL: 02/24 21 11 80

e best: KISS was back!

working him out was too demanding. Once Ace walked up to me in the parking lot of the rehearsal hall and said, "I still don't have my weekly check, and if I don't get it by five o'clock today, I'm quitting the band." He always thought, and still does, that people are trying to cheat him. To Ace it was always a conspiracy to do him in.

Ace Frehley, more than anyone else in the band, seems to have a dark cloud over his head. He was and continues to be fearless in almost everything he does. In some ways, it is a quality I have always found fascinating, because I don't have it myself. Where I am overly cautious about my health, Ace is the extreme opposite. He would drink until he passed out. He has used enough drugs to kill a lesser man. He has always been and continues to be unrepentant about all of that. He never cared about the effect his behavior had on anything or anyone: on the band, his personal relationships, or his health.

I have to admit to being completely stumped. If someone were to jump off a building to commit suicide, at least he or she would have an audience. Ace prefers privacy, though—he never minded numbing himself alone. In fact, he seemed to relish the idea of going back to his room and knocking himself out. He would spend off days in his room and never come up for air. But despite all the self-destructive behavior, Ace is bright. He would tinker with little gadgets; he actually designed and built his own rocket shooting device for his guitar in the early days when the band was first touring. I was in the dressing room watching Ace solder wiring on his guitar for this effect, and as he turned to face me I saw him solder his thumb to the guitar. When he felt the pain, he screamed and yanked his hand away, but part of the skin of his thumb remained soldered to his guitar.

Ace and Peter both have managed to cheat death more times than I can count. When KISS opened up one of our early tours in Florida in the days when guitars were still connected to amplifiers by jacks (electric wire connectors), Ace was electrocuted onstage in front of the audience but rejoined us within a few minutes to finish the show. Peter was once hit with an M-80 firework that was thrown onstage and was knocked off his drum riser. He had to be taken to the hospital. After he returned, the show went on. Ace has been chased by the police at speeds of 100 mph and has walked away from crashes reasonably intact. He and Peter have both been in a number of terrible accidents and should have been killed. But Paul and I had put up with much of that throughout the years, and we were prepared to deal with it again.

Before the Tiger Stadium tickets went up on sale in 1996, Doc McGee wanted to do a press conference in New York. And he had this idea doing it at the New York Public Library, on Forty-second Street and Fifth Avenue. I understood his rationale—he wanted a place that was easily accessible to all the national press—but I didn't want that locale. Libraries had nothing to do with KISS. Instead I suggested that we go to the United Nations, which could represent KISS's global reach. Doc liked that, but he couldn't get the right permits. Then I remembered that in 1981 Diana Ross had gone onto the USS *Intrepid* aircraft carrier for a small press conference. I suggested to Doc that we do a KISS press conference on the *Intrepid*, which is permanently moored in the Hudson River, on Manhattan's West Side. Even though it was raining, the event was a huge success—Conan O'Brien introduced us, and we managed to attract television and press from fifty-two countries. When we took questions, I made sure that we had big signs in front of us with our names. Ace thought I was crazy. He thought everyone knew who he was. I had to explain to him that some countries didn't have any idea who KISS was anymore. Amazingly, at the press conference itself, Ace came off fine. Better than fine, in fact—he was very charming, very self-effacing.

Those moments of good behavior were rare, though. We took over Cobo Hall in Detroit, where we had recorded *Alive!*, to rehearse for the Tiger Stadium show. Peter, Paul, and I, plus the road crew and everybody else, got there and got settled. While we were unpacking, someone came up and told me that Ace had not yet made it to Detroit. This was to be the first day of rehearsal for our biggest tour in almost two decades, and he couldn't get there on time. We booked him another flight, and he missed that one too. Then we booked a third one, which he also missed. When Ace finally walked into rehearsal and said something about how hard it was to pack, I basically tore him a new asshole. I told him he was a loser, that this was his last chance to get on his feet. I told him that he should be ashamed of himself, keeping the entire band and crew waiting. "If you can't do the job," I said, "get the fuck out."

Ace exploded right back at me and told me to go fuck myself. Then he left. When he was gone, Paul turned to me and asked me to smooth things over. "He'll listen to you," he said. So I had to swallow my pride and go out there and say in a gentle tone, "Look, Ace, whatever else is going on in your life, you owe it to your fans to show them that you can still be a great guitar god." This appealed to him, and he came back and started rehearsing. It didn't stop him from showing up late at other times, though.

◆ ◆ ◆

At around this same time, I wanted a band biography to be written for the reunion tour, and I wanted someone famous to do it. I tried to get Stephen King, but he was unavailable. Then I tried Steven Spielberg, but he was also unavailable. Then I thought about Bob Guccione, the editor of *Spin*. At that point, *Spin* was every bit as big as *Rolling Stone*. So even though we had once sued Guccione for printing and distributing an illegal and unauthorized KISS magazine in the 1970s, he took my call and we chatted. He agreed to write the bio, which would be a short thing, like a press release. Along the way I told Guccione about our reunion tour and the fact that we were getting back together. I wanted him to put us on the cover of *Spin*. He thought it was a good idea, although he wasn't sure it should be the whole band. He wanted a cover picture of me alone. While talking to him, I saw a larger opportunity, and the ideas just started flying out of my mouth. I ended up pitching him on a collectors' edition set of four identical KISS covers, one for each of us. "The KISS fans will want to buy all four of them," I said.

When the four solo covers of *Spin* came out, I brought them into rehearsals at Cobo Hall in Detroit, before our first performance, to show Ace and Peter that I was pushing the band, not myself. As long as I live, I'll never forget Ace's reaction. He picked up his solo cover and said, "I fucking hate this. This sucks. I'm leaving the band." And he walked out. He later came back calmer and explained that he didn't like his photograph. By the end of the day, he was looking around and asking us if we really thought his picture looked okay. Subsequently I learned that Guccione had printed 60 percent Gene Simmons covers and 25 percent Paul Stanley covers. The remaining 15 percent was divided between Ace and Peter covers. It was not the equal printing everyone thought it was.

The first leg of our reunion tour lasted 193 shows and ran over two years. It was a triumph in every way. At the end of 1997, we were playing in New Jersey, and Dick Clark, ever the gentleman, asked us if we would ring in the new year. We had become the number one touring band. (Number two was our good friend Garth Brooks.) The reaction was so tremendous that for the millennium New Year's Eve, Dick Clark decided to rebroadcast the footage.

◆ ◆ ◆

For all the wonderful feeling that passed between the band and the fans, the old problems were cropping up again. You think people will change. You hope they will change. You expect them to mature, to learn from their mistakes. But they don't. Ace would constantly ask questions about the number of people showing up at the concerts. These would be concerts in places we had played before, and the halls and stadiums hadn't changed in size. But he wanted to know whether anybody was hiding any tickets. Astonishingly, Ace was oblivious to the fact that he had a flat deal. If nobody showed up or if it sold out, he still got the same amount of money for each show he played. If he didn't play, he didn't get paid. I kept repeating that to him, every time he asked. I didn't understand why he was agonizing over it. Then I found out that he wasn't just asking me. He would ask Doc, our manager, "How many people showed up tonight?" And Doc would say, "Oh, I don't know. Maybe fifteen thousand people." Then Ace would produce a piece of paper from the concert hall, a schematic that showed the seating arrangements. On the bottom it would say "Capacity, 19,000." And he would bring me the paper and shake his head and say, "See, more lies." Keep in mind, it said "Capacity." But it was just like Ace to ignore that, or not to know what *capacity* meant. It seemed as if he didn't understand the difference between capacity and attendance, or that because our stage show was so big we had to kill three or four thousand seats.

Peter, for his part, retained a frustrating inability to understand press coverage. Articles would appear about the band, and Peter would be furious at me. He'd come up and confront me and say, "What the fuck did you say about me here?" I would take a look, thinking that maybe I had been misquoted. I hadn't: before the interview, the reporter had written his introduction, and maybe he would mention that Peter had known drug problems or had been bankrupt. This was the writer's voice, not mine, but to Peter it was the same thing.

Now that the band had reunited and I was spending more time with Peter and Ace, I was starting to see the effect twenty years of heavy drug and alcohol use had had. Ace had lost much of his memory. He has been quoted in magazines and has said directly to me that he literally doesn't remember entire decades of his life. I would like to think of that as a rock and roll exaggeration, but I have seen much evidence of memory loss. For example, Ace would come up and tell me a joke and then come by a little later and try to tell me the same joke again, but not remember how it went.

Peter also suffered from memory loss, but the difference between the two has been striking. There would often be moments of clarity on Peter's part when we were on tour. He would tell me how he had gone wrong and that this would be the first day of the rest of his life. He was tired of fighting his demons. He was tired of trying to show the world that he was a badass. He had been through two divorces that broke him spiritually and financially. He would speak very openly about wanting to change, and for some of the tour it was fun being around him. He would aid us in trying to keep Ace on the straight and narrow, saying things to Ace like, "You're a father. What's your daughter gonna say? I've been through the same stuff you've been through. It doesn't work. I don't want to go back to playing clubs, do you? It's time to straighten up." Unfortunately, it didn't work.

Later on, when Peter's insecurities kicked in and he saw that he had made millions of dollars from just one tour, he started to wonder why he hadn't made more, despite the fact that the contract he signed outlined exactly what, when, and how everyone was to be paid. When he got like that, he would team up with Ace and he'd be back to the Peter who had tortured me from the beginning.

I guess I shouldn't have been surprised when this happened. Peter was just too unpredictable. I had witnessed his unpredictability firsthand throughout our years together. For example, Peter once shot my television set. While he was trying to separate from his first wife, I let him use my apartment so he could hide out with his Playmate of the Month, whom he seemed crazy about. I gave him the key and the run of the house. When I came back, I noticed that my six-foot television screen seemed bigger and newer. It was. It was now a seven-foot television screen. When I looked behind the screen, I saw that part of wall had been repainted. I found out that Peter and this woman, who would become his second wife, had been watching TV. Peter, for some reason, had his 357 revolver out. When an actor's face appeared on the screen and he heard his girlfriend had known the actor, he shot the screen. It wasn't the first time he had done something stupid with a gun. When the band was on hiatus over the holidays during Peter's first marriage, he shot the tree out from under his first wife as she decorated it.

Ace and Peter may have tended toward this kind of behavior, but their weaknesses were exacerbated by their management. Both of them were still managed by George Sewitt, and he was, more and more in my opinion, acting the role of the band's management. I had, in no uncertain terms, told him not to do this. When we were playing the MTV Music Awards at the foot of the Brooklyn Bridge, I saw George give directions to some New York policemen. I went over to him and said, "George, stop it." Unfortunately I think he was under the direction of Ace, who kept telling him do whatever he could to promote him, rather than the band. At the end of the day, Sewitt almost got Ace and Peter into a nightmarish financial situation. I urged Ace to get some help—although I'm not a financial adviser, in my opinion it looked like a sinkhole that would give out and leave Ace holding the bag. When he did get some outside advice, they told him that it was the worst deal they'd ever seen. Ace and Peter parted company with Sewitt, and they soon sued each other. There are still claims pending.

After the split with George Sewitt, Ace and Peter started to separate. Peter, because he straightened up a bit, would often see how Ace showed up late or didn't show up at all. He would sometimes turn to me and say, "Don't get angry with him. He's bombed." Other times he would turn to Ace in a meeting and say, "You can't bullshit a bullshitter. You're high. I can see it in you." A number of times I was surprised by Peter's honesty and clarity.

As Ace lost Peter as his buddy, he withdrew. Despite Peter's drug past, when he did come back to the band after 1996, he was for the most part straight. He showed up and tried to do his work, although his attitude was always that of a complainer.

Jay Leno did a bit on the *Tonight Show* where he was interviewing us about being a member of KISS—he was asking us if he could be the fifth member.

In time KISS was called upon to deliver another album to the record company. When I say KISS, I mean Paul and me. We were the only real members of the band. Ace and Peter were not signatories to the contract. Bob Ezrin, who had been with us before in good times *(Destroyer)* and bad *(The Elder)*, started working on a new album, which we called *Psycho Circus*. But after a while, it became obvious to us, and to Bob himself, that he was too busy with his Internet company. During the initial rehearsals, he didn't think his contributions were as good as they should have been, and he took himself out of the picture. Then Bruce Fairbairn, a producer who had been successful with bands like Aerosmith, Bon Jovi, and Loverboy, among others, came to meet with us in Winnipeg, Canada. We explained to him that it was going to be a nightmare. Needless to say, from the beginning to the end, he was tortured by Ace and Peter, who tried yet again to change the contract and didn't show up for most of the record. We had to use Tommy Thayer, Bruce Kulick, Kevin Valentine, and others in their place. Bruce got us through the process and helped us to make a good, solid KISS record, one that debuted at number one in many countries around the world. Unfortunately, within the year Bruce Fairbairn was found dead in his house in Vancouver. That was the last KISS studio album, and it may be the last one ever. We have enough unreleased material to keep fans satisfied for quite some time, in the form of rarities, demos, and so forth, but it would take an earthshaking event to get us back into the studio. In the current market, there's no real place for a new KISS album, and I'm not interested in making an album that doesn't succeed.

During that *Psycho Circus* period, I had another once-in-a-lifetime experience when I hooked up with Bob Dylan and ended up cowriting a song with him. We weren't put together by anyone else—I just looked up Dylan's number, called his manager, and said that I had long been an admirer. I had never spoken to Dylan, never met him. He came to my guest house in Beverly Hills, and the whole experience was very cordial. I spent about two minutes telling him how important he was to music in general and to me personally. He's a very easygoing guy, but he doesn't say much. Then we sat down, picked up acoustic guitars, and traded licks back and forth. He had something I liked, I had something he liked, and so on. When we recorded the demo, he was nice enough to come down to the demo studio. Since then I have been begging him to write the lyric, and he keeps telling me that I should do it. Can you imagine that? Bob Dylan is telling me to write lyrics.

◆ ◆ ◆

The 1998 *Psycho Circus* tour kicked off at Dodger Stadium, the first 3-D tour in history. You got your ticket and you got your glasses, which at various points in the show would make it seem three-dimensional off the screen at the back of the stage.

Between concerts we flew on our own Gulfstream jet with all the amenities. We stayed in the best hotels, and when we had a day off in Texas Ace decided to visit his Texas cousins. They actually resembled him but spoke with drawls, like the Beverly Hillbillies. They were nice enough and said that Ace would stay with them on their farm. I imagined Ace on horseback, but I didn't want to think too much about it.

Later I heard Ace was in the hospital and word got out that he had shot himself. It seems Ace decided to go shooting—with an Uzi, an Israeli machine gun designed to shoot hundreds of rounds per second. There was a time when it was the fastest and deadliest weapon of its kind. Apparently, from Ace's explanation, one of the bullets backfired and a piece of shrapnel lodged in his chest. When he felt better, I asked him why he went shooting with a machine gun in the first place, and he actually responded, in so many words, "Yeah, well, if you Israelis knew how to build a machine gun, this never would have happened to me."

Ace generally needed diversions. He had flown in a body-guard to keep him company. Ace's reasons for companionship, be it girlfriend or bodyguard, were usually to get him ice for his drinks, pack his bags, or be his playmate when he was in the mood to cause mischief.

While we were at the same hotel where he had the machine gun incident, he bought paintball guns and he and his bodyguard shot at each other inside the hotel suite. Afterward we found out that the suite was a complete disaster. The walls and furniture were covered with paint; a blanket had apparently been dropped in a bathtub full of water, for God knows what purpose. The hotel banned KISS from all Four Seasons hotels nationwide. It took some doing to explain to the hotel that only one of us had the mental capacity to actually conceive of having a paintball fight indoors and that that person would be most happy to pay for the damages. The hotel quickly gave Ace a bill of approximately ten thousand dollars. He countered by saying he would sue them for any number of reasons. This was classic Ace. Everyone was trying to get him. He was the innocent victim.

This feeling of persecution depressed him. He couldn't understand why his domestic life seemed to be in such turmoil. He couldn't understand why the government was after him for unpaid taxes. He couldn't understand why Canada always made him go through such a ritual before they let him into the country. The fact that the rest of the group had to wait around for hours while we pleaded with the Canadian government that Ace's drug busts were a thing of the past was completely lost on him. Ace always blames the government, or fate, or anything or anyone but himself when things go wrong.

We were touring the world but not having a good time doing it. The chemicals had started to handicap Ace even more and he had a girlfriend who seemed to tolerate willingly this lifestyle. Peter, too, succumbed to his inner demons. He went back to being the Moaner, the nickname given to him by a former road manager.

We still had a few tricks up our sleeves, though, or at least I did. I called Hugh Hefner, who is a friend of mine, and told him I was in discussions with *Penthouse* for a KISS cover and that I wanted to let him know about it because we were close to a deal. He told me to forget *Penthouse* and he would put the group on the cover of *Playboy* if we had an angle. I suggested "The Girls of KISS." The photos and article would be about the female KISS fans who delight in going to our shows, showing us their breasts, and throwing their undies and bras onstage. He loved it. Under the wonderful guidance of Marilyn Grabowski, the word went out and about thirty beautiful girls came, undressed, and put on their KISS makeup. We had the kind of photo session guys can only dream of.

When *Playboy* appeared on the stands in March 1999, I was on the cover alone with four girls. The band, especially Ace and Peter, believed it was another one of my schemes. They had expected and demanded to be on the cover.

When *Playboy* was about to come out, KISS had the coveted spot on the Superbowl telecast seen around the world by a billion people. Five hundred and fifty girls in KISS makeup joined us as we lip-synched "Rock and Roll All Nite." Our fireworks and rockets were extra-charged, since the sky was the limit, and we showed the Superbowl and the world how it should be done. We were the openers. After KISS, Cher sang the national anthem. We saw each other later that night and reminisced about the great times we had had. She had just come off the biggest single in her career and was feeling great.

While we were at the Superbowl, I arranged to meet with Linda and Vince McMahon, the owners and creators of the World Wrestling Federation. I pitched them the idea of a KISS wrestler called the Demon ("I've been to hell and back"). I told them that we could follow it up with the Starchild, who was too pretty for his own good but could kick butt, and so on. Then we could introduce female versions of KISS, Lady Demon, Wildchild, and so on, and then KISS kids. While I was negotiating the licensing and merchandising slices we wanted on the back end, I was also talking to World Championship Wrestling, the rival wrestling outfit. In the end I took the better of the two deals and went with WCW. It was a win-win situation for us because KISS retained all licensing and merchandising rights: WCW did all the work and we reaped all the rewards.

The debut event for the Demon came as we were at our wit's end by the end of the tour and about to call it quits. We flew to Las Vegas to play one song, "God of Thunder," at the MGM Grand for the debut and made an enormous amount of money. It seemed like it should have been the easiest thing in the world, but with Ace and Peter nothing was ever easy. The misery of it was like pulling teeth.

Paul and I talked and finally decided to go out and do one more tour and then call it a day. This wasn't such a crazy thought. The comeback, which began in 1996, was always a five-year plan—emotionally for me and Paul, and by contract for Ace and Peter. By the end of 1999, it was becoming very clear that, physically, neither Ace nor Peter could endure too much more. And Paul and I didn't know how much more of them we could stand.

We really didn't have much more to prove, either. By 1999 KISS had scaled the heights. We had been on the cover of *Forbes* magazine, had broken every box office record, and stood proudly right behind the Beatles in the number of gold record awards by a group. We had gotten our own star on the Hollywood Walk of Fame. We were wax figures in the Hollywood Wax Museum. We had done what we had always dreamed of doing. And although I had been very frugal all my life, I was now, for the first time, loosening the purse strings.

Times had certainly changed. I had bought a car. I had bought property. I had cautiously dug my roots into the ground. I had two gorgeous kids who looked up to me. I was living with a living doll. But one thing hadn't changed—I still wasn't married. I had taken flack for that from friends, usually women. But it was the only way I knew to feel safe. I didn't want to fall into the trap of simply living my life by society's or anyone else's rules.

As I said earlier, I really wanted my kids to have both of their parents' names. I did not want Shannon to take on my last name; I find it insulting to women that they would agree to throw away their last names and assume their husbands'. Like property. "This is my car, this is my wife." I wanted none of that. I wanted Shannon to be her own person, decide her own destiny, and go after every whim and desire she ever had, without having to check with "the man."

As much as I was trying to fight the conventional nuclear family, here I was, crazy about the mother of my kids. As of this writing, we have been together for eighteen years. We have yet to raise a hand or our voices to each other. We often wonder if there is something wrong with us. We never fight, about anything.

So I let my guard down further and dug my roots deeper. I

decided to build a 16,500-square-foot home, with enough room for everyone and my work. It would have four levels on two acres with trees, a tennis court, and a waterfall. Building it would take three years. In the meantime, we had a farewell tour to complete.

◆ ◆ ◆

The farewell tour kicked off in Phoenix, Arizona, on March 11, 2000. The stage set was a bigger, bolder version of the reunion tour, with three huge screens and two huge KISS logos. It was an over-the-top version of what we had been doing for twenty-five years. We opened with a film about the band, then moved right into "Shout It Out Loud." The set was a strong mix of greatest hits and new material, the songs fans wanted to hear. I'm not sure if anyone believed that it was really a farewell performance. People were crying in the audience, but maybe it wasn't because they were never going to see us again—maybe it was because Ace and Peter were playing so badly. As the tour went on, it became clear to me that the decision to make this tour the last one was not only smart but maybe inevitable. Musically, it was the worst we had ever been. But the amount of fan worship was tremendous. Many of the fans were celebrities. Russell Crowe came out to Austin, Texas. L.L. Cool J flew out to see us.

The farewell tour also found KISS solidifying its marketing deals—in fact, we took the opportunity to push our corporate connections to a new level. To my mind, one of the most interesting things about the band was the fact that we were never afraid to admit that we were in the rock and roll business. From the beginning, from 1973, I was less interested in respect, which can be here today and gone tomorrow, than in brand. Did people have enough interest in what we did to go out there and buy something associated with us? From the beginning Paul was always more interested in credibility. I knew that credibility was fleeting. You can argue from now until the end of time whether something or someone is respected, but one thing you can't argue with is sales.

I think fans sometimes sided with Paul. Some of them perceived our obsession with marketing ourselves as characters to be sort of juvenile. Way before anyone else was doing this, we stuck question-naires in our albums. We wanted to know where the fans lived and what magazines they read. If we were going to take out an ad in a magazine, we didn't want to take it out in the wrong one. One way to find out which magazines people read is to ask them. My aware-ness of these practices went back to my childhood, to my own days as a pop-culture fanatic. Since I loved Superman, I would certainly watch the TV show and buy not only the comic books but anything that Superman endorsed. The same held true for Disney. Disney is not just the theme park and cartoons—it is anything you can imag-ine, from pillows to pajamas to videos. Mickey Mouse started out as a cartoon, then became a part of America. Whether Mickey Mouse is respected or not is such a small issue. When you're too big to argue with, you make your own rules. Is Elvis credible or not? Who cares? The question is moot. You may think Santa Claus doesn't have any credibility. But at a certain time of the year, he rules. That's what I wanted for KISS: to make such a big impact that authenticity or credibility would be beside the point.

At around this time, Pepsi approached us with an idea for a broad music-based TV marketing campaign that would use artists from all different kinds of music: from country to rock and every-thing in between. The commercials would star Hallie Eisenberg, a child actress, and include a country segment, where she sang with a country singer, a soul segment where she sang with Aretha Franklin, and so on. Pepsi approached us at the end of 1999 and at the beginning of the so-called farewell tour. While we were in Phoenix, we filmed it. Not only did VH1 come down and shoot the beginning of the farewell tour, but the day before, we spent about ten hours on the same stage filming the commercial.

They only showed it a few times, and then as a corporate deci-sion Pepsi started to show the country version of the commercial instead. The problem was that when the Pepsi people did a test with their own focus group, it was 90 percent for us and only 10 for coun-try. So they came back and started to play the commercial again. At the same time, ABC decided to use "Rock and Roll All Nite" as the theme music for its fall schedule.

The Pepsi deal was only the most recent in a long line of corporate associations. The very first one was for a KISS Honda bike, kind of a Japanese Harley-Davidson. Many corporations around the country were scared of an association with us. We have no illusions about our corporate identity—we're like any other corporation. Some rock bands are delusional. They say they're a people's band, but even they don't perform for free. Whether you have long hair or razor blades in your eyeballs, you're a corporation. KISS broke all the rules and ended up on the cover of *Playboy* and *Fortune*. We've never made any bones about the fact that the American dream is about not only fame but also riches. Money does make you a happier person. It's not everything, but it's better to have more money than less. Americans by and large feel a little awkward talking about money or showing it off when they have it. That's why the richest men in the country walk around in jeans. When a band that has sold millions of records walks onstage in jeans, it's every bit as much a costume as KISS's costumes. Each outfit is carefully designed to elicit a certain reaction.

I'm here to tell you it's all good. We don't hide behind that mask. We worked hard. Bands have come out and said that we're corporate while they have integrity, and they can point fingers, but the IRS makes no distinction. When you make money, it's called earned income. As a rock band, you are a business, and you have to seize every opportunity to promote your product.

◆ ◆ ◆

In the winter of 2001, as we were getting ready to embark on the Japanese and Australian leg of our farewell tour, Peter demanded a new deal. But we had a contract with him and weren't willing to meet these new terms. Peter held his ground and told us that we could take it or leave it. We left it. At the end of the day, Peter Criss is still the very same guy who, even before our first show at the Diplomat Hotel in 1973—a show where we scratched and clawed to get people there—was ready to quit the band. Why? Because he was disappointed that his best friend, Jerry Nolan, had a record contract. In 1980, on our first Australian tour, we played to stadiums full of people. Peter missed that tour. And here we were, going back to Japan and Australia in March 2001, kicking off at Tokyo Stadium, and Peter would miss that tour as well. Eric Singer rejoined KISS in the catman makeup.

Amazingly, during this final tour, I witnessed at least one miracle—an amazing change in the behavior of Ace Frehley. Maybe it's because he had a new girlfriend, who seemed wonderful. Maybe it's because he was finally growing up a bit. Whatever the reason, I'd never seen Ace more responsible. He showed up on time, played his instrument, and helped out. Perhaps it was because Peter was not there and Eric Singer, the sweetest guy in the world, was. The company you keep matters. But through Japan and Australia, Ace was a joy to work with.

With all this drama, with all the personal struggle and complicated feelings, the farewell tour ended up being the number-one tour in the world, based on calendar years. We started in March, but we were consistently selling out huge venues. It's comforting to know that you can end on top even after almost three decades.

✦ ✦ ✦

I feel a sense of accomplishment from our merchandising deals. I feel a sense of accomplishment seeing fans around the world putting on makeup that imitates what we invented almost thirty years ago. But in the end, the most satisfying part is still getting up on a stage and playing KISS songs that fans have come to love, from "Strutter" to "Deuce" to "Rock and Roll All Nite."

Soon KISS will hang up its boots and its studded codpieces. We'll take off our makeup. And when we walk off the stage for the final time, it will be bittersweet.

To be honest, there are some things I won't miss. The reunion tour brought us back to square one, both in rediscovering the simple pleasure of playing in a band and also in putting up with the headaches of band members who didn't see us as a unit.

I firmly believe that people have the right to behave as they wish. I have never thought I was anyone's guardian or protector. But for decades I saw substance abuse problems intensify every insecurity, spark unreasonable anger, and fog Ace's and Peter's ability to make intelligent decisions. As the farewell tour winds down, it's clear to me that KISS will never realize its full potential, because while the band was originally conceived as a four-wheel-drive vehicle, we often had to drive on flat tires. On the other hand, we've also gone where no band has gone before. We've survived the punk movement, the new romantic movement, the thrash movement. We've survived every movement you can think of. We walked weird, we talked weird. We certainly looked weird. And what genre we came from is anybody's guess. We owe our allegiance to the spirit of early rock and roll. The point was uplift. We wanted to capture the spirit and energy of bands we had never seen onstage.

We wanted to go where no band had gone before.

We wanted our fans to be proud of us and leave our concerts with big grins on their faces.

We wanted to stand guilty as charged by the poor, deluded critics who thought they were insulting us by charging that we made complete spectacles of ourselves. You're damn right we did.

We wanted, finally and most important, to let our fans, the KISS Army, know that they were the only reason we were doing this, that when they came to see us live and heard our call to arms—"You Wanted the Best, You Got the Best. The Hottest Band in the World, KISS"—they would know in their hearts we wouldn't let them down.

KISS will continue. Maybe not in the way you expect, but it will live on. There will be a KISS cartoon. There will be KISS theme parks. There are already, as you read this, KISS Kaskets. (They say you can't take it with you. I say you can.)

My mother taught me to dream big. "Reach for the sky," she would say. And to her I owe everything.

And to America, sweet America, thank you for making a poor little immigrant boy's dreams come true.

The rock star and his lady.

THE DEMON STRIKES AGAIN! IN THIS NEW CHAPTER, GENE TAKES YOU BEHIND THE SCENES OF THE *DESTROYER* RECORDING SESSIONS AND REVEALS SURPRISING DETAILS ABOUT THE MAKING OF THIS CLASSIC KISS ALBUM.

By 1975, KISS had broken all the rules—and records. We never had a hit single, and yet our double live album KISS *Alive!* had gone multi-platinum . . . in an era when live albums simply didn't sell. We not only broke through with a live album, but with a double album to boot.

god of thunder
of DESTROYER

The mystique had grown beyond even our own expectations. We had become our stage personas—the Demon, the Starchild, and so on. Offstage, we were forced to hide our faces. Photographers were constantly trying to photograph us without make-up: there was a $25,000 price tag on my head. In some ways, we were trapped by what we had created.

Initially, it was fun, but in short order, it became difficult. We couldn't go out in public without security. Bodyguards were often asking people to hand over film.

the making 1976

Differences within the band started to come to the surface. Paul was more the "classic rocker." He wanted to be a rock star. Period. Ace and Peter had those notions as well, but they were never able to really verbalize just what they were all about.

I wanted KISS to be the best of all worlds. I loved comic books. I loved horror movies. I didn't have preconceived notions about rock bands, and quite honestly, didn't care. It wasn't enough to tour and be a recording artist. Somehow, KISS should be about all these other areas as well.

I may have been the impetus behind getting the band and management to start thinking about a Frank Frazetta piece of art for our forthcoming *Destroyer* album. Frazetta was the finest of the sci-fi/fantasy painters, best known for painting all those *Conan the Barbarian* covers. I was a major fan. I asked the art department to reach the Frazetta estate. They contacted his wife and when we found out

Here we are hanging over the Empire State Building in New York City in 1976. We wanted the picture to be edgy, so we foolishly climbed over the guardrail and hung precariously close to the edge. It may look like we're posing comfortably, but soon after the photo was taken, all of us jumped back over to safety. That was the one and only time we ever posed there.

the price tag, it was too much—
we would need to find someone
else. Ironically, we hit upon a
cousin of Frazetta's, Ken Kelly,
who was known to me through
his *Creepy* and *Eerie* magazine
covers.

Kelly and the band met to
discuss the concept. I remember
suggesting we should be
depicted in a Marvel Comics
pose—like the Fantastic Four.
So, there we were, a rock and
roll band, depicted on their new album without guitars. It was a
major statement—we stood out from all the other bands. It said, in
effect, "We are more than the guitars we play." It was the pivotal
moment that sent a message out to millions of fans and press alike—
we were also superheroes.

The first version of the cover was done during the middle of
the recording process. We stopped recording mid-record and went
off on tour. We also decided to change the outfits. So, by the time we
finished *Destroyer*, the cover of the album depicted us wearing the
wrong clothes. Ken Kelly had to go back and paint on the new costumes.

Bob Ezrin was brought in to produce us. He was Canadian and
had been successful with the Alice Cooper albums. Needless to say,
we were fans of his work. He brought with him something we had
never seen before: he had vision. He knew before the album was
recorded what it should be. He rearranged songs. He cowrote half-
finished songs. He told Peter how to play his drums. He literally
came up with the melody line for the entire solo of "Detroit Rock
City." He made Ace play every note and stick on the harmony parts.
He suggested my bass line in the song. Neither Ace nor Peter was
thrilled with the notion that some outsider was now telling them
what to play—but the results speak for themselves.

All the major decisions on the entire record—the sound loops, the children's choir, the kids on "God of Thunder" (Ezrin's kids, by the way), the string-based "Beth," and the song order—were completely Ezrin's.

The car crashing at the beginning of "Detroit Rock City" was a sound effect Ezrin brought in. Initially, some of us thought it was a bit melodramatic. Though we knew movies used sound effects with songs, we simply never thought about using the sound of crashing cars to open a song. But while recently listening to Shangri-La's "Leader of the Pack" . . . sure enough, I heard a motorcycle crash in the background.

"Beth" was written by Stan Penridge, mostly. It was credited to Peter Criss, Stan Penridge, and Bob Ezrin. In truth, Peter didn't play a musical instrument (drums are a percussive instrument) and I have never seen him write a single song. Peter may have contributed a line of lyric or two, but after hearing the original Penridge demo tape of the song, it's clear who came up with the original song . . . which, incidentally was called "Beck," as in Becky.

As a side note, Peter was having a hard time getting the vocal performance down. His pitch wasn't to Ezrin's satisfaction. Ezrin made the band leave the studio to give Peter a chance to concentrate. Eventually, the track was done and we all stared at each other. There were no guitars played by the band on it, there were no drums on it, and Ace never showed up to play his part. In a very real way, "Beth" is simply Peter singing alone. There is not another piece of KISS on there. We didn't know if it would upset the fans.

The first single was "Detroit Rock City." The B-side was "Beth." In those days, the other side of a single would feature another song. Usually, it would be the song you could never imagine as a hit single, because you didn't want to compete with yourself for radio airplay. "Detroit Rock City" was not a hit record. We were all shocked to learn that radio stations were turning the record over to play "Beth." It became our biggest hit at the time. It also won the People's Choice Awards—tying, by the way, with "Disco Duck."

"God of Thunder" was written by Paul. Most people think I wrote it. It was originally recorded in demo form at Magnagraphics Studios in New York on 8-track with Paul singing and a disco beat.

Ezrin rearranged the song, slowed it down, and suggested I sing it instead. Paul, to his credit, was very receptive. Both Paul and I would offer our songs to be sung by Ace and Peter. Paul in particular, gave a few songs to Peter to sing. "God of Thunder" became my signature song for years. In what must have been an inspirational moment, I decided I should throw up blood during the beginning of the song, so that I could look the part.

   Destroyer was released and initially stalled at sales of around 890,000 copies. We were on tour and although the fans came out in droves to see their heroes, the record just stood still. Then "Beth" became a hit and everything around us exploded. We were invited to do the *Paul Lynde Halloween Special,* which meant national television exposure. We appeared on the show with Margaret Hamilton,

KISS appeared on ABC's *Paul Lynde Halloween Special* in 1976. A highlight was appearing on the show with Margaret Hamilton, the Wicked Witch from the original *Wizard of Oz.*

the original witch from the *Wizard of Oz*. We also noticed that the world had changed. All of a sudden, you could walk down the street and people would be walking by wearing KISS T-shirts. We had arrived!

Ezrin's recording style was leagues beyond anything we had seen. In some ways, it seemed like a throwback to a previous era, but in other ways, it was clear he knew what he wanted and how to get it. Records are recorded by separating all the different elements into tracks. You could move a fader and only hear the guitar, or the snare drum. Once everything was recorded (on a 24-track machine), you then added effects like echo or chorus and mixed it down to a stereo mix. What you hear at home is a mix. Ezrin would record two or three guitars, add effects, and submix them—which means there was no turning back. He would commit to a sound very early on. It further solidified the notion in my mind that he had a vision.

Destroyer also marked the first time we tried experimentation. Peter's drum set was set up in the loading area in back of the studio for one of the tracks. His drums faced an open elevator shaft. Microphones were placed close to the drums and at the end of the elevator shaft. That way, the sound would come back like thunder. Peter was separated from the rest of us, so a video camera was set up to film him. This was still at the early stages of video, so it all seemed very like science fiction to us. On one of the takes, Peter stopped playing and when we looked up, there was a guy carrying out the garbage into the elevator nearby.

"Flaming Youth" was probably the most difficult song to record. It was composed of a title Paul had (which he lifted from a band we had opened up for, called Flaming Youth), a verse and chorus that Ezrin, Paul, and I tossed back and forth, and a bass riff I had from an old song called "Mad Dog." Ezrin put all the pieces together and then threw a bizarre time signature at us—which was torture for a basic drummer like Peter. Peter never counted bars of time. He had never done it and, in fact, didn't understand the fundamentals. Ezrin had to start from the beginning. Where was the "one" and where was the "two"? And then he had to teach Peter, in particular, what a bar of music was—how long it lasted and how one counted it. He also tried to crystallize what a chorus and a verse were. All this education made Peter very irritable. It was also very time intensive. We were used to going into the studio, not thinking too much about technicalities, and just doing it. We had never encountered anything like this. KISS was a rock and roll band. We were unschooled, self-taught musicians. We got through the song, but it had to be done in pieces and then edited together.

"Shout It Out Loud" was written in Ezrin's apartment. Paul and I had gone over to play new material. Ezrin sat down at the piano; Paul had a guitar and suggested a few changes. When there was a basic verse idea, I suggested "Shout it out loud," as in "Shout it, shout it, shout it out loud." This wasn't a unique idea. Wicked Lester had recorded a song we never put on the album called "We Wanna Shout It Out Loud," written by Cook and Greenaway. The demo was originally done by The Hollies. They never used it. We

When photographers were in the pit in front of the stage, they couldn't get a closeup of my face if I was standing, so I often dropped to my knee to pose. The problem was getting back up—it wasn't all that easy with eight-inch platform heels and the extra pounds of studs and armor.

tried to record it, but it never made it to the final stages. I had always loved the notion of shouting anything . . . as in "Shout" by the Isley Brothers.

"Shout It Out Loud" seemed like a natural follow-up to "Rock and Roll All Nite." Where "Rock and Roll All Nite" proudly proclaimed "I Wanna . . ." as the key idea, "Shout It" brought the fans into the party: "Well the night's begun and you want some fun . . . ."

"Great Expectations" was a song I had written initially about the band. The orginal lyric went something like "You watch Paul playing guitar, and you see what his hand can do and you wish you were the one he was doing it to . . . and you watch me singing this song and you *know* what my mouth can do, and you wish you were the one I was doing it to . . ." Ezrin thought the song was too self-serving if it talked about the band. Although "Beth" was very clearly about the band: "Beth, I hear you calling, but I can't come home right now, 'cause me and the boys'll be playin' all night." I would have preferred to have the band names mentioned in the song. I had fondly remembered Beatles songs and hearing "Take it, George."

When *Destroyer* came out, KISS became the biggest band in America. We went from opening up for other bands to headlining at Anaheim Stadium in California with opening acts like Bob Seger, Uriah Heep, and Ted Nugent. We had billboard and television commercials. Coming soon were the KISS make-up kits and lunch boxes.

While almost every record we recorded in our thirty-year history has elements I would change, in retrospect, *Destroyer* is an album I wouldn't change. I might do away with the sound loop at the top of the first song, but other than that, I wouldn't change a thing.

KISS has played thousands of concerts. We have added and dropped songs from the set list purely as a response to what the fans seemed to like. *Destroyer* has stood the test of time. More than any other record we ever recorded, it probably defines what the band is and what it stood for. The songs on it, "Detroit Rock City," "Shout It Out Loud," "God of Thunder," and others, continue to be a staple of our live shows.

DISCOGRAPHY

KISS (Casablanca, 1974)

Hotter Than Hell (Casablanca, 1974)

Dressed to Kill (Casablanca, 1975)

Alive! (Casablanca, 1975)

Destroyer (Casablanca, 1976)

The Originals (Casablanca, 1976)

Rock and Roll Over (Casablanca, 1976)

Love Gun (Casablanca, 1977)

Alive II (Casablanca, 1977)

The Originals II (Japan only,
  Casablanca, 1978)

Double Platinum (Casablanca, 1978)

Gene Simmons (Casablanca, 1978)

Ace Frehley (Casablanca, 1978)

Peter Criss (Casablanca, 1978)

Paul Stanley (Casablanca, 1978)

Dynasty (Casablanca, 1979)

Unmasked (Casablanca, 1980)

Music from "The Elder" (Casablanca, 1981)

Killers (released abroad, Casablanca, 1982)

Creatures of the Night (Casablanca, 1982)

Lick It Up (Mercury, 1983)

Animalize (Mercury, 1984)

Asylum (Mercury, 1985)

Crazy Nights (Mercury, 1987)

Chikara (Japan only, Polystar, 1988)

Smashes, Thrashes and Hits (Mercury, 1988)

Hot in the Shade (Mercury, 1989)

Revenge (Mercury, 1992)

Alive III (Mercury, 1993)

KISS My Ass (Mercury, 1994)

MTV Unplugged (Mercury, 1996)

You Wanted the Best . . . You've Got the Best! (Mercury, 1996)

Greatest KISS (Mercury, 1997)

Greatest Hits (UK only, Mercury, 1997)

Carnival of Souls: The Final Sessions (Mercury, 1997)

Psycho Circus (Mercury, 1998)

Detroit Rock City soundtrack (Mercury, 1999)

KISS boxed set (Mercury, 2001)

Alive IV (yet to be released)

PHOTOGRAPH CREDITS

Front endpaper: Neil Zlozower, copyright ©1998

TEXT PHOTOGRAPHS

page ii: Laurel Martin-Jacobs

page ix: Bob Gruen

page 81: Raeanne Rubenstein

page 86: Waring Abbott

page 90–91: Neil Zlozower

page 93: Lydia Criss Catalog

page 94: Neil Zlozower

page 102: Waring Abbott

page 105: Bob Gruen

page 106: Reproduced by special permission of *Playboy* magazine. Copyright ©1976 by Playboy.

page 109: Barry Levine/KISS catalog

pages 126–127: Bob Gruen/KISS catalog

page 131: Fin Costello/KISS catalog

page 132: Bob Gruen

page 137: Bob Gruen

page 141: James Fortune

page 163: Reprinted with special permission of King Features Syndicate.

page 188: Reproduced by special permission of Columbia Pictures. Copyright ©1984 by Columbia Pictures.

page 198: Reproduced by special permission of
Columbia Pictures. Copyright ©1984 by Columbia Pictures.

page 203: Reproduced by special permission of
Playboy magazine. Copyright ©1996 by Playboy.

page 206: Copyright ©1988 by The Kiss Company.

page 209: Copyright ©1986 by Paul Entertainment.

page 248: Bob Duda/KISS catalog

page 260: Barry Levine

page 264: Richard Creamer

page 266: Neil Zlozower

page 268: Warring Abbott

INSERT PHOTOGRAPHS

INSERT 1

page 4: Ed Rottinger/KISS catalog

page 5, inset: Bob Gruen

page 7: Michael Lippman/KISS catalog

page 8: Copyright ©1978 KISS catalog.

INSERT 2

page 1: Courtesy of *People* magazine. Copyright ©1978 Time Inc.

page 2, bottom: Barry Levine Studios/KISS catalog

page 3, top: Ross Halfin/Idols

page 3, bottom: Gene Kirkland

page 5, bottom: Bob Duda/KISS catalog

page 6: Reproduced by special permission of
Playboy magazine. Copyright ©1999.

page 7: Reproduced by special permission of
Playboy magazine. Copyright ©1998.

All other photographs and illustrations are courtesy of the author.

INDEX

ABOUT THE AUTHOR

GENE SIMMONS has acted in movies and television, written and produced albums for other recording artists, managed the recording careers of, among others, Liza Minnelli, and was founder and president of his own record label, Simmons Records/RCA. He recently launched his movie and television producing career with *Detroit Rock City* for New Line Cinema, and is also the creator and publisher of his own magazine, through Sterling/Macfadden, called *Gene Simmons' Tongue*. Gene Simmons lives in Beverly Hills. Visit him at KISSonline.com.

more KISS!

With more than 250 photographs—most being published in this book for the first time—Gene Simmons and Paul Stanley take us on an intimate tour of the early days of KISS. An unprecedented insider's look at the days and nights of the band—onstage and off.

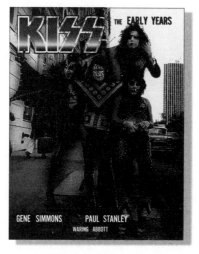

Kiss: The Early Years
0–609–81028–6
$24.95 paperback (Canada: $37.95)

THREE RIVERS PRESS • NEW YORK

Available from Three Rivers Press wherever books are sold.
RandomHouse.com